FINE WINE
EDITIONS

THE FINEST WINES OF

TUSCANY

AND CENTRAL ITALY

A Regional and Village Guide to the Best Wines
and Their Producers

NICOLAS BELFRAGE MW

Foreword by Hugh Johnson | Photography by Jon Wyand

UNIVERSITY OF CALIFORNIA PRESS
Berkeley | Los Angeles

University of California Press,
one of the most distinguished university presses in the United States,
enriches lives around the world by advancing scholarship
in the humanities, social sciences, and natural sciences.
Its activities are supported by the UC Press Foundation and by
philanthropic contributions from individuals and institutions.
For more information, visit www.ucpress.edu

First published in
North America by
University of California Press
Berkeley and Los Angeles, California

Fine Wine Editions
Publisher Sara Morley
General Editor Neil Beckett
Editor Stuart George
Subeditor David Tombesi-Walton
Editorial Assistant Vicky Jordan
Designer Kenneth Carroll
Layout Rod Teasdale
Map Editor Eugenio Signoroni
Maps Red Lion
Indexer Ann Marangos
Production Nikki Ingram

Cataloging-in-Publication data for this title is on file with the
Library of Congress

ISBN 978-0-520-25942-3 (paper : alk. paper)

Manufactured in China

10 9 8 7 6 5 4 3 2 1
15 14 13 12 11 10 09

Contents

Foreword

by Hugh Johnson

Fine wines detach themselves from the rest not by their pretensions but by their conversation—the conversation, that is, that they provoke and stimulate, even, I sometimes think, by joining in themselves.

Is this too surreal a thought? Don't you exchange ideas with a bottle of truly original, authentic, coherent wine? You are just putting the decanter down for the second time. You have admired its color, remarked on a note of new oak now in decline and a ripe blackcurrant smell growing by the minute, when a tang of iodine interrupts you, the voice of the sea as clear as if you had just parked your car on the beach and opened the door. Picture the Gironde, the wine is saying. You know the slope with its pale stones and its long gray view. I am Latour; how can you forget my siblings with their family taste of sweet iron? Keep me on your tongue and I will explain everything: my grapes, the sun I missed in August, and the baking September days up to harvest. Is my strength draining away? Then I am old, but all the more eloquent; you see my weak points now, but my character is clearer than ever.

He who has ears to hear, let him hear. The vast majority of the world's wines are like French cartoons, *sans paroles*. Fine wines are thoroughbreds with form and mettle, even on their off days or when they are outrun. If a seemingly disproportionate number of words and, naturally, money are lavished on them, it is because they set the pace. What do you aspire to without a model? And far from being futile, aspiration has given us, and continues to give us, more thoroughbreds, more conversation, and more seductive voices to beguile us.

Just 20 or 30 years ago, the wine world was a plain with isolated peaks. It had crevasses, not to mention abysses, too, but we did our best to avoid them. The collision of continents thrust up new mountain ranges, while erosion turned barren new rock into fertile soil. Do I need to mention the clambering explorers, the pioneers who planted at high altitudes with aspirations that seemed presumptuous at the time? If they started by making wine with little to say, those who persevered found a new grammar and a new vocabulary, to add its voice to conversations that will soon, it seems, be worldwide.

Even among the most established there is continual change, as their language produces its own literature, and its literature new masterpieces. Far from being regions where everything has been discovered, everything said, and every decision taken, the classic regions of the wine world are where the finest tuning takes place—where it is financially rewarding to go to the greatest efforts and explore in the greatest depth every elusive nuance that soils and techniques can offer.

In Bordeaux and Burgundy the fine-tuning has been going on for centuries, and there is no reason to think it will ever end. Tuscany presents the opposite picture: a wine culture reaching back into antiquity but advancing little, or only in fits and starts, until very recent times. We can speculate that Medici feasts were not irrigated with anything undrinkable, and Chianti is recorded as the name of a wine, possibly a white wine, in the 15th century. English noblemen of the 18th century appreciated Tuscan wine, principally sweet Moscato. In the 19th century, when Florence was momentarily capital of the newborn state of Italy, great efforts were made to make its local wines worthy of its status.

Either a prosperous middle class, though, or an established export market is vital to advance quality in wine, and with its aristocratic estates and its peasant sharecroppers, Tuscany had little of either until the 1960s. It is the past 40 years that have seen the Tuscan wine renaissance—if revolution is not a better term. Its authors are still active, and the ideas they propagated are still developing. Tuscany has progressed from making folkloric country wines to fine-tuning some of the world's most resonant reds. It is the New World within the Old, questioning, experimenting all the time, with ever-rising standards within parameters still being refined.

Preface

by Nicolas Belfrage

This book may be approached like a Tuscan meal. The first part (chapters 1–6), the antipasto, presents a quick history and general background information on Tuscan and central Italian wines, plus a more in-depth look at the area's geography, viticulture, and winemaking; a bit rich, perhaps, or abundant, but gets the gastric juices going. The second part, the *primo piatto* (which is always the centerpiece of a Tuscan *pranzo*), is all about the production zones, the finest producers, and their wines, the best of which are indicated by a star. The third part, the *secondo piatto* (often a bit of an anticlimax after the flights of the *primo*), takes a look at related matters such as vintages and wine-and-food pairing, and, for *dolce*, provides ten lists of ten wines or wineries that I consider top in their category.

It is important to note, however, that unlike the Tuscan meal, the different parts of the book do not have to be taken in ritualistic order but may be consumed separately—there is no need to plow through the whole of the chapters on grape varieties and winemaking practices before proceeding to the heart of the matter, though if you do, you might find the information provided useful when tackling subsequent chapters. Nor, even, need the profiles be read consecutively, though to do so will help one's understanding of the zones and subzones from which they spring. The third part, like the first, may be looked at separately.

All selections are subjective, though I like to think that, over a quarter of a century specializing in Italian wine, there may also have crept in a measure of objectivity about what's good. I have tried not to be dogmatic but to present producers with different approaches and ideologies, even if I do not necessarily

agree with them. I greatly regret not being able—for reasons of time and space (pardon my metaphysics)—to include certain producers, especially those whose wines well merited inclusion and who were only too willing to cooperate. I tried to home in on those I knew well or reasonably well, and in an area like central Italy, where there are so many wineries, it is impossible for one person to get around to visiting them all, however worthy they may be. At some point I have visited almost all of those represented, and I think I have met them all and obviously tasted their wines. Those noted under "Finest Wines" are, in keeping with the definition used for this series, those that I think are most worth writing about, be it for their absolute quality, some other intrinsic interest, or value.

I will no doubt be taken to task for including certain producers I represent commercially or have done at some point in a longish career as a buyer, retailer, importer, and broker of Italian wine. But I decline to apologize for this since, as I have said elsewhere, the writing side of my life has been helped immeasurably by the opportunities afforded by commercial activities, just as the commercial side has been a great enabler of and motivator for research. So yes, my people, past, present, and future, are in here, if only because, by definition, I believe in them—or I wouldn't be dealing with them. But as I say, I have tried—as I always try, no doubt not entirely successfully—to be as objective as possible with my writer's hat on.

So, *salute!* Or should I say, *buon appetito*?

To Will, Gabe, and Sacha: tomorrow's team

SENÇA PAVRA OGNVOM FRANCO CAMINI·
ELAVORADO SEMINI CIASCVNO·
MENTRE CHE TAL COMVNO·
MANTERRA QVESTA DONNA ISIGNORIA·
CHEL ALEVATA AREI OGNI BALIA·

Renaissances in the Land of Vines

When I first started taking an interest in Italian wines, in the mid-1970s, it seemed unthinkable to some that the word "fine," let alone "finest," might ever be applied to these overproduced, underripe, inconsistent, oxidized, occasionally acetic, and in various other ways faulty products. For most (but not all) of these wines, the only purpose in life was to be piled high and sold cheap, or to accompany mediocre food in second-rate Italian restaurants scattered across the globe in the wake of the Italian diaspora.

Although it seems obvious in retrospect, very little awareness seemed to exist in snobbish wine circles (and there were, and are, some very snobbish ones indeed) that, while Italy may not be firing on all its vinous cylinders at the moment, there had been an age, if not several ages, of Italian wine glory. During those times, among other things, the Italians—once better known as Romans—were teaching the French, Germans, Spanish, and Portuguese a thing or two about wine.

One has only to consider the history, the geography, the passion, and the artistic perfection of the country that the Ancient Greeks called *Enotria Tellus* (land of vines) to realize that Italy, even when she may have slipped into the very pits, has at least the potential to rise again to greatness and take on the world, including the greatest wine snobs of them all: the producers of Bordeaux classed growths and the leaders of the Champagne houses, together with their British counterparts. It was these Bordelais and Champenois that I was fleeing when I decided to make a specialty of Italian wines, while seeking to join the British wine establishment, in order—in the subversive tradition of my family—to undermine it from within.

But that is another story. What I want to chronicle briefly here is the story of Italian wine—in particular, central Italian wine—warts and all, with

Left: Carefully tended vineyards feature prominently in Ambrogio Lorenzetti's *Allegory of Good Government* (c.1348)

a view to demonstrating why the contempt of the wine snobs of the '70s, while justified on the surface, was fundamentally misplaced.

From religious ritual to noble viticulture

In the seminal work on Italian grape varieties, *Dei Vitigni Italici*, Professor Antonio Calò tells us that "the vine arrived in the Italian peninsula, probably brought by the Etruscans, before the 9th century BC."[1] The Etruscans, suggests the professor, were probably Phoenicians (though the identification is contested by other scholars), who had learned the art of fermenting grapes in order to produce a rare beverage used in religious rituals. Archeologists have found wine-related pottery on the island of Elba, off the Tuscan coast, from the Phoenician age. Since that time, unlike places farther east, which came under Islamic and hence prohibitionist rule from the 7th century on, wine and the vine have been essential to the civilization of the peoples of central Italy, enhancing the quality of everyday life and playing a role in the mysteries, through Etruscan, Roman, and Christian times, in an uninterrupted line right up to the present age.

There is clear evidence—in Columella, for example—that winemakers of the Roman era were aware of the importance of position, exposition, and grape variety in determining the character and quality of their product. After the fall of Rome, the rulers of Italy continued to take an interest in the esoteric side of wine, as is evidenced by the writings of the minister of the Lombard king Theodoricus, Cassiodorus (whose most famous contribution was a description of the making of Verona's famous Recioto, both red and white—a description that mirrors closely the vinicultural methods employed today). In the so-called Dark Ages, it was the monks who took fine wine under their wing, no doubt partially to comfort them for the lack of other essential pleasures of human existence. Following the monks' lead, there developed in the wealthy towns of central and northern Italy what Calò terms a "bourgeois viticulture," followed in its turn by what might be called a "noble viticulture" of the castle-dwellers. Of course, the vast majority of wine was made by peasants, for accompanying the meal and in preference to water of dubious hygiene, but that did not deter the wealthy from seeking to produce wines that would stand out from the herd for their quality.

Renaissance testimony

Perhaps the first wine pundit was one Pier de' Crescenzi, who in 1303 published *Ruralium Commodorum*, in which he identified certain grape varieties that are still in cultivation today, such as Albana and Tribanum (Trebbiano). According to Calò, while the intellectual understanding of fine wine grew during the next three centuries, as is evidenced by various publications, at the production level there was a reduction of effort to make wines of quality, especially as wine came to be used like money for the payment of land rent and even calorific sustenance. Of course, it is difficult for us to be sure about this, since unlike the amazing artistic

treasures that survive in abundance from this period, we have no direct evidence concerning wine quality and are obliged to glean what we can from the extant literature referring to the organoleptic aspect of wine, of which there is precious little.

Indeed it would be a little surprising if, during a period such as the Florentine Renaissance, when artistic receptivity was at a historic high, people of means (of which there were plenty) should not have taken care to provide themselves with the finest possible ingredients for their meals. We do know, for example, that the great 15th-century philosopher Marsilio Ficino insisted on quality wine for his table—and probably for the discussion sessions among cultured friends, sometimes referred to as the convivium. A century after Ficino's death in 1499, Andrea Bacci published his *De Naturali Vinorum Historia*, in which he gave the names of several dozen top wines of various regions, even identifying certain quality grape varieties of the south, such as *i Greci, le Vernacce, gli Aglianici...* Bacci quoted a 15th-century contemporary of Ficino, the Florentine author Cristoforo Landino, who in his commentary on Dante's *Divina Commedia* asserted that the Valley of Chianti "has always been a most fertile source of excellent wine." And Bacci himself describes the wines of Florence and the Valley of Chianti as follows: "Every place appears splendid and worthy of admiration for the accurate manner in which the fields and vines are cultivated." There are wines of every sort, he says, and he praises particularly "the splendid reds of the hills of San Cassiano." Bacci also speaks highly of "the vineyards of Montepulciano, from which are derived the most select wines, robust, and having a lively red color." These wines were, it seems, often sent to the potentates in Rome (mostly at the Vatican) "in the hope they will take account of this gift." Indeed, another wine voice of this epoch was Sante Lancerio, *bottigliere* (wine

Above: Lorenzo the Magnificent de' Medici (1449-1492), at whose Florentine court worked Michelangelo and Leonardo da Vinci
Right: Much of the Tuscan landscape, as here below Montepulciano, has changed little since Renaissance times

Above: Pope Paul III, who was convinced of the superiority of Tuscan wine, depicted here with his two grandsons; Titian, 1546

steward) to the Pope, who reported Paul III (1534–49) as dismissing French wines by saying they may be good for raising French spirits, "but in Rome they are not gentlemen's wines."

The 18th and 19th centuries: quality to quantity
The first quality denominations for Tuscan wines—possibly for any wines in the world—were cited in a decree issued in 1716 by Grand Duke Cosimo III de' Medici, in which four delimited geographical production zones were recognized as having the exclusive right to use their respective names: Carmignano, Pomino, Chianti, and Valdarno. Shortly before this, Bartolomeo Bimbi had tacitly recognized the importance of biodiversity in his paintings (today hanging in the Galeria Palatina in Florence) of a broad selection of grape varieties currently identifiable in Tuscan vineyards. Similar paintings, of various fruits, including peaches and lemons as well as grapes, hang in the Medici villa at Poggio a Caiano.

That Tuscan wines were thought good enough for export was evidenced by two papers delivered during the 18th century at Florence's Accademia dei Georgofili; one, by Ubaldo Montelatici, on foreign trade and how to increase it and ensure further successes; the other, by Adamo Fabbroni, on the conservation of wine in the context of export.

The final years of the 18th century saw a growth of wine academies in various parts of Italy, empowering a surge of mainly viticultural research in the 19th century. A simultaneous popularization and vulgarization of wine was partly to blame for qualitative decline, however, and while the English were raising their game in respect of transporting French, Portuguese, and Spanish wines from Mediterranean coasts and islands (including Marsala from Sicily), Italian table wines became less attractive to producers as an export proposition, having mainly low-priced local bulk markets to satisfy. As early as 1773 a Tuscan scholar and physician called Villafranchi complained that growers had fallen into the error of "caring more for quantity than quality." Another commentator, Francesco Lawley, noted: "[The peasants] grow those varieties that give greater quantities of grapes, ignoring those that produce little but that are the only ones that would give high quality to wine."

But the number of grape varieties present in Tuscan vineyards did not diminish significantly. It was estimated in the 19th century that as many as 150 varieties existed in vineyards in the province of Florence alone; and even today, in certain places, many examples can still be found bearing significant individual characteristics—if, indeed, they are not different varieties altogether. Research into these varieties is hotting up in the various relevant institutions, and some interesting results are emerging or can be expected to emerge (about which, more later).

Above: Grand Duke Cosimo III de' Medici, whose decree of 1716 identified four quality wine zones, including Chianti

Phylloxera and *cultura promiscua*

It is becoming a bit tedious, perhaps, every time one writes an introduction to modern Italian viniculture, to have to harp on about the hard times of the late 19th century and the first two thirds of the 20th; but, for the sake of completeness, it cannot be avoided.

So, toward the end of the 1800s, Italian wines were struck by a triple disaster: oidium, peronospera, and phylloxera—all conditions harmful to *Vitis vinifera*, and all imported in one way or another from outside of Europe, adding to the problems (from insects, parasites, animals, and bad weather) that already existed. The first two are fungal disorders, capable of devastating entire vineyards; the third—as is generally known today—is a root-chewing aphid powerful enough to kill every vine in Europe, just as the Dutch elm beetle more recently wiped out virtually all of Europe's elms. Those who had established a market for quality wines (the French, Portuguese, Spanish, and Germans, largely, as we have seen, thanks to the British) managed to weather the storm, finding sprays and grafting processes able to stem the deadly tide. But those who were already vulnerable tended to sink into a slough of despondency, and this is pretty much what happened to Italian wine in the 20th century, right up until the 1960s and '70s.

Moreover, the Italian economy was in a pretty dire state, not helped by involvement in a couple of world wars, following the second of which inflation was rampant. In such conditions, there was not much of a home market for finer products and therefore little basis for an export market.

But perhaps the most telling constraint on fine-wine production was the agronomic system that prevailed in Italy right up to the 1960s: *mezzadria*, or sharecropping. Until this system was abolished in the 1950s (though it survived well beyond this time), it entailed handing over a percentage of a smallholder's production to the landowner in lieu of rent. And since wine was a sellable commodity, a significant proportion of what was paid was in vinous form, or at least in the form of grapes.

In these circumstances, the smallholder would in most cases, if not all, practice subsistence farming, whereby the majority of what remained to him was needed for the upkeep of his family rather than for resale. And it all had to happen in a hectare or two (roughly 2.5–5 acres), so that specialized viticulture was out of the question. The name of the game, much to anglophones' amusement, was *coltura promiscua* ("promiscuous cultivation"). Until the 1970s, the "only areas where a specialized viticulture was practiced were the hills near Faenza [in Romagna], the upper Chianti zone, and the Montalcino area."[2]

It is probably impossible to give an exhaustive list of the crops that were planted in these limited spaces, but they included various fruits (apples, pears, cherries, olives, of course), vegetables (tomatoes, beans of various sorts, leaf vegetables, artichokes, onions, garlic), herbs, pulses, and importantly, grains such as wheat, maize, and barley, some of which served as fodder for such animals as chickens, guinea fowls, ducks and geese, pigeons, rabbits and hares, pigs, and even—where pasture land was available—sheep, goats, and cows. Not to mention the inevitable hunting dogs and rodent-controlling cats.

As for the vines, they were—and, in not a few cases, still are today—supported on vertical posts, mostly in the form of trees. This was an ancient system of training derived from the Etruscans (indeed, it is known as the "Etruscan model"), who for their part had not limited their choice of support to stunted poplars of the sort you can still see today but let the vines run up trees, with numerous ramifications perhaps dozens of feet long, bearing large numbers of fruiting nodes all on the same plant. In these circumstances, with a limited number of vines per hectare (vines tended to be planted very close together within rows, with large distances between rows to accommodate the alternative plantings) and each vine expected to compete for soil nutrition with various other crops and to bear multiple kilograms of fruit, it was not easy to avoid the austere and unripe characters that could only be compensated for by prolonged aging in large, old barrels (often of local chestnut, rather than imported oak). This, of course, led to oxidation at best; acetification, or "rotten stave," at worst. It was not easy to get a wine that anyone but a self-sufficient producer and his family were willing to drink, let alone to pay for.

Slow recovery from *fiasco*

Recovery from the deeply ingrained habits of the *mezzadria* system was not rapid. The majority of landowners, in repossession of their lands, which they might not have set foot in for generations, turned to specialist viticulture to exploit their resources. However, they had little, if any, clue as to what to do next other than to call in an agronomist and an enologist, or a combination of the two—provided they had the money. Even so, they had little choice but to plant the volume-producing clones that the nurseries wished to peddle them, partly because quality clones were little understood at that time, and partly because the nurseries were, or thought they were, merely following the market.

Another option was massal selection—taking the observably best material from their own vineyards and using cuttings. But this solution, often a very good one, required a lot of time and patience, first to identify the best material, then to graft it on to phylloxera-resistant America rootstock and wait for it to produce a valid crop.

In any case, the market was generally unwilling to pay for superior quality, so a certain volume of production was necessary to retain viability. The typical Tuscan red, even white, of the mid-20th century was sold at low prices in the picturesque wicker flask (*fiasco*) that once gave the world so many rustic lamps. True, the best wines were marketed in Bordeaux-shaped bottles, often an unattractive brown in color, but at the other end of the spectrum, most sales to local consumers were *sfuso* (bulk)—in *bottiglione* (extra-large bottle), *damigiano* (demijohn), or even *fusto* (cask). This crisis in the enological sector lasted right through into the 1980s.[3]

It was a combination of factors that ushered in the steady rise of Italian wine quality, which has been on a mainly upward curve now for several decades.

Right: Under *mezzadria*, olives and other crops were cultivated alongside vines, resulting in dark times for Tuscan wine

VENDITA VINO e OLIO
WINE AND OIL FOR SALE
WEIN UND ÖL ZU VERKAUFEN

VINO OLIO
GENERI
ALIMENTARI

ENOTECA

CANTINA

BALSAMERIA

KEYS ARE AVAILABLE ... OTECA. THANK YOU.

The abolition of *mezzadria* and the introduction of specialized viticulture were certainly influential, but so was the establishment, in 1963, of the Italian wine law, with its French-inspired DOC (*denominazione di origine controllata*) system for the control and delimitation of production in particular locations. Other elements of the great leap forward included a massive improvement in the technique of winemaking and of the technical equipment involved. Giant steps were also made in the development of fruit quality, which is obviously at the heart of wine quality (*see chapters 4 and 5*).

Perhaps the most famous and influential of all changes has been in the psychology of the people growing the grapes and making the wine. From being almost ashamed of their product half a century ago, Italians have come to take pride in their work and to believe in their destiny as the premier wine-producing nation on earth.

Gastronomic culture and globalization

Good or bad, wine has always played a central role in the gastronomic culture of the people of central Italy. Until very recently, a meal without wine was unthinkable. (Breakfast is not a meal; it is a punishment for waking up. But if you can make it to midday, you will find the time spent in Purgatory was worth it.) Wine was like bread—a "must-serve." On the other hand, the taking of dry table wine outside mealtime was, and is, almost unthinkable, unlike in countries of the north, where alcohol is primarily consumed on its own, or at most with a snack. And Italian people tend to like wines that harmonize with food (which they take *very* seriously) rather than those that take over from food. They call this latter type *impegnativo* ("demanding") and reserve them for special occasions. Your typical central Italian peasant will not necessarily enjoy a Robert Parker 95-pointer; 85 will do him nicely. Wine, traditionally

Left: Fine-wine production may have become more specialized, but consumption still has an integral link with food

in these parts, is nothing precious—it is an everyday commodity. The aristocracy may not agree, but even they will tend to favor simpler wines when there are no guests to impress. The aristos, though, even if they do wield a disproportionate amount of influence, are numerically in a small minority.

So the great leap forward, in a sense, was aimed at export markets rather than at native Italians themselves. In these days of globalization, this is not a problem, and producers can express themselves at much higher levels of alcohol and extract—and price—than they would were they catering mainly for a local audience. It is this upper sector of the market, of course, for whom this book is written. But one should never forget that the essence of wine, for an Italian, is in the bottle that he places on his table, not what he admires for winning *tre bicchieri*.

Notes

1. Antonio Calò and Angelo Costacurta, *Dei Vitigni Italici* (Matteo Editore, Treviso; 2004).

2. A Pecile, G Tempesta, and F Burroni, "An analysis of the genetic evolution of the Sangiovese population based on availability from nurseries from 1970 until today," in ARSIA II, *Il Sangiovese vitigno tipico e internazionale: identità e peculiarità* (Agenzia Regionale per lo Sviluppo e l'Innovazione nel settore Agricolo-Forestale, Florence; 2006).

3. In the words of Ginevra Venerosi Pesciolini of Tenuta di Ghizzano: "In the 1980s, the agriculture, but above all the viticulture, of our territory was in a state of deep crisis. Overproduction of grapes led to inertia in respect of obtaining quality wine. Prices were derisory even if justified, and did not even cover costs. Many of our neighbors grubbed up their vines, and some ended up selling their estate. It was then that my father Pierfrancesco decided to swim against the stream and to invest in the vineyard and the winery in order to try and make a quality leap."

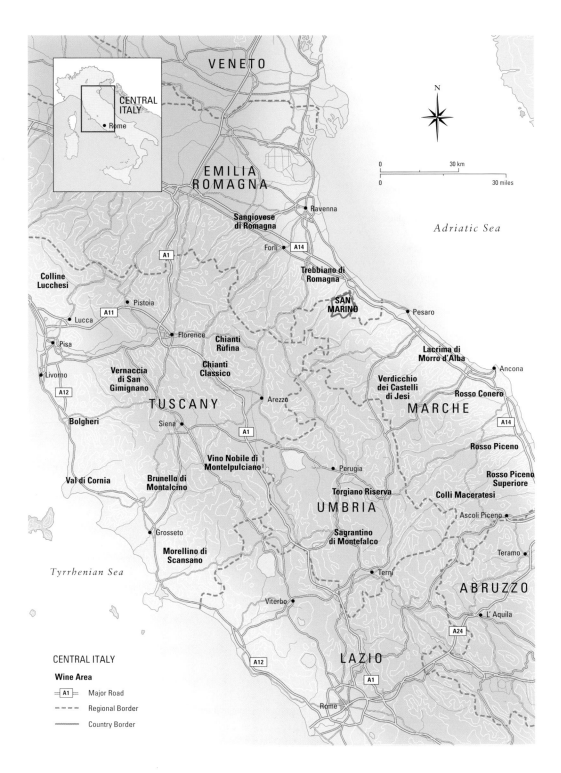

Terroir in the Sangiovese Belt

For the purposes of this book, we have defined Central Italy as consisting of the regions of Tuscany, Umbria, and Le Marche, plus the southern/mountainous part of Romagna, which is the eastern part of the region of Emilia-Romagna. We could have included Lazio and Abruzzo, but we felt that to do so would take the focus off what is arguably the most important element in the wines of this area—the Sangiovese grape variety, about which much will be said and to which many references will be made in later pages. Indeed, the book might have been titled *The Finest Wines of the Sangiovese Belt*.

Our zone, as the word "central" suggests, lies more or less in the middle of the country, between the German-speaking north of Italy, Alto Adige, and the more Arab-influenced deep south, as represented by Sicily (the southern tip of which is indeed south of the northern tip of Africa). It lies roughly on a latitude with such prized wine-producing zones, to the west, as southern France (Languedoc and Roussillon); northern Spain (Rioja and Galicia); northern New York (Finger Lakes); southern Ontario (think icewine); and Oregon (Pinot country); and, to the east, the Dalmatian coast, northern Bulgaria, southern Romania, and Georgia. A brief comparison of the very different styles of wine being produced in these various areas confirms, if confirmation were needed, that latitude is only one of a number of factors in the makeup of that complex concept, terroir.

Geographical and geological factors that must be taken into account in this context include altitude, exposure, soil composition (drainage and nutrients), and the proximity of bodies of water or weather-altering features such as mountains. And these, of course, are linked with climate and macroclimate. Actually, all these factors and more are summed up in the final wine—and more so in wines that, without

eschewing nurture, rely more for their character or "quality" on nature (as distinct from some of the rather contrived or formulaic wines increasingly on offer today). These, the wines of terroir, are what are under consideration in the present book.

Climate: Mediterranean meets continental

In broad terms, the zone we are looking at enjoys a Mediterranean climate—the sea, whether Tyrrhenian or Adriatic, being never very far away, except toward the Apennine ridge in eastern Tuscany and in landlocked Umbria, where the climate is more continental. A grape like Sangiovese will perform best where Mediterranean meets continental. In warmer climes, such as the Maremma, it can be quite jammy and flabby; in colder ones, as around Montepulciano, it can be irredeemably tough and astringent.

The perfect year will bring plentiful snow to the Apennine peaks and a good sprinkling of rain in winter to build up the underground water table without flooding. It can get very cold in Florence in winter, trust me—a lot colder sometimes than in London. Spring will be mild to allow the buds to develop steadily, without bursting out and rendering themselves vulnerable to late frosts. These constitute a threat until well into April and can destroy a crop before it gets going, as it did in places in the highly touted year of 1997. One positive effect of climate change is that frost damage occurs less and less frequently—and anyway, growers are increasingly alert to the dangers of planting vulnerable varieties in high-risk places. A negative effect is the steady reduction of snow on the high slopes.

Flowering will happen in late May or early June, depending on the weather and the variety. From this time on, summer heat will take over, and the two main hopes are, first, that it will rain from time to time, but not too torrentially, to keep the plant from desiccation; and second, that the heat will not be so intense as to stop the plants from photosynthesizing.

Left: *In media res*. The diverse regions of central Italy have in common the country's most widely planted grape variety

The *invaiatura* (change of color) of the red grapes has historically been a haphazard affair, even within a particular, if notoriously inconsistent, variety such as Sangiovese. Much depends on clones, production levels, and sites. But ideally it should have finished by mid-August. Climate change is tending to bring it forward, and work on clones and viticultural practices has reduced the time span over which the color turn takes place.

September is the crucial month, and the grower hopes for warm, sunny days and cool nights. These shifts in temperature render the grapes more aromatically complex and give them a greater chance of balancing their sugar content—which these days tends to be excessively high, as distinct from unsatisfactorily low 30 years ago—with their phenolic content, which tends to happen later, by which time the grapes' sugars may be too high and the acids too low. Brief rainfall is acceptable (in our perfect year), and it may even be beneficial for purposes of freshening things up, but it must not endure for days, because this is the time when botrytis may attack the more vulnerable, riper, thinner-skinned grapes and, in poor conditions, run wild through a vineyard.

Needless to say, freaks of weather—such as hailstorms, which can devastate one vineyard while leaving its neighbor untouched, or tornadoes, such as occurred in Rùfina for the first time in 2002 (I nearly got killed)—have no part in our perfect year. Alas, with climate change, such freaks are becoming more common, while the average temperature gradually increases decade by decade, presumably until such time as the native grapes will have to be replaced by other more heat-resistant varieties.

The harvest, of course, should take place in warm but not hot sunshine, so that the grapes keep cool on their way to the winery, and should be over by mid-October. This is not only for the fruit's sake but also for that of the pickers. Happy pickers are efficient pickers.

Altitude: Bacchus loves the hills

Altitude is a great compensator for latitude. At a given latitude, you can have plantings from sea level to more than 3,300ft (1,000m) or anywhere in between, and the natural timescale for the vine's numerous transformations will vary enormously. To take an example from another zone entirely—Mount Etna, in Sicily—some of the finest, most delicate, Burgundy-like reds of Italy today are being made at 2,600–3,300ft (800–1,000m), from Nerello Mascalese grapes, whereas down in the plain, the reds of Nero d'Avola come as black as tar and half as thick. In the present case, there are mountains in all four of our regions—Apennines and others—rising to well over 6,500ft (2,000m). Sangiovese succeeds from around a minimum of 650ft (200m) up to around 1,650ft (500m). White wines can work at up to 2,300ft (700m). Some of Bolgheri's most prestigious vineyards, for example (Sassicaia in part, Ornellaia, Cà Marcanda, Le Macchiole, and Guado al Tasso), are near sea level. Some of Chianti Classico's finest estates—Castello di Volpaia, Castello di Ama, Collelungo—are 1,300–1,650ft (400–500m) high. But all the star-studded wines of Bolgheri are from Bordeaux grapes, while Sangiovese at this altitude rarely rises above the mediocre.

Exposure: south by southwest

Altitude goes hand in hand with exposure as an influence on fruit quality, and there are two considerations here. First, clearly, is the angle of the vineyard in relation to the sun's rays. The ideal, for a variety, like Sangiovese, that needs plenty of light is a south-facing slope that exposes the vineyard to the sun from dawn to dusk. Southwest or southeast are the next-best options, but the sun's rays will not be quite so direct. The degree of the incline of the hill also plays a part: The steeper the incline, the

Left: Sangiovese benefits greatly from sunlight, so south- or southwest-facing vineyards help ensure maximum exposure

more direct the exposure. Second, an open hilltop with no windbreaks will help keep fungal problems and insects at bay, thanks to the constant breeze; and of course, such sites will recover first from any drenching. But this is just plain common sense. Central Italy—being largely hilly, except where it is mountainous or where there is a river running through—has a multitude of sites suitable for high-class viticulture. The wonder is, how in the past did they manage to situate so many vineyards so badly?

Soil: *galestro* and *albarese*

To go through all the soil types that exist in wine-growing sectors of our area would be tedious, and

Above: The rolling hills that dominate the landscape afford propitious sites that rise above the fog and mist

in any case this is not a geological tract. Suffice it to remind readers that there are two considerations in respect of soil: drainage and chemical composition. Drainage refers to the ability of the soil to retain water or otherwise. In the ideal scenario there will be sufficient porosity in the soil to avoid excessive soaking of the vine's feet, but not so much that all the water filters away, leaving nothing for the vine's roots to sip in a dry summer. Generally speaking, soils will be a mix of types, probably in layers, and the important thing is that the plant's roots should be able to penetrate deep, to be able to withstand extremes of temperature and lack of water, as well as to bring up to the grapes a mix of nutrients from the various levels. Such penetration is obviously impossible where there is solid rock too near the surface, or thick clay.

Specifically with regard to Sangiovese, the ideal soil will be limestone-based, with a balanced content of clay and schist, perhaps a bit of sand (but not too much), and not too low a pH, so not too acidic. The most widespread soil type of central Tuscany is called *galestro*, a schistous, crumbly rock type combining elements of clay and marl. This is particularly predominant, but far from ubiquitous, in Chianti Classico, which is one of the factors that unites this large and diverse growing zone, though *galestro* is also found elsewhere—for example, in Rùfina and Montalcino. Another soil type frequently found in Tuscany and Umbria is called *albarese*, a calcareous soil that comes in a more granular or more solid form (some mighty boulders have been extracted from vineyards being prepared for planting). In Bolgheri, that little Bordeaux, the best soils consist of layers of sand, clay, and gravel.

As for chemical composition, these days any grower worth his salt will have a chemical soil analysis done for any prospective vineyard. This will inform him as to whether the site is suitable for this grape or that—whether, for example, the soil is predominantly acidic or alkaline—and give him pointers as to what nourishment he should provide (chemically or organically) and what rootstock he should employ. Too many vineyards in the past, as already indicated, were planted in unsuitable sites (one of the major reasons why Sangiovese has performed so erratically), and the process of identifying promising sites will continue for some decades. This is known by Italian agronomists as *zonazione*—the identification and possible classification of the most suitable zones for growing a given grape. For its part, Sangiovese, according to Professor Mario Fregoni of the University

of Piacenza, can never be of high quality when grown in a soil that warms up quickly. This is why, he says, it can never be great from the Maremma; nor, for that matter, from California or Australia. But he reckons New Zealand could still succeed with the Tuscan prodigy.

Mountains: Apennines and Monte Amiata

We have mentioned them in relation to altitude, but mountains can also offer protection from extremes of weather or simply act as rainmakers. An example of the first is the Apennine ridge running west to east along the northern border of Tuscany, cutting off the worst of the *tramontana*, the cold wind that blows across from the north in the direction of Emilia-Romagna. But the Apennines are not the only mountains of central Italy. A major one-off is mysterious Monte Amiata, in the south of Tuscany, which helps, by attracting much precipitation, to keep Montalcino the driest part of the region—one secret of Montalcino's meteoric success.

Bodies of water: lakes, rivers, and seas

The proximity of bodies of water is well known to act as a mitigating factor of climate. In Tuscany, as already mentioned, the most important example is the Tyrrhenian Sea (as the Mediterranean to the west of Italy is known). Indeed, the Maremma (the Tuscan coast) enjoys remarkably mild winters compared with inland Tuscany and has even been compared, weather-wise, with California, which is much farther south in latitude. Inland, the River Arno and, in Umbria, the Tiber, act as regulators. Umbria may be a long way from the sea, but it also has three important lakes in Trasimeno, Bolsena, and Corbara. On the northeastern side of the Apennines, there is the Adriatic (as the Mediterranean to the east of Italy is known).

Right: The physical structure of the soils can vary widely, even within a single estate, as here at Caiarossa in the Maremma

By the Blood of Jove

Of the various quality factors in wine, most would agree that the most important is the grape variety. Certainly there is no doubt as to which grape is the most significant in central Italy. Some say it is ancient, emerging from the primeval forests of Tuscany (or Romagna?) thousands of years ago, since when it has been the rock upon which the major wines of central Italy have stood. Others claim it goes back no more than four centuries and was still of minor importance only 300 years ago, being a relatively recent cross between a Tuscan variety and one from southern Italy. Some, while admitting its tendency to alter in character according to terroir, say it has retained its fundamental DNA structure throughout. Wine journalist and researcher Luca Mazzoleni maintains that, while this is broadly true, it is merely a "population of grapes, rather than a consistent and homogeneous variety of *Vitis vinifera.*" Some criticize it as being hopelessly inconsistent from year to year, vineyard to vineyard, plant to plant, even berry to berry, with a "vast and disconcerting morphologic/phenotypic variability [that] inevitably results in varietal wines featuring notably diverse organoleptic traits" (Mazzoleni again). Others swear that, planted in the right place, with the right training and the right vine material, it can be quite reliable. Some say it gives wines relatively light in color, and that such color as it does have turns to orange early on. Others maintain that it is perfectly capable, in the right conditions, of a hue deep enough to satisfy even the most color sensitive of modern critics. Some say it gives wine capable of lasting a century. Others say it rarely improves beyond a decade. Some say it is the greatest grape of Italy, one that deserves membership of the exclusive brotherhood of world-class varieties that includes Cabernet Sauvignon, Merlot, Pinot Noir, and Nebbiolo. Others dismiss it as nothing special, capable of good table wines, never great.

"It," of course, is Sangiovese, and whatever else it may have been or may be now, today it is undoubtedly Italy's premier grape variety—certainly in terms of area (over 70,000ha [173,000 acres], or around 10 percent of total plantings in Italy) and ubiquity, being present in at least 16 of the 20 regions and playing an obligatory role in some 90 DOC(G)s (quality wine zones; *see pp.54–55*).

While other grape types prevail in other parts of Italy—Nebbiolo, Barbera, Dolcetto, and Freisa, among others, in Piemonte, for example—Sangiovese is totally dominant in central Italy, being the main grape in more than 25 DOCs of Tuscany, where it covers around 40,000ha (99,000 acres), or some two thirds of the total vineyard space. It is almost the only black grape in Romagna (approximately 6,000ha [15,000 acres]); easily the most popular variety in Umbria; and at the forefront quantity-wise, if not quality-wise, in Marche. It is also, with Barbera, the most planted grape abroad, in places like California, Australia, South Africa, Argentina, and even France (in Corsica).

Origins and synonyms

Most, not all, commentators agree that the first mention of Sangiovese in ampelographic literature came in 1590, in Gianvettorio Soderini's *Trattato sulla Coltivazione delle Viti*. He called it "Sangiogheto," describing it (according to Professor Calò) as a vine "juicy and chock full of wine," and "a vine that never fails." Skeptics might find this an odd thing to say about a vine that, in its modern form (or forms), fails all too frequently. Later mentions include one by D Falchini, who referred to "Sanvicetro" in 1720 (Calò, Costacurta, et al have shown that the grape today known as Sanvicetro is most frequently a different cultivar, though Sanvicetro may also be, and may well have been, a synonym for Sangiovese); by Cosimo Trinci, who in 1726 wrote of "San

Right: The calm appearance of the illustrated grape masks the mystery still surrounding Sangiovese's origins and potential

A. Kreÿder

Imp. F. CHAMPENOIS, Paris.

San Gioveto

Zoveto" in his *Agricoltore Sperimentato*; and by Cosimo Villifranchi, who wrote of "S. Gioveto" in his *Oenologia Toscana*, after which the mentions became more frequent.

Speaking of synonyms, Sangiovese has a whole host of them. Sangiovese is the name you will come across in Romagna, but in Chianti Classico today you are as likely to come across Sangioveto as Sangiovese, except when you are in Montalcino, where they call it Brunello, or in Montepulciano, where it goes by the name Prugnolo Gentile, or in the Scansano zone of southern Maremma, where it is Morellino. Among many others, perhaps the most interesting is Calabrese. A few years ago, researchers at the Istituto Agrario di San Michele all'Adige in Trentino used DNA evidence to prove that an obscure variety called Calabrese di Montenuovo, found in Campania but believed to be of Calabrian origin, is one of the "parents" of Sangiovese, the other being the Tuscan Ciliegiolo. Jose Vouillamoz, one of the researchers, has hypothesized that this crossing took place spontaneously (being before the era of human intervention in grape crossings) sometime before the year 1700. He pooh-poohs the generally held opinion that Sangiovese is an "ancient" Tuscan variety on the grounds that there is no scientific proof of it. One would need to point out, however, that neither is there scientific proof that this crossing did *not* take place hundreds or thousands of years ago, given that next to nothing is known of Calabrese di Montenuovo and not a lot about Ciliegiolo.

Other synonyms include Cardisco, Ingannacane ("fools the dog," because he eats what he sees as a ripe grape and gets a mouthful of tannin and acid), Nerino, Nielluccio (in Corsica), Pignolo, Prunello, Uvetta—the list goes on.

There are several theories regarding the origin of the name Sangiovese. The most poetic is *sangue di Giove* ("blood of Jove"), but that may be a bit fanciful. Could it, perhaps, derive from San Giovanni (St John, the patron saint of grape growers), where

Giovanni is mixed with *giovane* (meaning "young") on account of Sangiovese being an early-budding variety? Or could it come from the Romagnan *sanzves*, meaning "yoke," in the same way that the variety called Schiava indicates enslavement (the plant being rigidly trained)? Since nothing is certain in this department, I will stick with Jove's blood.

Other major black varieties

Because Sangiovese is overwhelmingly dominant in central Italy—especially Tuscany—other black varieties play at best a minor role. Minor, perhaps, but the role is crucial nonetheless, Sangiovese always, until very recently anyway, having been used in blends with other varieties. We shall look at blends in subsequent chapters. For now we are concerned with the identity and significance of central Italy's lesser varieties.

Alicante Also known as Cannonau, but best known as Grenache, this grape is increasingly in demand in southern Tuscany as a blender with Morellino/Sangiovese. It is not to be confused with Alicante Bouschet, also found in these areas, which is a cross of Alicante with Tintoria x Aramon.

Canaiolo Nero The name—so we are informed in Calò, Costacurta, and Scienza's *Vitigni d'Italia*—probably derives from the Latin *dies caniculares*, the "canicular (very hot) days" between July 24 and August 24, when Canaiolo undergoes *invaiatura* (veraison). As early as the 14th century, "Canajuola" was praised by Pier de' Crescenzi as "a most beautiful grape, good for conserving," and Professor Mario Fregoni tells us that until around 1700 it was Tuscany's "principal grape variety," followed by "San Gioveto, Mammolo, Marzemino, Canaiolo Bianco, and Abrostine" (ARSIA II, 2006, p.23).

In the Ricasoli blend of the mid-19th century (*see chapters 4 and 5*), Canaiolo plays a necessary if secondary role to Sangiovese, and it remained the

Canaiolo Nero

of Spanish origin of fairly recent introduction; others (more credibly, assuming the DNA evidence to be correct) consider it to be of ancient Tuscan lineage. It is used today mainly in the southern section of Tuscany, in the province of Grosseto, and occasionally, as in the case of the San Lorenzo of Sassotondo, it is vinified *in purezza* (unblended).

Colorino If Canaiolo's star is on the wane, Colorino's is in the ascendant. It is said to be of ancient Tuscan lineage, but these days such claims are not always unshakable. Historically, indeed currently, it was used principally to add color to chronically light-hued, Sangiovese-based wines—hence the name. In this role it has experienced a recent surge of interest, as growers pull away from using Cabernet Sauvignon or Merlot for a similar purpose (*see chapters 4 and 5*).

Colorino is used increasingly widely in Chianti Classico and Vino Nobile, as well as in the DOCs of Lucca (Montecarlo and Colline Lucchesi) and, farther afield, in Umbria and Le Marche.

Lacrima di Morro d'Alba The name may suggest Naples (Lacrima) or Piemonte (Alba), but this lightly aromatic variety is actually found mainly today in the vineyards of a small commune in Le Marche called Morro d'Alba. The color is deep and purple, tannins are soft, and acidity is moderate, so the wine is normally destined for early drinking, perhaps lightly chilled. Emerging from almost total obscurity about ten years ago, Lacrima is steadily building a dedicated following.

Malvasia Nera This is a member of the extended, not necessarily closely related family of Malvasias, the name being a corruption of Monemvasia, a port in Greece's Peloponnese peninsula, from where the various Malvasia varieties, or at least wines, traveled to Italy (mainly Venice) from the 13th century on. Most Malvasias are white and neutral in aroma, but

most important blending grape for Chianti until the 1990s, when effectively, if not explicitly, it was overtaken by Cabernet and Merlot and reduced from mandatory to optional status in major Tuscan wines such as Chianti Classico.

Today, Canaiolo still plays a supporting role in a number of Tuscan and Umbrian wines, but it is too light for the modern market, so one almost never sees it in 100 percent varietal form, except occasionally in Romagna under the name Cagnina.

Wines in which Canaiolo may feature include, apart from Chianti Classico: Vino Nobile di Montepulciano, Rosso di Montepulciano, Carmignano, Montecarlo, and Torgiano.

Ciliegiolo DNA research carried out in the early years of the 21st century, at the Istituto Agrario di San Michele all'Adige in Trentino, has established not only that a "relationship of the first grade" does exist between this grape and Sangiovese, but that it is almost certainly one of Sangiovese's parents (the other being an obscure grape found in Campania called Calabrese di Montenuovo). Some say it is this semi-aromatic black version, more prevalent in Puglia than in Tuscany, is used by some in Chianti Classico and the province of Arezzo to lend a bit of spice and exotica to their otherwise unremarkable Sangiovese-based wines.

Mammolo This grape is said to be of Tuscan origin. First mentioned by the Florentine politician Gianvettorio Soderini in 1600, it has been used historically, as presently, in blends to give a bit of floral uplift to the nose, the word meaning "violet" in Italian. It may be found in a number of wines, usually at between five and ten percent, but its area of greatest influence today is Montepulciano.

Montepulciano This is one of the great black grapes of Italy, belonging more, however, to Abruzzo in the center south and to a lesser extent to Le Marche than to any of the other parts of our zone. Its origins are unknown, though it has been surmised with some justification that the name derives from the Tuscan town of Montepulciano, with which there used to be a lively trade across the Apennine ridge from the 14th century. In this context, it is important to underline that there is definitely no close relationship between the grape now called Montepulciano and that employed in the Nobile di Montepulciano in Tuscany (Sangiovese, locally known as Prugnolo Gentile). But that does not necessarily mean that it did not come from Tuscany, as has often been claimed in the past.

These days, a great deal of Montepulciano from Abruzzo is said to make its way into Tuscan wines, though no one will admit it. It is the ideal blender with Sangiovese, contributing depth of color and richness of extract to feeble Tuscan brews, without taking over aromatically in the manner of Cabernet, Merlot, or Syrah. Why then, one might wonder, do the Tuscans not plant it and incorporate it officially into their *uvaggi* (grape mixes)? As you can imagine, it has been tried, but for some reason (presumably

because Montepulciano requires that bit more warmth), it has never really succeeded. So the illicit trade continues, to no one's desperate regret.

Sagrantino Outside Tuscany, but well within central Italy, are two outstanding grape varieties: Montepulciano and Sagrantino. The latter's growing area has, until very recently, been limited to the surrounds of the small town in Umbria called Montefalco. Its origins are not well known, nor is the etymology of its name, but what is certain is that it was facing possible extinction as recently as 30 years ago. Before the late 1970s, it had never been cultivated as a varietal grape but was represented in *uvaggi di vigneto* (vineyard grape mixes) as a blender, whose purpose was to add color and tannin to thin, overproduced Sangioveses.

Today it is increasingly produced *in purezza* as Sagrantino di Montefalco DOCG, dry or *passito* (from semi-dried grapes, sweet and rich and massively tannic), this latter being the form it took prior to rediscovery. This may account for the name, which suggests use in a "sacred" context. It is also blended with Sangiovese in Rosso di Montefalco DOC (maximum 15 percent). Perhaps it should be used more widely in central Italy for blending purposes, because it is a very noble variety, a little of which goes a long way. But that would entail the changing of various regulations—something both Montefalcans and Tuscans might, for different reasons, be reluctant to undertake.

Lesser black varieties
Abrostine is a Tuscan variety being researched (as are Abrusco, Foglia Tonda, and Pugnitello) by academics of the University of Florence at the experimental vineyard of San Felice and elsewhere.

Abrusco, a deep-colored member of the Lambrusco family, has been in Tuscan vineyards at least since the time of Soderini, who mentioned it in 1622.

Above: Of the many international grape varieties now making their presence felt, Cabernet Sauvignon is the most influential

Aleatico is a Muscat-like variety found mainly in Puglia and Lazio but also, to a small extent, in Tuscany's southern Maremma and on the island of Elba. Probably introduced by the Greeks, it goes mainly into the making of aromatic sweet wines.

Ancellotta is an anthocyanin-rich variety used in Romagna and Tuscany to deepen the color of Sangiovese-based blends.

Bursona Longanesi is similar to Ancellotta but is used only, as far as I know, in Romagna.

Colombana Nera is used in the blend of the wine

Colli di Luna from the northwestern extreme of Tuscany, where it borders on Liguria.

Foglia Tonda, from more southern parts of Tuscany, is a sturdy grape now making something of a comeback from obscurity in the province of Siena.

Pugnitello is a Tuscan grape of good color and fruit character. It is non-aggressive and therefore suitable for blending with Sangiovese.

Vernaccia Nera has two very modest claims to fame. First, it is the grape of the generally unremarkable red sparkler called Vernaccia di Serrapetrona, in Le Marche. Second, it is mercifully totally unrelated to Vernaccia di San Gimignano.

Major white varieties

In Tuscany, red wines are far more important than white, especially if you exclude the sweet Vin Santo. This cannot be said of the other three zones we are looking at, each of which boasts a particularly successful white grape. Such being the case, we will begin with the others.

Albana Possibly of Roman origin, this undoubtedly Romagnan variety was first mentioned by Pier de' Crescenzi of Bologna in 1303. It can make wines sweet or dry, but the dry versions tend to suffer a bit from anonymity. The sweeties, on the other hand, can be glorious, whether from grapes dried off the vine (as traditionally) or on. Zerbina's Scacco Matto ("checkmate") is the finest example.

Grechetto The Greco "family" is fraught with confusion. In DNA terms, one version (say Greco di Tufo) may have nothing to do with another (Grechetto), but going by the name, they may both (all?) be assumed to be of Greek origin. Umbria's Grechetto is mainly used as one of the ingredients, indeed the principal ingredient, of the *uvaggio* *di vigneto* (vineyard grape mix) that is Orvieto, conferring aroma and finesse. It does, however, stand increasingly often on its own and can reach considerable heights of quality, ranging in style from crisp and light to full and slightly scented. In Tuscany, it is usually called Pulcinculo ("flea in the bottom"), because of a tiny black dot it has on its nether regions.

Malvasia del Chianti This grape has accompanied Trebbiano Toscano in Tuscan vineyards for centuries and, like Trebbiano, was part of the Chianti blend as proposed by Baron Bettino Ricasoli in the mid-19th century. Like Trebbiano, it is no longer obligatorily used in Chianti, though it continues to play a minor role in several minor Tuscan and Umbrian DOCs (such as Orvieto). Overcropped, as it has traditionally been, it offers little in the way of aroma, but with careful management it can supply a wine with a hint of perfume and, as such, is capable of enhancing a dry white wine and, in particular, a Vin Santo.

Trebbiano Toscano By far the most common white variety in Tuscany is this one—though unlike Sangiovese, it is losing ground quickly as growers field-graft it out, in favor of more interesting varieties. Its main historical purpose was to furnish large volumes of indifferent white plonk, middling volumes of blending wine (for a long time, though no longer, it was an obligatory part of the Chianti DOC), and small volumes of dried grapes for the making of Vin Santo, of which it has been—and remains—the main grape, together with Malvasia Bianca and Sangiovese. The most prolific member of a broad family, the Tuscan Trebbiano also passes by the name of Procanico in Umbria, Passerina in Le Marche, Ugni Blanc in southern France, and a host of other monikers. Its one plus point is firm acidity, which helps make Vin Santo of a lively style. Unfortunately, it is almost entirely lacking in flavor.

Verdicchio Le Marche's pride and joy is a member of the otherwise inglorious Trebbiano family, and it has been shown, by DNA testing, to be the same as Trebbiano di Soave, otherwise known as Trebbiano di Lugana. Verdicchio is a versatile grape, capable of successfully making anything from basic dry whites, up through oak-fermented single-vineyard crus, to complex dry whites for laying down. Nor are its sparklers and stickies at all bad. Its origins are unknown, and there is little record of it before the end of the 19th century, but it has undoubtedly made Le Marche its home, especially the two DOC zones of Castelli di Jesi and Matelica.

Vermentino Presumed to be of Spanish origin, though displaying genetic similarities to Hungary's Furmint, this grape has thrived mainly in warm coastal areas such as Tuscany's Maremma and Liguria. Its most accomplished appearance is in Sardinia's Vermentino di Gallura DOCG, but it is capable, with proper handling, of achieving discreet quality levels in Tuscany—specifically in Colli di Luna, Lucca (Colline Lucchesi and Montecarlo), Bolgheri, and southern points.

Vernaccia di San Gimignano How this grape came to acquire membership of Italy's most prestigious wine club—that of DOCG—has always been a mystery to me, given that the wine has difficulty rising above the pedestrian level. No doubt the tourism attracted to the famous town of towers has something to do with it. Even so, it does have some credentials as a fairly ancient grape, having received a mention (in the communal archives) as long ago as 1276. This Vernaccia, whose name like that of other Vernaccias of Italy, derives from the Latin *vernaculus* ("of local origin"), has no other connection at all with said others and has not, in all this time, spread even to other parts of Tuscany.

Vermentino

Lesser white varieties

Ansonica is more prevalent in Sicily, where it is called Inzolia, but it may also be found in Tuscany's southern Maremma—specifically on the Isola del Giglio, where it makes dry, non-aromatic whites or may form part of a blend.

Bombino Bianco is used varietally or in blends in northern Marche and Romagna, where it is also known as Pagadebit ("pays the debt") for its ability to churn out good quantities of respectable dry whites.

Canaiolo Bianco can be found in various parts of Tuscany, often blended with Trebbiano and Malvasia, but is best known as the Drupeggio that must make up a minor part of Umbria's Orvieto blend.

Maceratino is considered part of the Greco group and is mostly found in the province of Macerata in

Le Marche, appearing among other things as Bianco Piceno or Bianco dei Colli Maceratesi.

Moscato Bianco, or Moscato di Canelli (in other words, the Moscato of Asti), is grown with some enthusiasm in certain pockets of Tuscany, mainly (today) Montalcino, where, under the name Moscadello, it is more often found in *passito* form than in *frizzante*. Either way, it is sweet.

Passerina, reckoned to be closely related to Trebbiano Toscano, is mostly found in Le Marche in a blend with other whites.

Pecorino, despite being mostly associated with Abruzzo, is also found in Le Marche and Umbria. It is capable of very considerable heights of quality as a crisp and somewhat complex dry white, not without Burgundian characteristics structure-wise, if different aromatically. It is definitely worth a try if you can find it. Alas, standard works on the etymology of Italian grape names make no attempt to explain its curious name, but do not expect it to remind you of goat's cheese.

Trebbiano Romagnolo, according to the Romagnans, is a special version of Trebbiano that, however, suffers no less than the Tuscan type when overcropped. Kept under control, it can make quite a refreshing wine, still or sparkling. It forms part of several DOCs, including Trebbiano di Romagna.

Verdello is likely related to Verdicchio rather than to Portugal's Verdelho. Its main presence is in Umbria, as part of the blend of Torgiano Bianco and Orvieto.

International varieties

French and, to a lesser extent, German grapes have thrived in central Italy for decades, if not centuries, though their apogee was reached over the past 30 years or so. The characteristics of these grapes are well known, so it is not necessary to describe them here. Suffice it to say that Cabernet Sauvignon, Cabernet Franc, and Merlot are all present in strength, with Petit Verdot coming on quite strongly. Syrah has also made a fairly big impact; Pinot Noir, less so. Others, such as Gamay and Tannat, have been employed experimentally but so far not very successfully.

On the white side, Chardonnay and Sauvignon have made their presence felt, as have Pinot Grigio and Pinot Bianco and, to a lesser degree, Marsanne, Roussanne, and Semillon. Traminer, Rhine Riesling, and Müller-Thurgau have all been tried, but this is not the right latitude for Teutonic grapes.

The future

A little while back, I spent a day with one of Tuscany's most dedicated ampelographical researchers, Roberto Bandinelli of the Dipartimento di Ortoflorofrutticoltura of the University of Florence, who explained some of the work that he and colleagues are carrying out in various parts of Tuscany, often in conjunction with private producers. He said he preferred these to government agencies, because the private people care only about the final result, whereas the public entities require justification at every step of the process. There was no limit to the amount of work that could be done on grape varieties, he said, except in respect of funds and the willingness of researchers to work long hours with very limited financial return.

The most important, or at least the earliest established, of the experimental vineyards that Bandinelli was following is the so-called Vitiarium, at the large San Felice estate at Castelnuovo Berardenga in Chianti Classico, where the variety Pugnitello was developed from a state of near extinction. The Vitiarium is not large—13,000 sq ft (1,200 sq m)— but it contains nearly 300 varieties at 18 vines per type—a riot of shapes in spring and of colors in fall. There are several sections to the vineyard. One

is dedicated exclusively to different biotypes of Sangiovese, including Sangiovese Forte, Sangiovese Piccolo Precoce, Prugnolo Gentile, Morellino di Scansano, Brunello, and Brunellone. This work is being repeated for comparative purposes at other Tuscan sites such as Montepaldi near San Casciano and Cantine Leonardo at Vinci. Another section contains clones of Tuscan varieties like Trebbiano, Malvasia, Vernaccia, Vermentino Bianco and Nero, Canaiolo, Colorino, and of course Sangiovese. Yet another has non-Tuscan Italian grapes like Nebbiolo (which, he said, performed extremely badly here), Sagrantino, Montepulciano (to describe which as similar to Sangiovese is, according to Bandinelli, to be an *asino*, or "ass"), Cesanese, Cannonau, Negroamaro, Nero d'Avola, and Aglianico.

Perhaps the work that will have most impact, he explained, is on crossings such as Sangiovese x Pugnitello; Sangiovese x Abrostine; Sangiovese x Cabernet Sauvignon; Sangiovese x Syrah; and one that is already in production: Sangiovese x Teinturier. People like a change, Bandinelli says, and the young are always seeking something different.

This is just a brief sample of the dedicated work that is taking place in Tuscany at the present time in respect of varieties and clones. I should also mention the excellent program hosted by the Umbrian producer Caprai at Montefalco, in conjunction with the University of Milan, focusing on Sagrantino; or that studying Verdicchio in Marche. What one always has to remember in these matters is that research based on the vineyard is necessarily slow, since there is only one crop a year. One has to take account of vintage variation; one has to allow time for the vines to grow to some level of maturity; and one has to allow time for the wines to mature. It is not like the winery, where everything can be changed almost overnight, provided the money is there.

Right: Some otherwise lackluster grapes such as Malvasia del Chianti and Trebbiano Toscano can be helpful in Vin Santo

Tradition and Innovation

Anyone in the first or second decade of the 21st century intending to plant a vineyard in Tuscany or elsewhere in central Italy must ask himself a number of questions. The answers to these questions will impact directly on his costs of production and his potential for mechanizing the work in an age when it is becoming difficult to find competent field workers, let alone skilled ones. Most important of all, his decisions will have a major effect on the eventual quality of his product.

Location, location, location
Leaving aside the matter of which vinous zone to choose, this question comes down to details concerning exposure, suitability of soil, and vulnerability to, or protection from, extremes of weather, fungal conditions, pests, and so on— and, of course, suitability in relation to the chosen grape variety. So, for example, one would not normally plant Sangiovese at altitudes of more than 1,650ft (500m) or less than 650ft (200m), whereas the Cabernet/Merlot/Syrah contingent might be perfectly happy lower down. These are matters we have already looked at, so there is no need to revisit them. But there are still plenty of other considerations.

Clonal research and designer grapes
This is perhaps the most important consideration. Clonal research on Sangiovese has been going on

now for some 40 years—much less than on the great French varieties whose clones were sorted out, and reduced to a handful, long ago; but more, no doubt, than for any other grape in Italy. The situation is confusing for growers, who have been presented with a bewildering array of possible clones from the nurseries (today there are around 70 approved clones), to say nothing of all the as yet unapproved, heterogenous biotypes hidden away in the vineyards of central Italy, several hundred of which have been the subject of study for one university research group or another. It was known in the 1970s that existing vine material was inadequate for the production of top-quality wine, but it was only in the '80s, and more so in the '90s, that work got going in earnest.

On a DVD called *Sangiovese: Let's Get It Right*, created for Australian grape growers interested in experimenting with Sangiovese, Tuscan agronomist/enologist Alberto Antonini gives as clear and concise a presentation of the importance of clonal selection as one might hope for. He divides Sangiovese clones into those relevant to the past, the present, and the future. Those of the past featured big bunches, tight bunches (so that light and warmth had difficulty penetrating to the inner fruit, which remained relatively green and unripe), and large berries, inhibiting contact between the aroma and flavor precursors found in the skins

Below: The rebirth of central Italian viticulture has been from the ground—or below the ground—up

and the catalyzing chemical compounds found in the center of the grape. They incurred time spent in the matter of pruning and bunch-thinning, increasing costs for what was always likely to prove a mediocre product. An example of this would be the notorious, highly productive R10 clone, widely disseminated during the post-*mezzadria* (post-sharecropping) plantings of the 1960s and '70s, and still responsible for a very significant proportion of Sangiovese plantings in central Italy. Antonini goes on to point out that the main reason why Sangiovese has not caught on in other major wine-producing nations is because the clones have been so poor.

Sangiovese clones of the present are much less productive, cutting labor costs in respect of pruning, while producing better balanced fruit more capable of resulting in quality wine. Examples would be B-BS 11, developed by Italy's premier vine nursery at Rauscedo in conjunction with the famous Biondi-Santi vineyard of Montalcino; and R24, a Romagnan biotype shown in repeated trials to make less but better wine than R10. But they are still, in many instances, based on the "Sangiovese Grosso" model, according to which the best biotypes are large of berry, as distinct from the supposedly inferior "Sangiovese Piccolo."

The clones of the future are more likely to conform to what we might call the "Fregoni principle" (after Professor Mario Fregoni), setting ideal weights of 0.035 oz, 3.5 oz, and 350 oz (1 gram, 100g, and 1,000g) respectively for the berry, the bunch, and the yield per vine. These will get closer to the ideal of low berry weight with thick skins, loose bunch structure, and limited production per plant, yielding wines of deeper, more stable color, richness of flavor and fruit, and plentiful ripe tannins—plus, of course, being virus-free. Examples of these would be the clones developed in the course of the so-called Chianti Classico 2000 project, initiated by the Consorzio Vino Chianti Classico in the late

1980s and followed through by the universities of Florence and Pisa. These clones bear the romantic names CCL 2000/1 to CCL 2000/7. They are of the future because, while meeting the criteria desired, there is not yet enough mature wine to enable us to confirm their superiority. Other major clonal-research projects on Sangiovese include those of the University of Milan, the University of Bologna, and the Regione Toscana, in conjunction with selected producers. Rauscedo has been involved in a number of these projects, as well as conducting its own.

One principle that the aforementioned Professor Fregoni, among others, has highlighted is the need, even in a 100 percent Sangiovese vineyard, to plant a mix of clones of the variety, having different responses to soil and weather conditions and yielding fruit of different character. This is not only to give complexity to the eventual wine, but is also in order to compensate for the failure of one clone in a given year with another more successful, quality-wise or quantity-wise.

Of course, clonal selection has been happening for other varieties as well, such as Canaiolo, of which eight clones were studied as part of the Chianti Classico 2000 (CC2000) project. But the majority of trials started more recently and have proceeded at a much less intense pace. The only other black varieties of central Italy to receive anything like comparable attention in the clonal sphere have been Sagrantino and Montepulciano. On the white side, Marche's Verdicchio has received most attention, and for good reason in my opinion, since I believe it to be by far the best white grape of central Italy.

Rootstock: seeking the perfect match

As is commonly known, European vines have to be grafted on to American rootstock, which is generally resistant to the phylloxera aphid that would otherwise destroy the roots of *Vitis vinifera*. It is of fundamental importance that the rootstock selected be suitable for the climatic and soil

Above: Clonal research now strives for a low berry weight, thick skins, loose bunch structure, and limited yields per plant

Scalabrelli et al studied the effects of 13 different rootstocks (unfortunately not including SO4) on fruit quality, concluding that certain types increased the already exaggerated tendency of Sangiovese to hyper-vigor, with a negative effect on sugar production, while 110R, a Berlandieri x Rupestris crossing, enhanced sugar production while containing vigor.

Numerous other rootstocks exist, with different characteristics for different situations, and it is up to the planter to make sure he has the right one for the specific job in hand. This is not an easy task, but it is one with important ramifications, since one cannot replace a plant's root system by field grafting, as one can with the principal vine.

Planting density: reaching the right balance

Density is generally expressed as a number of vines per hectare (2.47 acres). In France there is, and has been for a long time, a tendency, particularly in the classic zones, toward high density—around 8,000–10,000 vines per hectare. Vines are planted 31.5–39 inches (80–100cm) apart in rows, with distances between rows of perhaps 47 inches (120cm). The thinking, as we have already seen with the Fregoni principle, is that dry extract drawn from the soil and sent to the fruit by the roots is more concentrated; sugars and acids are higher; tannins and coloring matter are more abundant; and the grape is generally more balanced when the berries are small, the bunches also small and not too compact, and there are not too many of them. The potential of the land to yield up its treasures is maximized when the distance between vines is short. But many limited-production plants should still add up to only a modest total production per hectare.

In central Italy, traditionally this has been far from the case. Referring only to specialized vineyards of the type one might have seen regularly in the period 20–30 years post-*mezzadria*—not

conditions in which the vine is to be planted, as well as being compatible with the fruiting stock selected. Much research has also been carried out in this area, with Sangiovese and other varieties. An example reported by Di Collalto et al (ARSIA I, 2001) found that Morellino (Sangiovese) attained higher sugar levels when grafted on to rootstock 110R, followed by 41B and SO4. 41B also achieved relatively high acidity levels and was less productive, so it was considered most suitable in this test.

A major test was carried out in the 1990s at the Pagliarese estate in Chianti Classico, as part of the CC2000 project for improving and understanding Sangiovese via various field tests.

"promiscuous" ones (though they still exist, especially at kitchen-garden level)—the distances between rows may have been 6.5–10ft (2–3m). The plants were (and still are, in places) groaning under the weight of their fruit, and the bunches were (are) big and fat, with swollen berries, still partially green in the middle of the bunch, even at vintage time (green tasting if not green looking). The distance between rows, incidentally, was (is) explained by the fact that the large tractors made at the time had to pass through. Today they are much more slimline and may be what the French call *tracteurs enjambeurs*, the Italians *macchine scavallanti*, which are high enough to straddle the vines.

As part of the CC2000 project, tests were carried out in the 1990s in relation to plant density. At that time, one would have expected something like 1,500–2,000 plants per hectare—sometimes fewer, and rarely more. Densities experimented with were 2,500, 5,000, 7,500, and 10,000 plants per hectare. The consensus, judging by the majority of plantings in recent years, seems to be that somewhere between 5,000 and 7,000 is right. Beyond this range, the economic advantages of higher density start being negated by the higher costs of labor and material (such as sprays), and quality does not necessarily improve. Moreover, there are still not many *tracteurs enjambeurs* in Italy.

Professor Antonio Calò (ARSIA II, 2006, p.318) reports that Bertuccioli et al ran tests that led them to the conclusion (in a paper published in 2000), that a medium-low planting density will probably lead to physiological imbalance in the vine and favor vegetation at the expense of fruit quality. For this reason, Calò considers attention to density to be a matter of great importance in the process of tending to Sangiovese. He further reports that, in 2000, Scalabrelli et al found that a density of 5,000 plants per hectare was most likely to favor equilibrium in the plant. Higher densities, they maintain, do not offer advantages in respect of quality.

Training and pruning: *alberello* vs Guyot

Professor Intrieri of the University of Bologna is quoted in an article by Professor Calò (ARSIA II, 2006, p.317) as making this important observation regarding Sangiovese: "The high fertility of Sangiovese canes' basal buds (those nearest the stem) offers multiple possibilities of choice regarding length of pruning and, consequently, forms of training." To put this in perspective, we need only consider Valpolicella's Corvina, whose poor fertility on basal buds has historically necessitated very long training in the pergola mode. Sangiovese, then, can be pruned in various ways, as Intrieri, describing his field observations, explains: unilateral or bilateral Guyot (with a long, annually renewable cane); or permanent cordon, pruned either long (Casarsa style) or short (as cordon spur, simple or double T-form, short or long Geneva Double Curtain, or simple curtain).

As far as training is concerned, the most common shape one sees these days—that is, in vineyards planted during the past, say, 20 years, prior to which the most favored was *archetto* ("little arch"), single or double—is cordon spur. With a mature branch running off at a right angle to the trunk, it has a varying number of canes led up from the main branch, depending on the extent to which the grower wants to limit production. Most growers seem to feel that this is the best compromise between quality production and maximum mechanization.

There are, however, two major schools of very different thought. One dismisses the cordon method and favors the Guyot method of training a new fruiting cane every year at right angles to the upright—a method that stands a better chance (they say) of reining in Sangiovese's strong natural tendency to production of vegetation. This is the shape generally preferred in France's classic

Right: The ancient *alberello* method of training has been reintroduced by several leading producers, including Zerbina

vineyards, and as one Tuscan agronomist asked, "Have you ever tasted a great wine that came from cordon?" The question is rhetorical, of course, and the implication is ignored by larger producers. But the thinking behind it does seem to be finding increasing favor among smaller growers, whose only recourse, given their costs of production, is to attract business through high quality.

The other method, preferred by a very few producers because of the labor involved, is the *alberello* (or "bush") mode, introduced by the Ancient Greeks in southern Italy. Professor Mario Fregoni is one of the enthusiastic supporters of this method (as he tells us in the April/May 2005 edition of *VQ: Vite, Vino & Qualità* magazine, p.96): "As long as one is aiming for Sangiovese wines of high quality, the rules must include high density of planting and a form of training that severely limits vigor. For this reason, for several years I have recommended the Greek *alberello* (free-standing bush), with two to three spurs planted in the *settonce* style, which permits densities of over 7,000 plants per hectare, forming rows in various directions, and therefore mechanizable in all directions, obviously with *macchine scavallanti* (*tracteurs enjambeurs*)." Fregoni goes on to praise the work of the Montepulciano producer Avignonesi, who at the time he was writing had 55ha (136 acres) planted to *settonce*, and "the qualitatively superior results compared with *spalliera* (cordon or Guyot at right angle to the stem, like a shoulder) lead one to pursue efforts with *alberello*"—which, he points out, was once widely used in Tuscany. He concludes: "It is not so much the degree of sugar that makes the difference between *alberello* and *spalliera*, as the degree of maturation, the more stable acidity, and the total amount of polyphenols and anthocyanins, which are notably higher in the *alberello*."

Left: Secateurs are often now wielded for green-harvesting and leaf-thinning, as well as for the vintage proper

Canopy management: the new buzz phrase

It has always been obvious that grape maturity is linked to heat, but the recognition that it is just as much associated with light is relatively recent. Probably the world's foremost expert in this area is Dr Richard Smart of New Zealand. In the mid-1990s, I visited several illustrious vineyards in Tuscany with Dr Smart, trying to sell them (for their own good) on the idea of taking him on as a consultant. But for the most part, frankly, they had no idea what he was talking about.

These days, canopy management (*gestione della chioma*) is a buzz phrase. As the name implies, it relates to how the leaves and fruit are arranged in relation to the sun's rays to optimize photosynthesis, respiration, and transpiration, and to protect fruit from excessive exposure. Alberto Antonini, one of the best traveled of Tuscan "flying enologists," makes the point in the DVD mentioned earlier that proper canopy management can have a major effect on fruit quality. Fregoni remarks that canopy management is all the more important where (as is generally the case in Italy) irrigation is forbidden except in dire emergency. He says that tests are ongoing at Soldera's outstanding Case Basse vineyard in Montalcino to ascertain what kind of interventions are needed, at the level of both canopy and soil, in order to avoid water stress in the plant, which can negatively affect photosynthesis.

Nonetheless, canopy management as a recognized viticultural discipline is still very much in its infancy in Italy, and we ought to be able to look forward to a marked improvement in fruit quality when it comes to be better understood and practiced.

Green-harvesting: sacrilege to new orthodoxy

Closely connected with canopy management is the removal of leaves and shoots to reduce vegetation, as well as the cutting away of already formed bunches to keep the production per plant within legal or quality limits. There was a time, not so long ago, when it was extremely difficult to persuade field workers to cut off fully formed grape bunches. It seemed sacrilegious to those (and they were many) who had known times of great economic hardship. Nowadays, on the contrary, producers take pride in the display of potentially fine fruit covering the ground between rows, sometimes in July or as late as August. But we are beginning to see something of a backlash: Some producers prefer limitation by more severe winter pruning or early bud removal —or indeed by canopy management—feeling, like the old-timers, that the sacrifice of actual fruit is in some way prejudicial to the plant. Various research programs are currently running in central Italy to study this problem in greater depth.

Seeding between rows: what and where to plant

Trials have been carried out, notably as part of the CC2000 project, on the effect of planting certain crops, like broad beans, between vineyard rows. This can have the effect of enhancing the nitrogen content of the soil (reducing the need for fertilizer, especially handy for organic producers), reducing vegetation in the plant, and discouraging erosion on steeply sloping vineyards. The CC2000 project concluded that the best crop for this purpose was red fescue (*Festuca rubra*). But it can be too much of a good thing if every row is planted, so the practice, where it is practiced, of seeding alternate rows seems to have been generally adopted.

The vintage: when and how to harvest

Different grapes ripen at different times, and this is one reason why the traditional *uvaggio di vigneto*—where three, four, or more vine types were planted together and harvested together in the same vineyard—was not a good idea. For its part, Sangiovese ripens between the middle of September and the middle of October, depending on climate, clone, and other considerations as discussed above. Central Italian growers reckon that climate change and other factors have brought forward the picking time by up to three weeks over the past 50 years.

There are several issues at stake here. One is machine-picking versus hand-picking. Sangiovese is said to be quite adaptable to machine-harvesting, thanks to the ease with which the berries become detached, and their resistance to bursting in the process. On the other hand, there is nothing quite like the human touch. Whatever system is employed, you will find the producer boasting of its advantages—and it would indeed appear that there are advantages, and therefore disadvantages, on both sides. On the plus side for mechanical harvesting, it is much faster, and you can do it at precisely the moment you choose, or the grapes choose for you, avoiding the hottest part of the day or clearing a vineyard rapidly when it is threatened by rain or mold. On the minus side is the high cost of the machine that stands idle for 11 months of the year, as well as the inability of machines to select, plus whatever subtle or not-so-subtle damage is done to the plant—a matter on which there are different assessments, according to which side of the debate you are on.

Another major issue is when to pick. In the old days, growers simply went by sugar readings. Today it is phenolic maturity (well-developed anthocyanins and ripe tannins) that most producers seek, even if it means going a bit beyond the peak moment of "physical" maturity—that is, sugar ripeness—with a subsequent loss of acidity and gain in eventual alcohol. This is one reason why there are so many massively alcoholic wines coming on to the market these days. It is also one reason why, as potent as they are, the best do not seem out of balance, having also gained in color, extract, and ripeness. Still, alcohol is alcohol, and it does what it does.

Right: Hand-harvesting into small containers is the preferred method of picking for most quality-minded producers today

Blends, Trends, and Techniques

So, the grapes are picked, and we pass from the first major stage of the making of wine, the viticultural, to the second, the enological. Two main themes arise, the first relating to enological technology and technique; the second, to something more quintessentially, and historically, Tuscan: the blend.

Blending: art, craft, and crime

Professor Mario Fregoni makes this point (in *VQ: Vite, Vino & Qualità* magazine, April/May 2005, p.92): "Sangiovese has always been considered a grape for blending. It enters obligatorily into the varietal mix of 88 DOCGs and DOCs, very rarely *in purezza* [on its own]. If one examines the evolution of the use of Sangiovese in Italian blends, one deduces that until the beginning of the 18th century, Canaiolo Nero was the principal grape, followed by San Gioveto [sic], Mammolo, Marzemino, Canaiolo Bianco, and Abrostine, with Trebbiano Toscano and Malvasia Lunga used mainly for the *governo* [*see p.51*]. It is only from 1832, in the time of Bettino Ricasoli, that the proportion of Sangiovese in blends begins to increase, arriving at 100 percent after World War II in the recent phenomenon of Brunello di Montalcino (previously a Chianti)."

We should perhaps recall that even a 100 percent Sangiovese wine such as Brunello should, in the prescription of Fregoni and others, be a blend of clones to compensate for the notorious changeability and unreliability of the grape.

This perception of Sangiovese as a blending grape is essential to an understanding of the development of Tuscan wines. In the mid-19th century, the aforementioned Baron Ricasoli, a major property owner in Gaiole in Chianti, as well as prime minister of Italy for a time, proposed what came to be known as the "golden blend" for Chianti Classico, which included a significant minority portion of Canaiolo as well as of Trebbiano Toscano and Malvasia (Bianca and Nera). The motive was to soften the austerity and asperity of Sangiovese on its own, especially from grapes that are not fully ripe (phenolically, as well as physically). It has been maintained that the Baron did not intend the white-grape element to be present in serious wines for aging, only in those for early or everyday drinking. However that may be, when this formula—complete with an option of including up to 30 percent of white grapes, with a minimum of 10 percent—became enshrined in the DOC *disciplinare* (rules) for Chianti Classico in 1966, there was consternation on the part of the better producers that the amount of white grapes admissible—indeed, enforceable—would dilute the wine, while the Canaiolo element and that of other permitted varieties (Colorino, Mammolo, Malvasia Nera) would not compensate sufficiently.

It was this dilemma that pushed quality-minded producers into what is sometimes termed "lateral thinking." This is the moment of the birth of that unofficial but very real phenomenon that since the 1980s has been called the "Super-Tuscan"—a term used by journalists (though not permitted officially) to denote a top-quality wine made according to principles that go against the letter, though not, many would maintain, the spirit, of the DOC laws.

Basically, producers such as Piero Antinori of Marchesi Antinori, Enzo Morganti of San Felice, Ugo Contini Bonacossi of Capezzana, and Sergio Manetti of Monte Vertine, not to mention Mario Incisa della Rocchetta of Sassicaia, decided sometime between the late '60s and the late '70s that if, in order to make top-quality wine, it was necessary to blend in grapes that were neither "recommended" nor "authorized" for their local denomination, to exclude grapes that were supposed to be blended in, and to "declassify" their wine to Vino da Tavola status (supposedly the lowest of the low), then so be it. The new wines these men produced were anything between pure

Left: While some winemaking techniques remain staunchly traditional, others keep abreast of developments worldwide

Sangiovese and pure Cabernet, via a blend of the two. But they all had in common that they were made from top-quality grapes; they were aged in French oak barriques; they were far from cheap, despite their lowly status; and they stood, with the exception of Carmignano, for which Bonacossi succeeded in acquiring DOC status, outside of the quality wine law.

When other growers—especially but not exclusively of Chianti Classico—saw that the prototypes were not only selling but stirring up increasing excitement in the world of wine, they followed suit. Cabernet, mainly Sauvignon, began appearing in every estate's vineyards, and because it proved a reliable provider of quality grapes, growers fairly boasted about their wonderful Bordelais. The trickle of the '70s became a stream in the '80s and a veritable torrent in the '90s, when Merlot and later Syrah and Petit Verdot caught on. Everyone and his brother seemed to be rushing to get on the bandwagon of increasingly high- and even ridiculously-priced wines, designed, with surprising success, to impress the most influential points givers in the USA and Italy. By this time, the Italian wine law of 1992 was in effect, forcing producers to abandon Vino da Tavola status in favor of the slightly less humble IGT (*indicazione geografica tipica*) denomination, on pain of not being allowed to display a grape name, place name, or vintage on the label—something unthinkable for a "vintage" wine. But it made little difference to the market, which went sailing on blithely. Alas, the Super-Tuscans were riding for a fall, and sure enough, soon after 9/11, the all-important US market imploded. Suddenly, from a position of amazing arrogance, the makers of high-priced "super" wines were on their knees, begging buyers to accept a variety of price-lowering offers.

At the time of writing (in early 2009), it is possible to detect a renewed interest in the Super-Tuscans—in part thanks to new markets opening up in Russia and Eastern Europe, India, China and the Far East, Brazil, and Mexico. But producers seem to be taking a more pragmatic approach to the market, depending less on their top wines to pay off the huge debts they incurred when they started building that state-of-the-art winery they had always wanted.

Meanwhile, there were two other developments in relation to blending. As a trickle-down effect from Super-Tuscans, the Bordeaux grapes plus Syrah began, from the 1980s, to appear as part of the blend of more mainstream wines such as Chianti and Vino Nobile di Montepulciano. This had a certain legitimacy, since there was in the *disciplinare* of most of the important DOCs a provision for the use of a small proportion of grapes, wines, or musts from alternative origins—all part of the perceived need of Sangiovese for help in the blending. It is undeniable that the Bordeaux grapes, which indeed seemed to thrive in the Tuscan climate, contributed to wines that were deeper and more stable in color, rounder and riper on the palate, and altogether more elegant than wines of pure Sangiovese (especially of the old clones) or of a Sangiovese-led blend. They were also, however, that much less typical of Tuscany. Bit by bit, and somewhat by stealth, the amount of Cabernet/Merlot/Petit Verdot/Syrah that may be used in the blends of Chianti or Chianti Classico or Vino Nobile crept up to 20 percent—at which level, most experts agree, the essential character of the Tuscan grape(s) is compromised, if not lost. And yet there were still producers who wanted to increase the permitted proportion of nontraditional varieties to 30 or even 40 percent. According to the contrary, pro-Tuscan school of thinking, it is a question not of quality but of authenticity. "You wouldn't want 20 percent Sangiovese in your claret, would you?" they ask rhetorically. According to this school, wines with a significant proportion of French grapes blended in should be IGT, not DOC(G).

This debate rather came to a head in 2008, when a handful of top-flight producers in Montalcino had

Above: Stainless-steel tanks became more prevalent from the 1960s and are now found in all shapes and sizes

could suffer a loss of image in the consumer's eyes, as well as losing an element of *tipicità* that, some would say, is essential for the maintenance of the unique image that any wine needs to nurture if it is to be described as "fine."

There is another type of blending, based on historic precedent. Until the 1980s, "Chianti" was allowed to include in its blend up to 15 percent of grapes, wine, or must from other regions—such as Abruzzo, whose Montepulciano grape/wine is an ideal partner for Tuscan reds, being deep of color and full of fruit, but without the distinctive aromas of the French varieties; or Puglia, whose Primitivo can add power to the weedy and weak, and whose Negroamaro can smooth the tannins and soften the acidity of Sangiovese. Theoretically, this blending has now been terminated, but everyone knows that it lingers on in the form of illicit practice, especially in a poor year like 2002 or a short vintage like 2007, when Sangiovese may need supplementing if not "improving." Presumably it will continue to linger until an irrefutable test exists to prove the presence in a wine of fruit that is not supposed to be there. DNA testing does not work on wine (only on solids like skins and pips) because of the distorting presence of alcohol. There has, however, been progress recently toward identifying varietal components of wine by studying the anthocyanin content combined with molecular analysis.

The advent of stainless steel and barriques

In other ways, the making of Tuscan/central Italian wines largely resembles the processes employed to produce high-quality wines anywhere else in the world. These methods can be reviewed in works on general enology, so I will stick to discussing those aspects that are peculiar to our area.

As has been noted, it takes a lot longer for change to happen in the vineyard than in the winery. In the latter, all it takes is a will to keep abreast, or keep ahead, of developments in the sector—and money.

their cellars blocked by the authorities on suspicion that they had blended grapes other than Sangiovese into their 2003 Brunello (officially on release from the beginning of 2008). The big difference between Brunello di Montalcino and Chianti or Vino Nobile is that Brunello, by law, is supposed to be 100 percent Sangiovese, so no blending is allowed at all. It should be said that producers involved in this problem—most of whom were cleared following declassification of considerable quantities of wine from DOCG to DOC or IGT—would have been blending in the same spirit as they did in the early Super-Tuscan years—that is, in the interests of quality (as they saw it) and not for reasons of economy. Nonetheless, the law is the law, and the wider implications for Brunello di Montalcino are that the whole denomination

Back in the 1960s, the decade when the DOC system began to influence Italian winemaking (and that influence was a lot greater than the system, for all its flaws, has often been credited for), Italy was way behind the then undisputed greatest wine country in the world, France, in its technical and technological approach to fine-wine production.

But there was an increasing amount of money around, as the wealthy of Italy and the rest of the world acquired properties in the beautiful Tuscan hills, and this money was poured into the reequipping and later rebuilding of wineries. From the characterful but somewhat unhygienic cellars of old Tuscany—with their walls covered by centuries-old mold, their cobwebs in corners, their ugly if functional concrete vats, and their massive, ancient barrels, often of local chestnut if not of Slavonian oak—gradually, then more rapidly, there emerged a vinous Tuscany of gleaming stainless-steel tanks and pristine barrels of the more classic 225-liter (barrique) or 500-liter (tonneau) size. Fermentation tanks became more and more sophisticated, with various ingenious devices to ensure optimum juice-solids contact, built to shapes designed to maximize color and flavor extraction.

The buildings themselves began to resemble temples more than wineries, with barrel rooms boasting arches and vaults of almost ecclesiastical design. The design was, of course, increasingly authored by famous architects, who ensured, among other practical measures, that the flow of wine should, as far as possible, be downward, according to the laws of gravity, rather than forced upward or laterally by pump. As in everything else, computers began inexorably taking over from humans. Temperature control was introduced almost everywhere—not just in the fermentation but in storage areas, too—and hygiene was taken off the list of secondary considerations and elevated (by some obsessives) to the level of religion.

The *maestro assaggiatore* and other consultants
Where did the inspiration for all this activity come from? A lot came from France, with serious post-*mezzadria* producers making pilgrimages to sacred sites like Château Lafite in Bordeaux and Domaine de la Romanée-Conti in Burgundy. Suddenly there was an awareness of high quality in Tuscan and central Italian wine circles that had not been there before, or hardly. Even if the new proprietors were amateurs in the field of wine, there were, from the early 1980s, ever more consultant enologists to advise on how to make "the world's greatest wine," at a price. The daddy of this breed might have been *maestro assaggiatore* ("master taster") Giulio Gambelli, still active at the time of writing, though well into his 80s, having begun as a consultant in the early 1940s. But Gambelli does not really belong to the brotherhood of modernist enologists, believing as he does in the old ways of very long maceration and, almost uniquely nowadays, no artificial temperature control during fermentation. Despite the condemnation this practice almost universally brings him, Gambelli can claim to be behind some of the greatest wines of Tuscany today—including Gianfranco Soldera's Brunello di Montalcino Case Basse and Sergio Manetti's groundbreaking 100 percent Sangiovese Super-Tuscan Le Pergole Torte.

The credit for being the father of the modernists goes to Giacomo Tachis, longtime chief enologist for the house of Antinori and still, in his 70s, consultant to Sassicaia and other top Tuscan names. Other consultants whose names have become almost mythical in the past 30 years or so are Maurizio Castelli, Franco Bernabei, Vittorio Fiore, Carlo Ferrini, and Attilio Pagli. There is also a growing host of younger men and women whose skill at making wines for other people almost matches the distances they notch up behind the wheel of their very racy automobiles.

Right: Some producers have come full circle, reverting from stainless-steel to cement or wooden vats for the fermentation

Red wines: maceration to maturation

The issue of length of maceration, in order to get the best—which may, but does not necessarily, mean the most—from the fruit, is as alive here as it is anywhere. Some believe in a brief maceration to avoid picking up harsh tannins, while others consider that a maceration period of five or six weeks is essential to the making of a fine wine for laying down. But most in central Italy will soak the juice/wine with skins for 10–20 days, with pumping over to break the cap, or punching down, mechanically or manually, and/or *délestage*.

The malolactic fermentation is almost universally induced for reds immediately following the alcoholic fermentation, usually by raising the ambient temperature and/or by inoculation. But it is also increasingly seen as an opportunity to fix the color, as well as to adjust the acidity, by natural means, and there is a large and growing consensus that this result is best attained by putting the wine into barrel immediately after maceration.

The barrels used today are overwhelmingly of French oak, increasingly of barrique or tonneau size, though other oaks like Austrian, Hungarian, or American are also found. The traditional large *botte*, of, say, 10 to 100hl plus, usually of Slavonian but increasingly of French oak, is back in demand, having suffered a longish period of rejection, by modernists anyway, as producers grow more sensitive to the complaint by one sector of the market that excessive wood aromas, like an overdose of Cabernet, can distort the essential terroir character of the wine and make for bland international anonymity.

Another container making a comeback is the glass-lined concrete tank. Many of these were destroyed in the early days of the '70s and '80s, when they were considered unaesthetic, unhygienic, or just old-fashioned. But since then it has been realized that they are useful both as fermentation

vessels and as storage tanks, thanks to their ability to moderate temperature and exclude oxygen, provided they are kept topped up ("like a giant bottle," one producer opined).

Minimum duration of aging is in several instances laid down in DOC(G) regulations. For example, Brunello di Montalcino must be aged at least four years from January 1 following the vintage, two of which must be in barrel (this used to be three and a half years). Size of barrel is not specified, but those who use small oak tend to stick to the minimum, while those using *botte* will often voluntarily aim for longer. IGTs, which are unregulated in this respect, are aged for varying periods according to the producer and the vintage, but 30 months would be the maximum (except for fanatics) and 18 months nearer the norm.

Books on Tuscan wines often make much of the so-called *governo all'uso toscano*, but today very few producers use it, probably because it is somewhat labor intensive and therefore adds to expenses. Having said that, it is a good idea in principle, endowing the wine with fuller body and a silkier mouthfeel—putting a bit of flesh on the bones, you might say. Basically, this process involves feeding into the already finished wine a small percentage (usually around 5 percent) of grapes that have undergone *appassimento*—that is, raisining by being laid out, or hung up, to dry, from vintage time until around December. This adds a bit of alcohol and, more importantly, a touch of glycerol, which accounts for the creamier texture. Perhaps it is a pity that it is not practiced more than it is.

Another thing that is being practiced less frequently these days is filtration. Unfiltered wines have been growing in popularity for a few years, and consumers tend to think of them as being more complete, more natural.

Speaking of "natural," another identifiable trend in central Italian wine production is toward the organic, or even biodynamic, methodology. This should usually result in wines that contain fewer additives, if any (in particular the dreaded "sulfites"), though organics/biodynamics refers more to what happens in the vineyard than in the winery.

White wines: aroma therapy

As for red wines, the dry and medium-dry whites of central Italy are made according to precepts applied to the making of similar wines elsewhere, and there is nothing particularly remarkable about them from a purely enological point of view. One could make much of the appalling mistakes of the not-so-distant past in respect of central Italian white-wine production—such as excessive exposure to oxygen at all stages from picking to bottling, or the once-hailed process called "hot bottling," a euphemism for pasteurization. But to what end? Today, all dry and semi-dry white wines of central Italy—of which there are some excellent examples, mainly from Le Marche and Umbria—are kept rigorously, as grapes, musts, and wines, in anaerobic conditions, as far as possible. Many have adopted the practice that originated in hot countries like Israel of harvesting only in the early morning, and dry ice is increasingly used for the cool maintenance of the grapes. Those who aspire to make a white wine of greater body and aromatic complexity are increasingly resorting to cryomaceration and/or keeping it on the fine lees with *bâtonnage* (lees-stirring) or similar techniques. Meanwhile, the excessive use of oak that bedeviled the more ambitious whites of central Italy until recently is being rolled back, with producers coming to realize, like Burgundian Chardonnay producers, that great whites fare better in used barriques than in new ones. Specific peculiarities will be looked at in the appropriate place.

Vin Santo: all the saints

This so-called holy wine is a Tuscan specialty that deserves closer attention in a section on enology. The historic wine—the origins of which go back at least to the Middle Ages and probably much further, and whose name may come from the Italian word for holy (*santo*) by virtue of its use in communion, or from *Xanthos*, referring to the Greek origin of the wine style—is by tradition the wine offered as apéritif to guests in central Italy. It is made in a variety of styles—from almost dry, to very sweet, from fully oxidized in the manner of Sherry, to almost reductive. The grapes for its making may be white (mainly Trebbiano and Malvasia) or partially black (Sangiovese and Canaiolo). In the case of Canaiolo, it is often called Occhio di Pernice ("partridge eye") due to its pinkish hue. They may be hung up for drying or laid out on mats, until December or perhaps even until March.

Vinification and aging of the wine is carried out in generally old or used barrels of varying sizes, from 50 liters (*caratelli*) up to a maximum of 500 liters, the barrels being filled to about four-fifths capacity to allow room for the fermenting wine to expand. The best Vin Santo is made in a barrel that contains what is known as *madre* ("mother")—the remains of the wine previously occupying that barrel. The *madre* can therefore include elements of very old material, and this is said to impart a particular character to that wine. Aging of Vin Santo can be an amazingly protracted process, and there are those who keep it in *caratelli* that are sealed at the beginning and never opened until the moment arrives for the racking, for more than ten years, though three to four years would be nearer the average. Obviously, every barrel's wine has evolved in that period differently from its neighbor, so the process of tasting and blending at the time of bottling is crucial.

Vin Santo should be made in accordance with DOC regulations, which now specify minimum alcohol levels between 15.5% and 17%, without fortification, plus varying amounts of residual sugar.

Right: Although the range of techniques used for Vin Santo is unusually wide, many of the best spend years in small barrels

From DOC to Super-Tuscan

The Italian wine law is modeled on the French AOC system and dates back to the 1960s. It is called DOC, an acronym for *denominazione di origine controllata*, or "controlled denomination of origin." There is a higher version of what the EU classifies as "quality wine," called DOCG, the "G" standing for *garantita*, so "controlled and guaranteed denomination of origin." The law as it stands has many flaws, but it does provide a discipline more or less to be adhered to for the production of any given wine—geographical origin, volume of grapes, percentage of wine from grapes, varietal makeup, sometimes winemaking technique, and permitted qualifications. Wines may be named for a place (Chianti, for example, is named for the Chianti range of hills in central Tuscany, while Bolgheri is named for a representative village); a grape variety and place (Verdicchio dei Castelli di Jesi); or a wine style and place (Vin Santo del Chianti, Rosso di Montalcino). The common factor is place, which may be large or small, even as large as a region (such as Montepulciano d'Abruzzo). Most region-wide denominations, however, belong to a lower category called IGT, or *indicazione geografica tipica* (such as Toscana), though here again, while rules governing volume and so on tend to be more lax, a place name of some sort is essential. Only in the lowest category, Vino da Tavola, is there no place name; nor is there allowed to be mention of any vintage or a grape variety.

In other words, the Italian system is based on that contentious concept, terroir, which leads on to the even more contentious concept of what Italians call *tipicità* (typicity). This is not the place to wax philosophical about what those terms imply (I have done that elsewhere). I am only trying to explain the Italian system, such as it is.

The big problem with a geography-based system, it turns out, is the proliferation of names that tend to arise from it, since every Tommaso, Riccardo, and Enrico of a mayor wants his little commune to be represented on the DOC(G) roll of honor. And since the Italians have been making "local" wine in every part of their very extended nation for some 3,000 years, there are a lot of church steeples (*campanili*) seeking recognition (a phenomenon called *campanilismo*). Until quite recently this would not have made a big difference to the marketing of wines, since most were sold locally, in bottle or in bulk (*sfuso*). Only a few names became nationally known, and even fewer could claim any international recognition: Chianti, Valpolicella, Barolo, Frascati, Orvieto...

But when Italian wine producers realized that not just Rome and Milan were potentially their oyster, but also London, New York, Buenos Aires, Moscow, Tokyo, and Sydney, *campanilismo* began to spread like cancer, and before anyone knew it there were almost 500 named wines in the three categories described above, all jostling for shelf or wine-list space. Now, it is hard enough for a Londoner or a Tokyoite to pronounce "Verdicchio" (should that be vur-DEECH-ee-oh or vur-DICKY-oh, or what? In fact, it's vair-DEEK-kyo). And if you're not sure how to pronounce it, dare you order it in a wine shop or restaurant? But to have to learn the pronunciation— to say nothing of the grapes, the wine style, the basic what-to-expect from wine X—to have to do that hundreds of times over... No thanks, I'll stick to good old varietal names like Chardonnay and Cabernet and PEE-noh-GREE-joe.

Into the breach, in its limited wisdom, has stepped the European Union. It has identified the problem all right—too many names, my dear Mozart—and has proposed to reduce all the DOCs, DOCGs, and IGTs to a total of fewer than 200 DOPs and IGPs (*denominazione di origine protetta* and *indicazione geografica protetta*). This new system is due to come into operation more or less at the time of the publication of this book, and it will be interesting to see what actually happens. One version has it that the existing denominations will

The classic label of the original Brunello di Montalcino, **Biondi-Santi's Tenuta Greppo**, with its DOCG status proudly displayed in capital letters toward the top

Tenuta San Guido's Sassicaia first appeared as a Vino da Tavola but was later brought into the DOC(G) fold through the creation of its own DOC, Bolgheri Sassicaia

A relatively humble IGT Toscana in terms of its label, **Tenuta dell'Ornellaia's Masseto** is another Super-Tuscan that enjoys a price and reputation out of all proportion to its official status

Isole e Olena's Cepparello is still marketed as a Vino da Tavola, even though the Chianti Classico regulations that originally prevented it from being sold under the DOCG have since been changed to allow pure Sangiovese wines

be allowed on to the label with the new ones (or is that instead of the new ones, for a period?), which sounds as though it will produce even more confusion than already exists. I won't go into detail here, but there is already more than enough scope for confusion (to say nothing of bad blood on the part of all those suppressed *campanilisti*) to be getting on with, so perhaps the only thing one can safely say at this time is, Wait and see.

As for this book, as you will have noted, we are sticking with the old system until we know what the new one really involves.

Other descriptors

Meanwhile, there are a few words that one will find on labels that have a greater or lesser significance. You can't just scribble any old adjective on the legal label and get away with it, such as super (as in Super-Tuscan) or *vecchio* (old), the latter of which used to be allowed for Chianti. The words you are most likely to come across are *classico*, *riserva*, and *superiore*. Classico means that the wine comes from the heartland of an area, before it got extended due to growers on the fringes wanting to cash in on an established name, as in Chianti Classico. Riserva generally means that the wine has been aged longer than the non-Riserva version, and there may be specifications as to maximum yields, containers used (barrels, bottles), and obviously time elapsed before the wine may be released. Superiore generally means riper grapes and higher alcohol, but in one case in our area, Rosso Piceno Superiore, it refers to a growing zone considerably more restricted than that of basic Rosso Piceno.

If the above is not very clear, frankly it does not matter. What matters is the intent of the producer—and this is something you can only judge by drinking his or her wine.

The concept of the cru

In this book I have used the French word cru, for which the Italian language has no equivalent. For a Frenchman, a cru (past participle of *croître*, to grow, and therefore something grown; in English, "growth") is a wine from grapes produced exclusively in a limited patch of earth of particular vocation. It can also mean that in Italy, so that a Chianti Classico cru would be a wine from the best vineyard or the best part of the vineyard (French premier cru or grand cru); but it can also indicate any wine of higher quality than the average, so a blend of the best bunches or the best barrels, or both. Nor need the wine's name be that of the vineyard or part of the vineyard from which it hails; it may be the name of a nearby landmark or even a dedication to a person (such as Percarlo, A Sirio, or Saffredi). To an Italian, a Super-Tuscan would be a cru, though not all crus are Super-Tuscans by any means. The main point, I suppose, is that unlike Riserva or Superiore, it is not an officially recognized term, and therefore, although one will come across it frequently, one will not find it on any legal label.

Statistics: value and volume

To put Italian wines generally, and central Italian wines particularly, in perspective, it might help to crunch a few numbers (for which I am indebted to Assoenologi, the Association of Italian Enologists and Enotechnicians). World production of wine in the three-year period 2004–06, the latest for which figures were available at the time of writing, was about 300 million hl, of which 170 million, a little under 60 percent of the total, were produced in the EU. Seventeen percent of world production and 30 percent of EU production was Italian. The average, in terms of millions of hectoliters, over the past five years, was 48, down from 59.2 between 1988 and 1997. The trend is still downward. In 2007, Italy produced a mere 42.6 million hl, the lowest amount since 1950. Between 1980 and 2008, the area planted to the vine in Italy was reduced from 1.23 million ha to 711,000ha. Given that there are around 700,000 producers of grapes in Italy, that comes to around 1ha per grower—a minuscule fraction of the equivalent figure prevailing in a New World country like Australia. Unsurprisingly, therefore, more than 50 percent of total production comes from cooperatives, though there are about 25,000 licensed bottlers with an average of five labels each. Of the national crop, 60 percent is red, about 35 percent is white, and the rest is rosé. Grape and wine-production turnover is worth around €13 billion, of which €3.5 billion worth is for export. A further €2 billion is accounted for by manufactured winery equipment, in which sector Italy leads the world.

In 2008, Italian wine production was 44.5 million hl, up 5 percent on the previous year. The share of Tuscany was 2.26 million hl, which (against the trend) represented a drop of 20 percent year on year. Tuscan wines thus represent about one twentieth of the total production of the 20 regions, though in value terms the percentage would be far higher. In quantity terms, therefore, Tuscany is

Above: Tuscany today produces roughly one twentieth of Italy's wine by volume but a far higher proportion by value

right on average, while in value terms she punches well above her weight. Le Marche at the same time produced a mere 870,000hl, way below the average, though again her contribution in value terms would be much higher. Separate figures for Umbria, and the quality section of Romagna (excluding the production of the Romagnan plains plus all Emilian production), are not available.

Chianti Classico

Chianti Classico constitutes the heart of Tuscan wine—arguably of Italian wine—so it is fitting that we start here.

The name "Chianti" has, since the early 15th century (if not before), referred to an extended zone stretching from just south of Florence to just north of Siena, and from Poggibonsi in the west to Gaiole in the east. It is an area of hills rising to about 2,600ft (800m) and valleys descending to around 650ft (200m), though almost all the serious viticulture happens at 800–1,600ft (250–500m). It is a place of sweeping vistas and breathtaking undulations, of which painters have always taken full advantage, with a rich and varied vegetation that includes oaks, chestnuts, and pines; cypresses, often in columns; vines, covering about 10,000 of a total 70,000ha (25,000 of 173,000 acres); olives; flowers galore, including the famous lily, symbol of Florence, and Mediterranean *macchia*. It is also a region that boasts a very distinctive architecture, in the form of *case coloniche* (traditional stone-built houses) and fortifications—indeed, castles—with features like crenellations and turrets that, to travel-conscious folk the world over, could only be Tuscan. The fortifications, one might add, were a necessary and functional feature of a land bitterly fought over for centuries, mainly by Florentines against Sienese.

The following are some of the key dates in the Chianti Classico story.

1716: A *bando*, or ruling, of Cosimo III de' Medici, Grand Duke of Tuscany, gave the zone exclusive right to the name "Chianti," the world's first controlled denomination, according to the *chiantigiani*.

1924: A group of 33 vineyard owners got together to form the original *consorzio* for the defense of

Chianti and create its brand, the now world-famous black cockerel, or *gallo nero*.

1932: The wine-producing zone of "Chianti" was extended to several other parts of Tuscany, to the disgust of the original *chiantigiani*, though theirs was recognized as the "historic" zone with a right to the epithet "Classico." The boundaries set then were virtually the same as those pertaining today.

1967: Chianti was elevated to the status of DOC, with the special status of the historic zone recognized by the addition of the word "Classico."

1984: Chianti, including Chianti Classico, became one of the first DOCGs. From this time, the blend was allowed to contain up to 10 percent of international grapes.

1996: Chianti Classico was recognized as being autonomous, with its own separate *disciplinare*, or set of rules. Sangiovese was allowed at 100 percent for the first time, while the optional addition of international grapes increased (tacitly) to 15 percent.

2000: The optional use of international grapes in the blend was again increased (still tacitly) to 20 percent.

2003: The Chianti Classico *consorzio* was "assigned responsibility for the monitoring of the Chianti Classico denomination," with control over all estates, regardless of whether or not they are members of the *consorzio*.

Right: The picturesque landscape of Tuscany, with its gently rolling hills, has enchanted artists and visitors for centuries

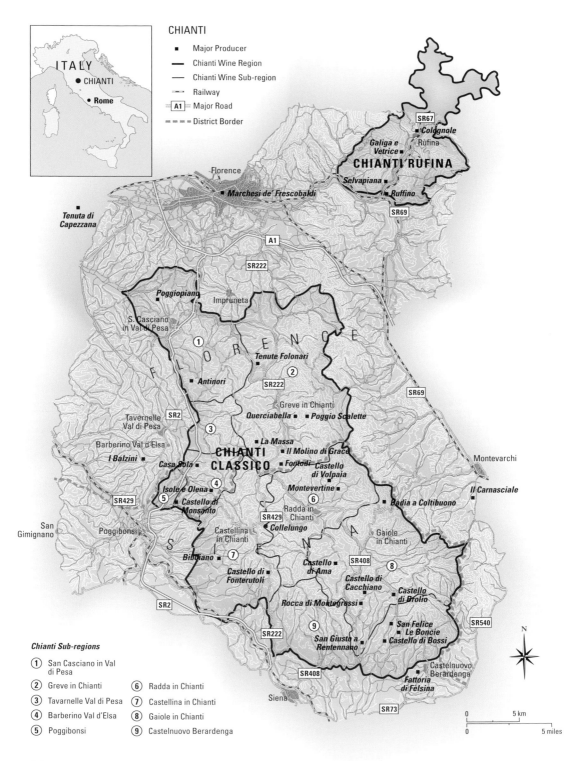

CHIANTI

- ■ Major Producer
- ▬ Chianti Wine Region
- ── Chianti Wine Sub-region
- ⌐ Railway
- [A1] Major Road
- ▬▬ District Border

ITALY

● CHIANTI

● Rome

Florence

■ Marchesi de' Frescobaldi

SR67

■ Colognole

Rùfina

Galiga e
Vetrice

CHIANTI RUFINA

Selvapiana ■

■ Ruffino

SR69

■ Tenuta di
Capezzana

A1

SR222

Poggiopiano ■

Impruneta

S. Casciano
in Val di Pesa

F L O R E N C E

①

Tenute Folonari ■

②

SR222

SR69

■ Antinori

Greve in Chianti

Tavernelle
Val di Pesa

SR2

Querciabella ■   ● Poggio Scalette

③

Barberino Val d'Elsa

La Massa ■

I Balzini ■   Casa Sola ■

● Il Molino di Graca

**CHIANTI
CLASSICO**

● Fontodi

Castello
di Volpaia

Montevarchi

Isole e Olena ■

④

Montevertine ■

SR429

⑤   ■ Castello di
Monsanto

⑥

Badia a Coltibuono ■

San
Gimignano

SR429

Radda in
Chianti

Il Carnasciale ■

Poggibonsi

● Collelungo

Castellina
in Chianti

S

Gaiole
in Chianti

SR222

Bibbiano ■

⑦

Castello
di Ama ■

E   N   A

SR408

⑧

SR2

Castello di
Fonterutoli ■

Castello di
Cacchiano ■

Castello
di Brolio

Rocca di Montegrossi ■

San Felice ■

SR540

SR222

⑨

San Giusto a
Rentennano ■

Le Boncie ■
■ Castello di Bossi

Castelnuovo
Berardenga ■

Siena

SR408

Fattoria
di Fèlsina ■

SR73

0   5 km

0   5 miles

N

Chianti Sub-regions

① San Casciano in Val
   di Pesa

② Greve in Chianti   ⑥ Radda in Chianti

③ Tavarnelle Val di Pesa   ⑦ Castellina in Chianti

④ Barberino Val d'Elsa   ⑧ Gaiole in Chianti

⑤ Poggibonsi   ⑨ Castelnuovo Berardenga

2005: The black-cockerel insignia began being applied to every bottle of Chianti Classico by way of the DOCG sticker.

2006: White grapes, as first prescribed by Baron Ricasoli in his mid-19th century blend, were excluded from the blend. (They were previously allowed up to a maximum of 6 percent.)

2008: By this time, the number of Chianti Classico producers had grown from the original 33 to more than 600, of which some 350 are bottlers, the rest selling grapes to one of the two major cooperatives (Grevepesa in Greve, or Chianti Geografico in Gaiole), or to one of the many private négociants of the area. A decreasing number also sells wine in this way, either as a matter of policy or because it is surplus to their own bottling requirements.

While on the subject of dates, it may also throw some light on developments in Chianti Classico to note that, over the past 40 years or so, there have been periods of great activity in the matter of planting new vineyards, alternating with periods of calm. Between 1950 and 1959, less than 1 percent of current plantings were carried out, this rising between 1960 and '69– the decade of the introduction of DOC— to nearly 7 percent. In the following decade, when the planting bug really got a grip, the proportion rose to over 30 percent (of current plantings). With so many vineyards recently planted, the numbers fell back sharply until the current decade (2000–09), which looks like overtaking the 1970s (a quarter of current plantings took place in the half decade from 2000 to 2004). The main reason for this is the vast improvement in clones, as well as advances in knowledge of rootstocks and plant density, as discussed in Chapter 4.

A number of wine types are produced in the Chianti Classico zone—the main one, obviously, being the eponymous Chianti Classico DOCG. At the time of writing, the maximum yield permitted is 75 quintals per hectare (1 quintal = 100kg [220lb]), or 52.5hl/ha, and 3kg (6.6lb) per plant. To qualify as Chianti Classico, a wine must contain 80–100 percent Sangiovese, with other grapes permitted up to a maximum total of 20 percent; these include native varieties such as Canaiolo, Colorino, and Mammolo, and international varieties like Cabernet Sauvignon, Merlot, and Syrah. There is, as we have seen, quite a debate surrounding this subject, the essence of it consisting in a split between those who would allow a higher proportion of internationals in order to make the wine more, er, international, and those who consider that any amount of foreign grapes is too much, since they risk distorting the unique aromas and structure of typical Tuscan wine. To me, it seems obvious that a fine wine must have a unique personality that transcends commercial considerations. To misquote, the market should come to Mohammed and not the other way around. There is quite enough wine made for the market, and that is not the role of fine wine.

A similar disagreement rages between traditionalist and modernist producers in relation to the use of oak in vinification and aging. In the (bad?) old days, casks tended to be large to very large and made of local chestnut or oak from a part of Croatia called Slavonia (not to be confused with Slovenia). As we have seen, a feature of the *rinascimento* of Tuscan wines has been a move toward smaller barrels, preferably of French oak. In my view, however, the case against Chianti Classico in barrique is by no means so cogent as that of Cabernet/Merlot in Chianti Classico, since, with skilled handling, barrique aging can give a wine much greater elegance and roundness without significant loss of *tipicità*.

There are two types of Chianti Classico: the version known commonly, unofficially, as *normale*, and that called (officially) Riserva. As the name suggests, Riserva is meant to be the finer of the two, and indeed it may not be released on to the market until it has been matured for at least 24 months, including three months in bottle, whereas *normale* may be released on October 1 following the harvest. Names like Vecchio and Superiore, which may be found on very old labels, are no longer permitted.

Apart from Chianti Classico DOCG, there is a certain amount of simple vino da tavola produced in the zone, as well as a modest quantity of dry white wine of unremarkable pedigree. There are also some excellent sweet wines emerging today, mostly called Vin Santo. But the most prestigious—and certainly the most expensive—wines of all from hereabouts are the IGTs, or so-called Super-Tuscans. The name suggests that these wines might come from anywhere in Tuscany, as indeed they do, but by far the most important zone for their production has always been Chianti Classico—precisely because of the too-restrictive laws governing the local DOC(G), as we have seen in Chapter 5. In a book on fine wines, the Super-Tuscans of Chianti Classico will inevitably feature prominently.

Chianti Classico is spread over nine communes: four in their entirety—Gaiole in Chianti, Radda in Chianti, Castellina in Chianti, and Greve in Chianti; and five partially—Castelnuovo Berardenga, Poggibonsi, Barberino Val d'Elsa, Tavarnelle Val di Pesa, and San Casciano in Val di Pesa. Those who have not been to Tuscany should know that two roads are crucial for a trip through the zone: the *superstrada* that joins Firenze Certosa and Siena, and which more or less skirts the western border of the zone; and the Strada Regionale 222, which runs right through the heart of the zone from Firenze Sud to Siena Nord. Here, however, we will go through the communes and their most prominent producers in alphabetical order.

Barberino Val d'Elsa
The Elsa is a tributary of the River Arno, forming a valley that runs south–north from below Colle

Val d'Elsa, through Poggibonsi, up to the Arno just west of Empoli. The commune of Barberino (bearing in mind that a *comune* in Italy often covers a significantly more extended space than the eponymous town) is one of those that straddle Chianti Classico and non-Classico—in this instance, in the center-west of the zone. Barberino itself is a town with an Etruscan past, but it also boasts an impressive medieval castle.

There are significant wine producers on both sides of the dividing line, which is mainly determined by soil differences between the two parts. Producers on the Chianti Classico side tend to put their main resources into classic grapes, in particular Sangiovese, making wines of good fruit definition but strong tannins. Those on the other side are more inclined toward international grapes and the rounded, deep-fruit style.

Castellina in Chianti
Castellina is one of the three (or four, depending on the version you go with) original communes of Chianti, and today it is entirely contained within the Chianti Classico borders. The Strada Regionale 222, a slow but extremely picturesque road that winds through the heart of the Chianti countryside, cuts right through it.

Castellina reveals itself to be a small but tasteful Tuscan town, the architectural integrity of which is unfortunately brutalized by a huge cement factory, constructed in the dark days of the 20th century, smack along the main road—and because the town is high up, the monstrosity can be seen from a long way away. I can never drive past it without thinking how much somebody must have got paid to allow such an eyesore to be thrown up in such an otherwise charming location.

Chianti Classico is the main preoccupation of growers here. Wines tend to be more elegant and

Right: Castellina in Chianti, fully within the Classico zone
Over: The idyllic hilltop village of Volpaia in Radda in Chianti

nervous from higher vineyards, chunkier and richer from lower down (toward Castellina Scalo).

Castelnuovo Berardenga

The town of Castelnuovo Berardenga lies just outside the Chianti Classico zone in the extreme southeast of the denomination, but the *comune* straddles both parts. Again, the difference is soil: Calcareous soil or schistous rock predominates on the Classico side; *creta senese* (mainly clay) is prominent on the Sienese side. Certain properties, such as Felsina, have vineyards in both zones.

The area is large and extends from Castelnuovo to San Gusme in the northeast and Vagliagli (a very difficult word to pronounce—try *va-lya*-LYEE), with lots of woodlands and rocky slopes, on the Classico side of the divide. Although it is difficult to generalize, wines are inclined to be forceful rather than subtle but capable, in the right conditions from the right producer, of protracted life in bottle.

Gaiole in Chianti

Gaiole is another one of the three (or four) original Chianti towns. It is quite a charming little place, tucked away in the depths of Classico, not far west of the eastern border of the zone consisting of the high Chianti ridge. This is a rugged, rocky, and much-wooded area, run through with narrow roads forever ascending and descending and especially bending. If Chianti has an area that is more Classico than thou, this is it. And within Gaiole, there is one subzone that achieves classier and more long-lived wines than elsewhere—and that is the village of Monti, whose environs contain some of the best estates of Tuscany—indeed, of all Italy.

Greve in Chianti

Some would say that Greve is not part of Chianti at

its most historic and classic, though the producers of Greve, unsurprisingly enough, would beg to differ. In any case, Greve is one of only four communes entirely within the bounds of Chianti Classico, stretching from Castellina in the south, almost as far as Florence in the north, with the Chianti ridge describing its eastern border. The town, on the Strada Regionale 222, is the nearest thing Chianti Classico has to a thriving metropolis. It has always been an important market town, and today it is also a center for tourism.

The wines of Greve are a very heterogenous lot, reflecting the varying soil, altitude, and macroclimate conditions of the rather large area but reflecting perhaps still more the diversity of the people who live here—or who, having a lot of money, have come to live here in recent decades.

As Gaiole has its famous *frazione* Monti, so Greve—the *comune*—extends to a town, Panzano, which some consider the center of classic Tuscan fruit quality, especially from that amphitheater of south-facing vineyards known as the *conca d'oro*. Greve's boundaries also enclose an area historically associated with high-quality Sangiovese (known as Sangioveto): Lamole.

Radda in Chianti

With Gaiole and Castellina, Radda completes the trio of communes that represent Chianti in its origins, going back to the Middle Ages—at least in the view of the Sienese. If anything, Radda is more wild and rocky and hilly than Gaiole, which may partly account for the fact that there are distinctly fewer very good producers in Radda than in the latter. Wines from here tend to represent the ultimate in elegance, lacking power, perhaps, but making up for it with perfume. The structure is such, too, that the wines can age well, though they are less known for their longevity than those of Monti.

San Casciano

Here, we are in the northwest corner of the Chianti Classico zone, the part nearest to Florence, in the hills on the right side of the Elsa Valley. This is another commune divided between Chianti Classico and non-Classico. Despite its size, San Casciano does not boast many top producers, though Antinori's principal cantina was situated here for several decades.

Below: An antiquated but admirably detailed road sign, testifying to the area's abiding attraction for tourists

Castello di Monsanto

The first impression one gets, arriving at Monsanto on a sunny summer's day, is that this could be the set for a modernized version of a Renaissance play. A beautiful, not-too-imposing *castello*, surrounded by flowering gardens, is set in a countryside of rolling hills, vineyards, olive groves, cypress trees—a sort of paradise in the Tuscan mode.

The wealth behind this superb estate—72 of its 206ha (178 of 544 acres) are planted to vines, of which 56ha (138 acres) are Sangiovese—derives from a thriving textile business in Lombardy. Aldo Bianchi, father of present owner Fabrizio Bianchi, bought the property in the early 1960s as a wedding present for his son. In those days, the main vineyard, Il Poggio, was a partially promiscuous plot with an *uvaggio di vigneto* that included Sangiovese, Canaiolo, Trebbiano, and Malvasia. It was, they claim, the first Chianti Classico cru.

In 1968, the white grapes were eliminated and the blend became more or less what it is now: Sangiovese plus 10 percent Canaiolo and Colorino. At the same time, Bianchi kicked out the old wooden vats in which the wine was still being made and stored, then bought one of the first, if not the first, water-cooled stainless-steel tanks in Tuscany. Other changes around that time included the destalking of the grapes, the elimination of the *governo* process, and the installation of new Slavonian oak barrels for the maturation. 1974 saw the inauguration of another quasi-revolutionary concept: a 100 percent Sangiovese cru using selected grapes from the Scanni vineyard, called Sangioveto Grosso, a Vino da Tavola later called Fabrizio Bianchi Sangiovese.

There have been gradual improvements ever since, Fabrizio taking time off from his textile business to come down and tend to the really important matter of wine at every pretext. Unusually for one in his situation, he did not call in a consultant but ran affairs himself, together with a resident

Right: Laura Bianchi, daughter of the current owner Fabrizio Bianchi, gave up her law practice to help run the estate

The Chianti Classico Riserva Il Poggio is unquestionably one of Tuscany's top wines. Its site should be a prime candidate for the Tuscan equivalent of grand cru, should any classification ever be made

enologist (currently, since 2001, Andrea Giovannini). Pressures eased for him when, in 1989, his daughter Laura decided to abandon her law practice and work full time at the winery, while her two siblings pulled the short straws and were given, some years later, responsibility for the textile business.

The 5.5ha (14-acre) Il Poggio vineyard was replanted from 2003 with 100 percent Sangiovese. As with all Monsanto's Sangiovese plantings, the replacement stock was from massal selection. Maceration length is standard to long—18–30 days, depending on the year—and aging lasts about 18 months in barrique (since 1997, prior to which a mix of barrique and *botti*; and prior to 1990, all *botti*).

The *barricaia* is in itself a work of art—a 250m- (820ft-) long, 6m- (20ft-) wide arched-roof gallery that looks as if it might be centuries old (apparently its shape is based on the "Etruscan arch") but was in fact constructed toward the end of the 1980s.

FINEST WINES

Chianti Classico Riserva Il Poggio
Unquestionably one of Tuscany's top wines, and its site should be a prime candidate for the Tuscan equivalent of grand cru, should any classification ever be made. I have participated in vertical tastings back to the 1960s on a couple of occasions and have been impressed not only by the way the old wines have survived, but also by the uncompromising elegance, rather than power, that the producer has maintained into modern times. The 1998 is particularly splendid of the older years. Recent vintages have been a bit oaky for my liking, but the underlying fruit is as magnificent as ever.
1968 Light orange/brown color. Low-key nose, but sweet if very evolved fruit on the palate, plummy and pruney, with smooth tannins and good acid. Fading now, but it still has some charm.
1977 More color than the above, still orange. Mature notes of plum and prune. Sweet fruit on the palate (cherry liqueur), leather and spice, good length and concentration. Holding on well, with time to go.
1982 Deeper, more youthful color. Fruit and leather, sandalwood on the nose. Acid firm, tannins ripe, chunky and elegant simultaneously. A wine of

balance, concentration, complexity, and length.
1988★ Still youthful, holding its color. Ripe, sweet fruit on the finish, plus a certain earthiness and a hint of balsam. Potent but elegant, grip and balance, berry fruits and spice—an exceptional wine.
1997 Hints of barrique, but otherwise a classic expression: firm tannins and acidity, with plenty of subtle fruit, spice, and leather aromas. Needs time.
1999 Deeper color but still bright, not opaque. Some oak (woodsmoke) as well as fruit on the nose. Firm but fine tannins, and rich, ripe, sweet fruit.
2000 Significantly lighter color, so no attempt at color for color's sake. Toasty notes are a bit dominant on the nose, but there is also some strawberry. Delicious, sweet, almost jammy fruit on the palate, perhaps more charming than classic.
2001 Color deeper. Some oak on the nose, but a nice concentration of fruit on the palate, with plum and cherry and hints of balsam. Concentrated and complex, yet elegant, with good acid and tannins, so could turn out to be a great bottle.

Fabrizio Bianchi Sangiovese IGT Toscana
Originally Sangioveto Grosso Vino da Tavola, this is still one of Tuscany's great 100% Sangioveses, and one of the few that demonstrate the aging potential of pure Sangiovese. The 1975 is still magnificent— meatier, rounder, and riper than the equivalent Il Poggio—and the 2001 will also live for decades. In a way it will have to, since the main vineyard of this wine was grubbed up after the excellent 2001 vintage, and the next year on release is 2006.

Other excellent wines include the **Chianti Classico Riserva** (since 1962) and **Nemo**, one of the first 100% Cabernet Sauvignons (from 1982). The basic **Chianti Classico** successfully combines the house style, which inclines toward austerity, as Barberino wines will, and more immediate drinkability.

Right: 1988 Il Poggio, a great vintage for this top Tuscan wine, which the Bianchi still make with few concessions to fashion

Castello di Monsanto
Total area: 206ha (544 acres)
Area under vine: 72ha (178 acres)
Average production: 450,000 bottles
Via Monsanto 8,
50021 Barberino Val d'Elsa, Florence
Tel: +39 05 58 05 90 00
www.castellodimonsanto.it

Il Poggio
1988
Chianti Classico
Riserva

Isole e Olena

It was in the 1950s that the father of Paolo de Marchi, a *piemontese* by origin, purchased the adjoining hamlets of Isole and Olena, in the Tuscan commune of Barberino Val d'Elsa, with their respective estates. Toward the end of the 1960s, with the *mezzadria* (sharecropping) system breaking up, the farm went through a troubled period. But with Paolo's entry into the business full time, in 1976, after agricultural studies in Turin as well as six months' training at a winery in California, the tide began to turn.

Not immediately, mind you. He arrived, accompanied by his Uruguayan wife Marta, with little experience in grape growing, less still in winemaking, and none at all in running a farm, so the early years were fraught, to put it mildly. But Paolo de Marchi has both the humility to acknowledge his ignorance and a thirst for learning. His humility still shines through, even now that his has become one of the most respected voices on Tuscan grapes and wines.

When asked a few years ago what it was that drove him—at a time when Sangiovese was considered unable to stand on its own, and Chianti was still seen as a blended wine—to produce a wine like his 100 percent Sangiovese called Cepparello, a veritable icon of its type, he replied: "I wanted to understand Sangiovese." Not in isolation but "here, in this soil. Sangiovese is our grape, and we must try to study it and understand it in varietal form" (this from the producer of some of the finest French-grape-based wines in Tuscany). Cepparello, a selection of the best grapes of the estate, could not be classed as Chianti Classico because the denomination at the time it emerged—1980 was the first vintage—was not applicable to 100 percent Sangiovese wines. And so it became Vino da Tavola, and subsequently IGT. It could now qualify for the DOCG, and indeed Paolo thinks of it as his true Chianti Classico Riserva, but it has established itself as IGT, and IGT it remains.

Right: Paolo de Marchi, the individualist but modest visionary whose passion for Sangiovese gave rise to iconic Cepparello

When Paolo de Marchi speaks, his humility shines through,
even now that his has become one of the most respected
voices on Tuscan grapes and wines

Paolo, who unusually for Tuscany remains his own chief agronomist and enologist, is a passionate and much-traveled advocate of small estates, maintaining that only the individual, hands-on producer can make truly exclusive wine. It must be based on an ensemble of factors that constitutes a whole unobtainable elsewhere. "The duty of the producer is to understand his territory. He must have a vision of origin in all its aspects."

These aspects, he says, include climate/weather; site selection and the position of the vineyards; clones and the manner of their selection; rootstock; planting density (he graduated from 3,000 to 5,000 and finally to 7,350 plants per hectare, two thirds of the 50ha [124-acre] vineyard having been replanted since 1987); training and pruning (he prefers Guyot to the more prevalent cordon spur)—the usual suspects. Most important for him, however, is the human factor. "I do things my way," he says. "My sons will do it their way, and it will be different."

One of the quality-influencing decisions that reflect his personal approach is that of generally

Above: A barrique sealed with red wax, to help reduce evaporation and oxygenation while the wine rests in wood

leaving the vintage late, to give the fruit plenty of time to arrive at full polyphenolic and grape-sugar maturity. "Sangiovese will always be a tannic grape," he comments, "but it makes a big difference if the tannins are green or ripe." Likewise, "it will always be an acidic grape; what you need is mature acidity in equilibrium." A long growing season also adds to complexity. "Why are the great classic wines from the north? Because a long growing season allows them to build up a residue of minerals and other elements from the earth, all of which add to the total picture."

Like all great wine producers, Paolo believes strongly that what you do in the vineyard is more important than what you do in the winery, though the latter is obviously not without importance, and here, too, he has his own style. He had his cantina completely overhauled in 2001/02, and today it is a mix of technology and commonsense tradition. On the whole, however, Paolo intervenes in the process as little as possible.

FINEST WINES

Cepparello IGT

This is improving all the time as its maker understands more about his material and puts his understanding into practice. Recognition has come in the form of being voted Wine of the Year (out of all the world's best) by *Wine Spectator* (1997 vintage), as well as being the cover wine for *Decanter* (50 Greatest Italian Wines) in 2008. A vertical tasting going back to 1988 indicated that it still needs work in respect of longevity, but at up to 15 years, from a top vintage like 1997 or 1999, where it displays all the earthiness and austerity of its commune, coupled with deep, layered, complex fruit, it can certainly be classed among Tuscany's outstanding wines, the rival of most Brunellos. The 1993—not a great vintage—is still showing very well, while the 1988, supposedly excellent, and multifaceted, is into a noble decline. Most recently I tasted with Paolo a range of vintages from 1991 to 2003. All of the wines (with one exception) seemed to reflect both the character of the property and the quality, actual and potential, of Sangiovese, when it is handled with devotion. But what seemed most impressive was the difference they displayed from vintage to vintage, underscoring the winemaker's stated desire to reflect the character of the year, even one as supposedly poor as 2002.

1991 Color is relatively evolved on the rim but still a luminous garnet at the heart. Less expressive and complex but holding up well for a wine of a lesser year. Tannins firm, drinking well.

1993 Color still reasonably deep and youthful. A balsamic hint on the nose, together with a touch of leather and ripe fruit. Rich, sweet fruit, quite long. Very attractive still, and will continue.

1997 The sudden fame brought by this wine caused Paolo many headaches (in terms of turning away or drastically reducing orders), but it put his estate and Cepparello specifically on the map for good. Deepest color. The nose is rich and opulent— redcurrant, spice, and herb. Delicious, ripe, soft, velvety fruit, outstanding tannic structure, holding but not impinging. Expressive, extrovert, and drinking now but will last for years. Not quite the all-round classic that the 1999 is, however.

1998 Attractive nose, clean and pure if not forceful. Very good fruit, but lacking the concentration of the 1999, the tannins a little bit too evident, with some astringency on the finish. Will age well, but not as long as the 1999. Very typically Sangiovese.

1999 ★ Relatively deep color. Complex nose of fresh fruit, graphite, and herbs. Sweet fruit on the palate, with firm acidity and a solid tannic structure. Not ready yet, but has everything it takes to develop into a great bottle, and to last for many years.

2000 The only one of the wines that appeared to fail, having what seemed to be excessive oak on the nose and finish. Tannins a bit drying, too.

2001 Cherry-berry fruit on the nose, repeated on the palate. Fresh fruit/acid balance with tannins fairly smooth. The firm acidity will keep it.

2002 Surprisingly, in this supposedly "off" year, Paolo decided to make his top wine, though in very limited quantity. The color is predictably light with a tendency to brick on the rim. Clean, fresh, and fragrant, almost floral on the nose. A bit light and nervous with zingy acidity, but the tannins are perfectly ripe. Finishes fresh and a little tart. It may not last long, but is very creditable. Paolo maintains that what the 2002 lacked in strength it compensated for in length.

2003 Nose not developed, but beautiful, sweet, cherry/strawberry fruit on the palate, with refreshing acidity. The tendency to jamminess (in this excessively hot, dry year) is also checked by the well-managed tannins. One of the best.

Chianti Classico DOCG [V]

Paolo believes this denomination is for drinking, not thinking, and his is consistently one of the most quaffable of the genre, while retaining the character of both the vintage and the estate.

Collezione de Marchi Cabernet Sauvignon, Syrah (l'Eremo), and Chardonnay IGT Toscana [2006 ★]

Paolo was one of the first in Tuscany to plant these more international grapes with a view to producing top-quality varietal wines—and in every case he has succeeded. Each of them, in any given year, is a contender for best wine of its type in Italy. And the competition (think of Gaja, Cà del Bosco, Sassicaia) is now pretty fierce.

Isole e Olena
Total area: 290ha (717 acres).
Area under vine: 50ha (124 acres)
Average production: 220,000 bottles
Isole 1, 50021 Barberino Val d'Elsa, Florence
Tel: +39 05 58 07 27 63
www.isoleolena.com

I Balzini

This is a cameo estate—not one of those that rises rapidly and falls back into obscurity, but one of those that started slowly and has been improving and polishing its act in stages ever since.

It all began in the early 1980s, when Vincenzo D'Isanto, after thorough searches for his ideal country home, bought I Balzini ("The Little Steps," named for the original vineyard whose vines were planted on small terraces) and started making wine *per gli amici* (for friends) who appreciated his idiosyncratic tastes. For although in a DOCG zone, on the Colli Fiorentini side of the commune of Barberino, Vincenzo had his own ideas as to how his wine should taste, and it was not as other Chianti Colli Fiorentini wines tasted at the time.

This is a cameo estate— not one of those that rises rapidly and falls back into obscurity, but one of those that started slowly and has been improving ever since

He planted some Sangiovese and some Cabernet (today the estate's most prevalent variety) and, helped by master taster Giulio Gambelli and enologist Andrea Mazzoni (who recently handed over to the talented young Barbara Tamburini), turned the resultant grapes into a 50/50 blend dubbed White Label, which met with considerable critical approval. In 1998, having planted a couple more hectares, he introduced Black Label, 50 percent Cabernet with 25 percent each of Sangiovese and Merlot. The current three-wine range was completed when, in 2006, Green Label was introduced, combining 80 percent Sangiovese with 20 percent Mammolo in a fresh Tuscan blend, with no oak aging, for early drinking (and, originally, with a glass stopper).

Meanwhile, Vincenzo had met and, in 1998, married Antonella, whose experience in PR came in useful when she decided, from 2005, to work full time for the azienda. This dynamic Sicilian lady has injected a whole new breath of life into the operation and is helping ensure that I Balzini, despite its modest size, is coming to be known in markets around the world.

FINEST WINES

Black Label
The estate's most serious wine, this is given a more prolonged maceration period than the White Label (up to 20 days), and is aged longer in French barriques (up to 15 months). The color of the 2004 was deep, with new oak wafting from the glass. On the palate, it was a big mouthful of bursting fruit, creamy and opulent, but perhaps a bit one-dimensional, and certainly more Cab/Merlot than Sangiovese, the latter contributing acidity more than anything in the aromas department. A "mighty wine," I noted, of the "American blockbuster type." But the structure and depth of fruit suggest that it will age well, which was borne out by the 1999: still very firm and lively, with plenty of fruit remaining, and the oak aromas and tannins well integrated.

White Label
This may be less dense and rich than the Black Label, but it is, to my taste, the better balanced and certainly more Tuscan-tasting of the two, the 2004 having fine Sangiovese acidity, sour-cherry fruit, well-handled tannins, and a relatively easy drinkability. The 1998★ was holding up brilliantly at ten years of age, when it was pretty close to its peak. A wine of balance, complexity, and depth, as well as being recognizably Tuscan, despite its considerable Cabernet content.

Green Label [V]
This is obviously the one to be drunk young—fresh, lively, and perfumed.

Società Agricola I Balzini
Total area: 10ha (25 acres)
Area under vine: 5.4ha (13 acres)
Average production: 50,000 bottles
Località Pastine 19,
50021 Barberino Val d'Elsa, Florence
Tel: +39 05 58 07 55 03
www.ibalzini.it

Casa Sola

This is, in a way, the typical, quality-conscious Chianti Classico producer of the late 20th century. It features an estate in the center-west of the zone (contiguous with Isole e Olena), purchased in a run-down condition by a family of titled northerners (the Conti Gambaro of Genoa) soon after the end of *mezzadria* (1960) and before DOC and the boom to come.

The vineyards were transformed in the following years from "promiscuous" to specialized. Chianti Classico as well as Riserva were produced from the 1965 vintage on, but not a lot else changed until the son, Giuseppe Gambaro, saw (in 1985) that Chianti Classico was on an upward trajectory and set about sorting things out, both in the vineyard and in the cantina. Small amounts of French grapes were subsequently planted in order to "improve" the blend. Today the vineyard's red grapes consist of 75 percent Sangiovese, 10 percent Cabernet Sauvignon, 5 percent Merlot, and 10 percent Canaiolo, in addition to the traditional white grapes.

In 1990, enological consultant Giorgio Marone, for a time chief winemaker at Antinori, came on board and began to bring some refinement to wines that had suffered from the fierce, mouth-puckering tannins of this dry, chalky-stony zone. In 2007, an expert in the viticultural conditions of the area, Piero Masi, late of Isole e Olena, was recruited to bring further improvement to the fruit with which Marone was working. Meanwhile, the family guard had changed when, in 2003, Giuseppe's son Matteo, a qualified agronomist, took over the reins of the estate, installing himself there full time.

Today the estate prides itself not on any revolutionary changes but rather on steady and consistent betterment of all sectors of production. "We have our idea of how to carry our business forward," says Matteo, "and we will continue to do so despite all fashions and tendencies of the passing moment, whether that affects the blend, the aging, or the methods of aging." That said, Matteo claims he has given up on pleasing all markets with a single style, and is contemplating splitting his Chianti production into modern and traditional versions.

FINEST WINES

Chianti Classico [V]
This *normale* version of the wine is a mix of Sangiovese and Canaiolo with about 6% of Cabernet and Merlot. The latter pair does enough to add ripeness and smooth tannins without obviously distorting the aromas. Maceration is 15 days (so quite traditional), and the wine ages for up to 18 months in 20hl *botti*.

Chianti Classico Riserva
The Riserva features around 10% Cabernet/Merlot with 90% Sangiovese. It gets a pre-fermentation soak, and maceration lasts about 20 days, with aging of about 20 months in a mix of *botti* and barriques. I may not agree with calling Chianti Classico a wine that contains 10% of Bordeaux varieties, but I cannot argue with the quality of the wine, which strikes a nice balance between firmness of structure and roundness of fruit, without sacrificing Tuscan typicity. [2004★]

Montarsiccio
The IGT Super-Tuscan, comprising Cabernet/Merlot at 90% and Sangiovese at 10%, is supposed to be the top wine, but I have never found it approachable until it is about eight years old.

Pergliamici
At the opposite end of the range is this pleasant quaffing wine (the name meaning "For Friends"), which contains Canaiolo and white grapes as of old.

Vin Santo
This traditionally made sweet wine is among the best of its type in Tuscany.

Casa Sola
Total area: 110ha (272 acres)
Area under vine: 30ha (74 acres)
Average production: 133,000 bottles
Frazione Cortine,
50021 Barberino Val d'Elsa, Florence
Tel: +39 05 58 07 50 28
www.fattoriacasasola.com

Castello di Fonterutoli

Fonterutoli is one of the noble Chianti Classico estates most steeped in history. The property, centered on an ancient Tuscan village some 3 miles (5km) south of Castellina, has been in the family of the Marchesi Mazzei since 1435, when the granddaughter of Ser Lapo Mazzei—a notary of the Carmignano district, as well as being the first person, as far as is known, to use the name Chianti in connection with wine (a white wine, apparently, in a document dated 1398)—married Piero di Agnolo di Fonterutoli.

Led by another Lapo Mazzei—still the proprietor of the estate, and for 20 years between the 1970s and 1990s president of the Chianti Classico *consorzio*—Fonterutoli was among the first in the dynamic final third of the 20th century to think quality. A program of replanting vineyards recently abandoned by *mezzadri* (sharecroppers) was initiated, and Bordeaux grape varieties were introduced for blending purposes from 1975. Meanwhile, aging methods based on small French oak were phased in. And all this before most in Tuscany had cottoned on to the fact that Sangiovese and its Tuscan partner grapes were, at least at that time, far too unreliable, and the large old chestnut barrels used at that time far too risky, to allow for regular production of wine acceptable to the market as drinkable, let alone good.

The improvement of the vineyards continued with increased vigor after Lapo's sons Filippo and Francesco got involved in the mid-1980s. Today, the vineyards, which are planted in five different subzones at altitudes varying from 650 to 1,640ft (200–500m), have a density of between 5,600 and 7,400 plants per hectare. They are planted with material derived partly from clonal selection and partly from massal selection from among Fonterutoli's best vines.

The new cantina, upon which work began in 2003, was clearly a matter of pride for Filippo Mazzei as he showed me around it in summer 2008. Designed by his architect sister Agnese to be not just functional but also as unobtrusive as possible in the middle of the Tuscan countryside, it is on three levels, dug into the hillside, so that humidity (indeed, running water from underground streams) and the coolness of the earth can be utilized, while enabling operations to be carried out to the maximum by gravity. There are sufficient small and medium-sized stainless-steel fermenters for well over 100 separate vinifications to be carried out at vintage time, reflecting the work they have done over the years on identifying parcels of particular character (for light quality, water availability, soil structure, and so on) amid the five subzones attached to the castle. These include the Caggio property purchased in 2006 from Ezio Rivella, ex-chief of Banfi. It is a feature of the vinification of these parcels that *assemblage* does not take place in most cases until shortly before bottling, under the direction of consultant enologist Carlo Ferrini. "And all," Filippo exclaimed, "for four wines."

"Our philosophy," he continued, "is the classic one of mixing grapes" (though not necessarily, it should be noted, using the classic Tuscan blending varieties). "I do not believe in 100 percent Sangiovese wines—one year they're great, the next they're worth nothing. It is also observable [and this is certainly true] that many who claim to do it, don't do it. In years like 2006 or 2004, okay, 100 percent Sangiovese is possible. In years like 2005 or 2003, it's difficult. In ones like 2002, it's impossible. I prefer to be consistent and to tell people exactly what I'm doing."

FINEST WINES

Castello di Fonterutoli
Of the two wines that vie for supremacy here, this is an upmarket Chianti Classico that blends Sangiovese from the finest vineyards—Belvedere and Siepi—with a "small percentage" of Cabernet Sauvignon. Its aim, often successfully achieved, is a marriage of power and elegance. It repays keeping,

Right: Filippo Mazzei, who has given new impetus to the family pursuit of quality along with his brother Francesco

and indeed becomes more "Tuscan" and less "international" as it ages. Its introduction, in the late 1990s, as a Chianti Classico DOCG, was a bold move whose purpose was to help the denomination claw back some of the reputation for quality that it had previously squandered. I gave the 2005 —not the greatest vintage—a good score for its concentrated but balanced palate, ripe tannins, and typical Tuscan acidity, the perfumes being a mix of Tuscan and international (cassis, oak). It finished, however, on a typically Sangiovese-esque sour cherry note.

Siepi
This Super-Tuscan (IGT Toscana), about two thirds Sangiovese, one third Merlot, is considered one of the highest expressions of its genre. It somehow achieves ripeness, roundness, and lushness with seriousness of structure and intent, aging beautifully over 15 years, as a vertical tasting in 2008 attested. For the present book I tasted the 2005★, which was plump and sweet, with rounded fruit on the palate yet with a good backbone of ripe tannin. The oak was excellently handled, as one would expect from an enologist as expert with barrique as Carlo Ferrini. It is distinctly more "international" than Castello, but then it does not pretend to be anything else.

Fonterutoli
This basic but well-made Chianti Classico blends Sangiovese, Colorino, Malvasia Nera, and Merlot.

Belguardo IGT Toscana
Fonterutoli has two other properties, one of which—Belguardo, in the Morellino di Scansano zone—falls within our remit. The 2005, a blend of Cabernet Sauvignon and Cabernet Franc, is typical of today's high-quality, international-style Tuscan wines—rich, ripe, and juicy, with dark chocolate and coffee-grounds, having the structure to age well.

Left: The barrel cellar in the impressive new winery, designed by Filippo Mazzei's sister Agnese and dug into a hillside

Castello di Fonterutoli
Total area: 650ha (1,606 acres)
Area under vine: 117ha (289 acres)
Average production: 710,000 bottles
Via Puccini 4, Località Fonterutoli,
53011 Castellina in Chianti, Siena
Tel: +39 05 77 74 13 85
www.fonterutoli.it

Bibbiano

There is now a slightly abandoned feel about this historic property (mentioned as Castello di Bibiune in a document dating as far back as 1089), with its magnificent but little-lived-in villa and semi-remote situation beyond Lilliano, on a side road between Castellina in Chianti and Castellina Scalo.

This is explained partly by the fact that the owners—brothers Tommaso and Federico Marrocchesi Marzi, in whose mother's family the estate has remained since 1865—live in Rome. But they do visit regularly (at least, Tommaso does) to sign checks and make sure that the staff are all doing their job.

Other regular visitors, thankfully for the wine, are Giulio Gambelli, consultant enologist here since the 1940s, who brings with him his illustrious taste buds; and Stefano Porcinai, a consultant agronomist-enologist of more recent vintage who, like several before him, was once head of the *consorzio*'s technical branch.

Of the tradition that Gambelli represents, there is the old-style cantina, now at the planning stage of reconstruction, I gather, but still, as I write, equipped with no stainless steel (well, almost none). For fermentation purposes, there are only those once-reviled glass-lined concrete vats that so many destroyed in the frenzied years of modernization, only to realize later that these containers have certain definite advantages.

Of the modern world that Porcinai represents, there is a bit of Merlot in the vineyard. There is also now equipment for ensuring temperature stabilization during fermentation (something Gambelli never bothered with), and there are the inevitable barriques, as well as the traditional Slavonian oak *botti*.

All of the vineyards were planted between 1966 and 1970 and partly replanted, with both massal-selection and commercially available clonal stock, between 1998 and 2005.

FINEST WINES

Chianti Classico [V]
This Sangiovese with 5% Canaiolo and Colorino is a delightfully traditional wine that has not changed much, it seems, since it first went into bottle with the 1969. Acidity is piercing at first sip, but the palate adapts quickly, especially since the tannins are well handled and the alcohol (13.5%) is well disguised. Archetypal, sour-cherry Chianti, bright and fresh, for lovers of the old style.

Chianti Classico Montornello
The single-vineyard, 95% Sangiovese with 5% Merlot, is less modernistic than it sounds, the Merlot having had minimum impact on Sangiovese's natural light color and characteristic sour-cherry and tea-leaf aromas. It makes you wonder how much other people, who claim to add only 5% Merlot/Cabernet, really put in. The wine is rounder and riper than the *normale* above—perhaps a bit more internationally acceptable, a bit less uncompromisingly Tuscan.

Chianti Classico Riserva Vigna del Capannino
Another single-vineyard wine, this is a special selection carried out only in the best years. 100% Sangiovese, aged in barrique, it is quite round and ripe but unmistakably Tuscan. [2004★]

A top-end Merlot-based wine, projected for imminent release, indicates the direction in which Bibbiano may be going. Lovers of old-style Tuscan Sangiovese had better get in stocks of wines 1 and 3 above while the getting is good.

The Chianti Classico is a delightfully traditional wine: archetypal, sour-cherry Chianti, bright and fresh, for lovers of the old style

Tenuta di Bibbiano
Total area: 220ha (544 acres)
Area under vine: 23ha (57 acres)
Average production: 85,000 bottles
Via Bibbiano 76,
53011 Castellina in Chianti, Siena
Tel: +39 05 77 74 30 65
www.tenutadibibbiano.com

Collelungo

The most remarkable feature of Collelungo is the average altitude of its vineyards, well over 1,650ft (500m), making it one of the highest, if not the highest, and latest-picked *aziende* in Chianti Classico. To add to the difficulty of getting grapes ripe at those heights, the soil has all the meanness and unfertility associated with Chianti Classico, with limestone and *galestro* and stones and rocks—if not boulders—galore, very little clay, and therefore excellent, if not too excellent, drainage. On the compensation side, the vineyards face mainly south and get plenty of breeze to relieve the heat and discourage molds and insects. And of course the planet is getting hotter, so altitude will be an increasing advantage. Meanwhile, they can play the "elegance" card, which they do, in spades.

Collelungo is one of the highest aziende in Chianti. Altitude will be an increasing advantage. Meanwhile, they can play the "elegance" card, which they do, in spades

"They" are Lorenzo and Monica Cattelan, a young married couple who bought the property from Brits Tony and Mira Rocca in 2002. Lorenzo and Monica hail from Vicenza in the Veneto and had no experience in farming but were attracted—as so many are—by the Tuscan countryside and the idea of running an already established *agriturismo* business and a wine farm on the top of the world. What they have done since is basically consolidate what Tony and Mira had developed, before, as Mira put it, "running out of steam," having taken over a farm in 1989 that, according to Tony, "had not been looked after"; indeed, they were not inclined to look after it viticulturally until the mid-1990s, when the *agriturismo* was up and running.

Today, following an extensive replanting program, leaving only 1.5ha (4 acres) of old vineyard, the Cattelans have more or less doubled the planted area to 20ha (49 acres), almost entirely with Sangiovese (plus a "very small" area of Merlot), at densities of up to 6,000 plants per hectare. Giacomo Cesari has acted as assistant to enological consultant Alberto Antonini since 2004, with Lorenzo himself lending a helping hand. A new cantina is planned. Meanwhile, wines are made in a classic-modern style, with a 2–3-week maceration, *délestage*, and pumping over, with malolactic and maturation in French barrique, and no filtration.

FINEST WINES

Chianti Classico
This is the bedrock of production—a wine that concentrates more on perfume than on body and displays the sour-cherry character of Sangiovese at its purest. It can be almost aggressively sharp, but delicacy and elegance shine through it.

Chianti Classico Riserva
Like the above wine, this is 100% Sangiovese, aged 12 months in barrique plus 12 months in bottle, compared with six for the *normale*. A selection of the best bunches in top years, it has correspondingly more richness and structure, but the perfumes of Collelungo are still very much in evidence. [2006★]

Chianti Classico Riserva Campo Cerchi
This single-vineyard wine also used to be 100% Sangiovese but since 2006 has had 5% Merlot, no doubt to deepen color and blunt the acidity's cutting edge. We can only hope that it does not compromise the striking purity of the wine.

Merlot IGT
An intense, raspberry/strawberry wine, with the characteristic house elegance.

Collelungo
Total area: 94ha (232 acres)
Area under vine: 20ha (49 acres)
Average production: 120,000 bottles
53011 Castellina in Chianti, Siena
Tel: +39 05 77 74 04 89
www.collelungo.com

Castello di Bossi

This large and impressive estate in the southeast corner of the Chianti Classico zone stands at an altitude between about 920 and 1,250ft (280–380m), where the wines tend to be fuller and earthier than their counterparts from the more central section of the zone.

The imposing *castello* has roots going back nearly a thousand years, though it was not completed in its present form until around 1500. The present owners, the Bacci family, clothing merchants of Florence, bought it from a family of Prato cloth manufacturers in 1980—not so much for its already fairly extensive vineyards, wine production being at the time pretty near the nadir of its cyclical movement market-wise, but more as a family retreat with an agricultural aspect. The wine they did produce was sold in bulk, and even now they bottle only the best for themselves.

As time passed, however, one of the sons, Marco, got bitten by the wine bug. By the middle of the 1990s, Marco was thinking big, not just in terms of size but of quality, too, and by 1997 he was involved in wine full time, leaving the management of the clothing business to his brother Maurizio. He realized the current structure was not at a level to achieve the quality he sought, and so he sacked the enological consultant and brought in another, the now-famous Alberto Antonini. Already, from 1995, Marco had initiated a 15-year program of renewal of the vineyards, replanting around 8ha (20 acres) a year, at up to 5,500 vines per hectare, with a range of proven Sangiovese clones and doing his best to match clone to soil. Previously, in the 1970s, under the guidance of maestro *enologo* Giacomo Tachis, there had been extensive plantings of Merlot and Cabernet, and these, too, entered the replanting program initiated by Marco.

In the winery, Marco's aim has been to keep right up to date with those technological innovations

Right: Marco Bacci, who left the family firm in Florence to transform the wine production at their country retreat

One of the sons, Marco Bacci, got bitten by the wine bug.
By the middle of the 1990s, he was thinking big,
not just in terms of size but of quality, too

that can do that bit more to translate quality grapes into quality wine—reequipping with the very latest stainless-steel fermenters; computerized temperature control; a system of breaking the cap by chains placed at the top of the fermenters. For aging, no doubt encouraged by Antonini, he decided on small oak for all reds, even Chianti Classico, but with an inclination toward low toast in order to avoid excessive oak character in the wine.

Not content with a large winery in Chianti Classico, Castello di Bossi purchased two other wine properties in the late 1990s: first in Montalcino, at Renieri, where 35ha (86 acres) were planted between 1998 and 1999; then in Magliano, in the Morellino di Scansano zone of the southern Maremma, where an equal area was planted at a higher density of up to 6,500 plants per hectare. In both cases, the principal variety was Sangiovese but with a good sprinkling of international and, in the case of Terre di Talamo (Magliano), white varieties.

FINEST WINES

Chianti Classico
This is the bread-and-butter wine. It tends, as in the most recently tasted 2006 vintage, to the chunky, earthy style common to this corner of the zone. There is plenty of fruit and structure, but rather less elegance.

Chianti Classico Riserva Berardo
Even fuller and more robust, certainly in its youth, this has proved itself capable of aging really well, with lots of sweet, evolved fruit, interesting tertiary aromas, and enough structure to keep it alive for some time yet. I gave high marks to the 2001★, 1997, 1995, and even the earliest vintage, 1993, not normally known for its staying power. More recently, the 2003, with plenty of fresh and stewed fruit but some harshness on the finish, scored less well.

Corbaia
One of the other two significant wines, both "international"-style IGTs: a barrique-aged blend of Sangiovese and Cabernet, from vines more than 30 years old. The 2003 has plenty of plum/prune fruit and an almost porty finish.

Girolamo
A Merlot from vines planted in the early 1970s, supposedly the first in Tuscany (at least from imported clones). The 2003 tends to muscularity, but there is lots of rich, plummy fruit.

Above: The current Castello di Bossi dates back to 1500, but a castle has dominated the landscape here for 1,000 years

Castello di Bossi
Total area: 650ha (1,606 acres)
Area under vine: 124ha (306 acres)
Average production: 600,000 bottles
Località Bossi in Chianti,
53019 Castelnuovo Berardenga, Siena
Tel: +39 05 77 35 93 30
www.castellodibossi.it

Fattoria di Fèlsina

It was in 1966 that Domenico Poggiali purchased this large property of Fèlsina, lying either side of Chianti Classico's extreme southeast border. At that time, the ancient estate, with roots going back a thousand years, existed mainly for the production of olive oil, wheat, grain, and other crops, as well as livestock.

Of vineyards there were scarcely 2.5ha (6 acres), and while Domenico and his son Beppe worked hard to renew and expand the vineyard and cantina over the next ten years, it was not until Giuseppe Mazzocolin came on the scene, following his marriage to Domenico's daughter Gloria, that things really took off. Or perhaps the real takeoff dated from

"People say Sangiovese is an impossible grape," says Giuseppe. "But how can you judge something you don't know? Sangiovese is a grape you have to live with"

1982, when Giuseppe—now full time, having traded in his career as a schoolteacher—made contact with Franco Bernabei, an acquaintance and fellow native of Veneto now working as a freelance enologist in Tuscany. Together they agreed to take not the easy route of planting the more obedient but non-indigenous Bordeaux varieties, as many were doing in those days, but to go the hard way with Tuscan's prodigal son, Sangiovese. "People say Sangiovese is an impossible grape," says Giuseppe. "But how can you judge something you don't know? Sangiovese is a grape you have to work with, live with, experiment with endlessly. Maybe 50 years from now we will be able to say that we understand Sangiovese as we understand Cabernet Sauvignon."

Between 1983 and 1985, Giuseppe, his brother-in-law, and their field staff, who had to be retrained from general agriculture to monoculture (or duoculture, if you include, as you must, olives,

another of Giuseppe's abiding passions), began transforming the Fèlsina vineyards. In the late 1980s and '90s, they embarked on a major replanting program, which is still ongoing, based on massal selection, virtually doubling plant density to 5,600 vines per hectare. The work took another quantum leap after they purchased the neighboring Pagliarese estate in 1995.

Giuseppe is always delighted to take visitors on a bumpy ride around his vineyard. He insists that his wines cannot be fully understood without a knowledge of the soil, exposure, climate, and light quality of the land from which they derive. He points out that, of his two pride-and-joy wines— Fontalloro and Rància— the former, despite various similarities with Rància (pure Sangiovese, same estate, very similar vinification and aging, apart from Fontalloro receiving slightly more maceration time and more new oak than Rància), needs to be understood in the context of the wines of Siena, being grown (two thirds of it, at any rate) on the sandy-clay soil with marine deposits typical of the *creta senese*; while the soil of the Rància vineyards is that chalky *alberese*, rocky and poor, typical of Chianti vineyards as far away as Rùfina, some 45 miles (70km) to the north.

Giuseppe's fascination for Sangiovese does not, however, prevent him from experimenting with several other grapes. He also produces, quite separately and with no blending, a pure Cabernet Sauvignon called Maestro Raro. Giuseppe's views on Cabernet are quite straightforward: It is a great grape variety in its own arena, as is Merlot, but it has got no business in Chianti, nor being blended with Sangiovese. "Even with 2 percent Cabernet," he insists, "one cannot have the experience of pure Sangiovese, whose greatest character lies in its evolution in bottle.

"We should shout this from the rooftops," he explains, "that if you're going to add these grapes, you'd better off going back to Trebbiano!"

FINEST WINES

Fontalloro and Rància

I was offered a fascinating vertical tasting of these two star wines, side by side, apparently the first time old vintages of Rància had ever been tasted alongside old vintages of Fontalloro. Both proved themselves to be sturdy wines, capable of *lungo invecchiamento*, Fontalloro generally having the greater structure and staying power, with perhaps a more earthy and more fruity character than Rància, and in general a greater staying power. Rància proved the more complex wine, lending itself less to straightforward enjoyment.

Descriptors applying to Rància tended more toward the vegetal, the spicy, the pruney (in older bottles), while freshness and fruit character were more in evidence with Fontalloro. Both wines were firm of acidity and had their fair share of tannins, but these elements seemed more noticeable in Rància than in Fontalloro. Both crus scored very well for character and consistency, Fontalloro coming out on top overall. The highest points for a single wine, however, went to 1990 Rància.

1983 Rància Aging, but with attractive herb and spice notes and pruney fruit.

1983 Fontalloro Fresher and more forceful than the Rància, appearing no more than half its age.

1985 Rància Mineral/iodine nose, pruney and leathery, with drying tannins and a fading finish.

1985 Fontalloro Strikingly fresh berry fruit, firm but ripe tannins, and truffles. Classic.

1988 Rància One of the weakest wines in the tasting: aggressive, drying tannins and vegetal notes.

1988 Fontalloro Fresh and fruit-driven, with coffee and spice notes. Mouthfilling.

1990 Rància★ The apotheosis of the Rància style: complex, truffle-pâté nose and savory palate, with beautifully balanced acid/tannin structure.

1990 Fontalloro Relatively closed and slightly tough, but still with some delightful, porty fruit on the finish.

1993 Rància and **Fontalloro** Rància just edged it in this unimpressive vintage. Both wines were hard, but Rància's saving grace was its herby, spicy nose.

1995 Rància Mineral and vegetal, without any great sweetness of fruit, but complex and still improving.

1995 Fontalloro Plummy, blackberry fruit on the nose, with a firm structure, chocolate, spice, and tar; nice complexity.

Left: Giuseppe Mazzocolin, a former school teacher, now engaged in *élevage* of a different kind with large, old oak *botti*

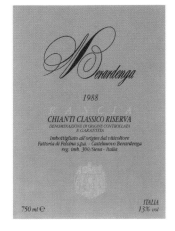

1997 Rància One of the best vintages: vegetal, mineral, garrigue; concentrated and still growing.

1997 Fontalloro The perfect contrast, with the accent on fruit: less complex but more seductive.

1999 Rància Floral, mineral, vegetal, with some cherry fruit; nicely balanced and well structured.

1999 Fontalloro★ Deep, rich, plummy fruit, with impressive structure. Still a long way to go.

2001 Rància and **Fontalloro** After four years, both wines are still in their shells: closed, hard, and lacking in charm. They have yet to express their differences, but the potential is there.

Chianti Classico and Chianti Classico Riserva

Of Fèlsina's other wines, the Chianti Classico and Chianti Classico Riserva (also made with 100% Sangiovese) tend to be among the gutsier representatives of their respective genres.

Maestro Raro

This sturdy Cabernet Sauvignon makes up in power and concentration what it lacks in elegance.

Fattoria di Fèlsina
Total area: 512ha (1,265 acres)
Area under vine: 62ha (153 acres)
Average production: 600,000 bottles
Via del Chianti 101,
53019 Castelnuovo Berardenga, Siena
Tel: +39 05 77 35 51 17
www.felsina.it

San Felice

This historic property may be owned by a massive international concern, Gruppo Allianz, and may also boast, apart from several major wineries, a superb Relais & Châteaux hotel, with a memorable restaurant, golf course, swimming pool, and so on. But it is run almost like a family concern, with the bosses of the various companies that have owned them letting the long-serving and highly committed employees get on with what they know best: growing grapes and making wine. In charge of the grapes since 1973 has been Carlo Salvinelli, while Leonardo Bellacini has been on board a quarter of a century, taking over as enologist from maestro Enzo Morganti after his death in 1994. A measure of how well employees are treated is the assertion by Leonardo that he could be earning three times his salary as a freelance consultant, but prefers the lifestyle here.

History abounds, there having been an important church, and no doubt some vines, here since the 8th century, and there is evidence of a medieval Pope ordering wine and oil from the estate. But we will fast-forward to 1967, when Enzo Morganti came from Tenuta di Lilliano to take over direction, producing from the 1968 vintage what was certainly the prototype of the Chianti-zone Super-Tuscans in the form of a 100 percent Sangiovese Vino da Tavola called Vigorello. Another of Enzo's innovations was to form an alliance with the academic world, to study nearly 300 indigenous vine types in the experimental vineyard called Vitiarium (*see Chapter 3*). Among the many flowerings from this research, in recent years overseen by the University of Florence's Roberto Bandinelli, has been the development and recent approval of a unique Tuscan grape that was heading for extinction. Pugnitello, so called because the bunch resembles a fist (*pugno*), is today San Felice's second most-planted variety (6 percent

Right: Leonardo Bellacini, San Felice's enologist for the past 15 years, at the entrance to its experimental vineyard, Vitiarium

*Enzo Morganti produced from the 1968 vintage what was certainly
the prototype of the Chianti-zone Super-Tuscan in the form of
a 100 percent Sangiovese Vino da Tavola called Vigorello*

of total vineyard space), used in at least one of their blends and even made varietally at a high level of quality. Work is also going ahead with a couple of other indigenous grapes, Abrusco and Abrostine, for which they have high hopes. They are carrying forward research into zoning—ascertaining the soil/climate characteristics of the various parts of their vineyard in order to understand better what rootstock and varieties/clones will be most suitable for replanting in any given location. They are also experimenting with plant density (up to 8,500 plants per hectare) and with different pruning and training systems (*alberello* and Guyot).

But it is not experiment for experimentation's sake. "We have been innovative," Bellacini explains, "when it has been necessary to challenge the absurdities of the law [mandatory inclusion of white grapes and Canaiolo; interdiction on pure Sangiovese]. Today we are in the forefront of those who want to put the brakes on"—in the sense of opposing the inclusion of significant volumes of foreign grapes in denominated Tuscan wines. Right on, Leonardo. (He looks like a movie star, too.)

FINEST WINES

Pugnitello IGT Toscana
This is perhaps the most interesting of San Felice's wines. First released in 2003, it is a pure varietal that combines deep and vibrant color ("Unfortunately," jokes Bellacini, "most people today drink with their eyes") and a fruity-peppery nose, with a dollop of fruit on the palate, savory-sweet and quite smooth in its tannins. The 2004 [V] is very distinctive and eminently drinkable, yet it will probably age well.

Vigorello
The wine that is meant to be the star, and that originated in 1968 as a pure Sangiovese, the first of its type outside Montalcino, is nowadays a blend of 45% Sangiovese, 40% Cabernet Sauvignon, and 15% Merlot. The 2003 has plenty of cassis fruit and firm tannins, and will no doubt improve with bottle age. But it is a bit too in-your-face Gallic for me. The Sangiovese gets a bit lost.

Poggio Rosso
This single-vineyard Chianti Classico Riserva (80% Sangiovese, 10% Colorino, and 10% Pugnitello), first vintage 1978, is a wine I have admired right through to the excellent 2004, mainly for its concentration and intensity of fruit, which can be irresistible. Unfortunately, many turn away from it because of the austerity of its tannins. An acquired taste, but the 2003 and (especially) the 2004 vintage ★ are worth the effort.

Chianti Classico Riserva Il Grigio
Somewhat down the scale from the above three wines, and first produced as a Chianti blend in the 1968 vintage, this has since the mid-1990s taken over where Vigorello left off, as a pure Sangiovese. The 2005 is perhaps the quality equivalent of good Rosso di Montalcino: well made, very typical of Sangiovese (firm acid, cherry fruit), and to be drunk within ten years.

Campogiovanni Brunello Riserva Il Quercione
San Felice also has a sizable vineyard, Campogiovanni, in the Sant'Angelo section of Montalcino, where it produces a good Brunello and an outstanding single-vineyard Riserva called Il Quercione. At ten years of age, this wine has intense, velvety fruit and a lovely finish, in no way compromised by oak. A final, revealing comment from Leonardo: "The quality of the grapes at Campogiovanni is notably superior to that at San Felice, where we have to work much harder." [1999 ★]

San Felice
Total area (Chianti): 635ha (1,570 acres)
Area under vine (Chianti): 140ha (346 acres)
Total area (Montalcino): 65ha (161 acres)
Area under vine (Montalcino): 20ha (49 acres)
Average production: 1 million bottles
Località San Felice,
53019 Castelnuovo Berardenga, Siena
Tel: +39 05 77 39 91
www.agricolasanfelice.com

Le Boncie

Giovanna Morganti, daughter of the late, great Enzo Morganti (who passed away in 1994; *see San Felice*) is undoubtedly one of Chianti's non-conformists. She never worked with her father, but he sent her to enological college in Siena, where she became inspired by a method of planting that had been widespread in Tuscany a couple of centuries earlier but that had virtually died out in northern Italy: *alberello*. And, of course, he left her and her mother this small but tasty property that he had received from a grateful San Felice.

After working with consultant enologist Maurizio Castelli for a few years, looking after customers such as Castello di Volpaia and Badia a Coltibuono, she began making her own wine in 1990, according to organic principles, using traditional Tuscan varieties like Colorino, Mammolo, and Foglia Tonda as blenders, though the proportion of Sangiovese is always very high (around 95 percent).

It was in 1997 that Giovanna finally gathered the courage to plant two thirds of her vineyard to *alberello*—7,500 plants per hectare. The system, she reports, is generally positive for quality but does have a downside, mainly in respect of labor. So when she planted again in 1999 (the final third of her vineyard), she reverted to Guyot training on wires.

Today, she is reluctant to say which system is better but maintains that *alberello* enhances consistency—an important consideration for notoriously inconsistent Sangiovese. "Every now and then I get fed up with *alberello*," says Giovanna, "but when a vintage like 2002 comes along, I'm grateful I've got it. It's a system you have to believe in thoroughly, otherwise you'll abandon it."

As for the making of the wine, she vinifies in open wooden *tini*, limiting the maceration to 16 or 17 days. She punches down by hand and aging lasts about 18 months in French oak *botticelli* (little barrels: so that's what Sandro's name means). No cultured yeasts or enzymes are added, the idea being to keep things as pure and natural as possible.

FINEST WINES

Le Trame Chianti Classico

This is the only wine that Giovanna Morganti produces commercially. The style, as I have described it elsewhere, is feminine—or perhaps elegant is a better word—unsurprisingly, as the azienda is high, at around 1,300ft (400m) and on stony, calcareous soil. Giovanna goes in for subtlety and suggestion, where more macho male types—like a nearby neighbor (not San Felice) who makes liberal use of the right of Chianti Classico producers to use Cabernet and Merlot, and is at a lower altitude, with more clay in the soil—might aim for muscle and power. The latter style may score better with some critics, but there is gathering evidence that consumers looking for the real Sangiovese are turning in her direction. This is one for lovers of subtlety (*trame* means intrigues). A vertical tasting going back to the mid-1990s gave evidence that her wines can also take bottle age.

1995 A "nervous" wine in the best sense, the acidity seeming a bit high, and body a bit on the thin side, but well-defined fruit, perfumed and pure, with good length.

1998 Not a great vintage generally but possibly Giovanna's best so far. The aspect is brilliant, lively cherry fruit on the nose, and the fruit is sweet and long and subtle. Clean, well expressed, very Chianti Classico, and probably capable of aging for 15–20 years.

1999 Deeper color, and inviting cherry fruit on the nose. Firm acidity, very sour cherry, very typical. Again the acidity is pointed, but elegant.

2000 Relatively soft, almost jammy fruit compared with the others, but it works. Forward and good in youth, but probably not a long-distance runner.

2001★ This *is* a long-distance runner: brilliantly defined sour-cherry fruit, clean and fresh, with firm tannins. Still 15–20 years of life left.

2002 Soft and easy to drink; shows what can be done with care and selection even in a poor year.

Le Boncie
Area under vine: 3.3ha (8 acres)
Average production: 13,000–14,000 bottles
Strada delle Boncie,
San Felice,
53019 Castelnuovo Berardenga, Siena
Tel: +39 05 77 35 93 83

Badia a Coltibuono

One of Chianti Classico's most historic and illustrious estates, Badia a Coltibuono has been in the same family since 1846, when, together with Fattoria Selvapiana in Rùfina, it was purchased by Florentine banker Michele Giuntini, great-great-grandfather of the current proprietors, siblings Emanuela, Roberto, Paolo, and Guido Stucchi Prinetti. Its history as a wine-producing estate goes back much further than that, however, having been a monastery in the Vallombrosan order since 1051—and we all know how religiously the monks cultivated their vines. It was Piero Stucchi Prinetti, father of Emanuela et al, who after the war shifted the balance of production from everyday Chianti to Riserva, and as long as I can remember (longer than I wish to say), Badia has been famous for its old riserva wines.

One of Chianti Classico's most historic and illustrious estates, Badia a Coltibuono has been in the same family since 1846, and is famous for its old riserva wines

Once upon a time, these wines were as likely as not to be brown in color and volatile on the nose, having been aged for donkey's years in huge, old, chestnut barrels. Until the mid-1970s, the traditional (that is, since the mid-19th century) vineyard blend was followed, consisting of Sangiovese accompanied by Canaiolo and Trebbiano/Malvasia. And it was not so bad. A recent tasting showed the 1970 Chianti Classico Riserva in a favorable light—white grapes, low alcohol level (12%), chestnut *botti, governo all'uso toscano*, and all. But they were missing a dimension, and the turnaround began when consultant Maurizio Castelli first came on the scene in 1979 (he left for a few years but is now back).

Bit by bit, the old *uvaggio di vigneto* vineyards, situated some 12 miles (20km) distant from the *badia* (abbey), in the sub-zone of Monti, were replanted to single varieties. The vast majority of these were Sangiovese, of various clones—indeed, the Stucchis were among the first to introduce a 100 percent Sangiovese wine, called Sangioveto (the Tuscan version of the grape name), from 1980. They adopted a massal-selection program using Sangiovese cuttings of different biotypes from the oldest vineyards (of which a significant number, up to 55 years old, have been left), but they were also careful to keep abreast of the latest discoveries in clonal research.

Since that time, there have been numerous developments at Coltibuono (which means "good crop"). Roberto, having taken a degree in enology at the University of California, became resident winemaker for a while, though he has recently departed in somewhat mysterious circumstances... Emanuela, the senior sibling, has since taken command. They have gone organic, about which Emanuela is very proud. They have built a 21st-century winery at Monti that not only is completely electronically and technologically equipped, but that works by gravity, so there is no need to force the wine through pipes—of which Emanuela is equally proud. They have started an experiment with maceration lasting several months, as in the old days, but the results are yet to be seen. And they have, in keeping with their commitment to their production zone (Emanuela was president of the *consorzio* for three years), introduced a new upmarket Chianti Classico wine called Cultus Boni.

FINEST WINES

Chianti Classico Riserva
This is the wine for which Badia has long been famous (the oldest bottle in their cellars is a 1937). Today it is about 90% Sangiovese plus Canaiolo,

Left: Emanuela Stucchi Prinetti, under whose leadership Badia a Coltibuono has converted to organic viticulture

sourced from the oldest vineyards, up to 35 years old, and aged 24 months in Austrian and French oak. A wine of elegance and breeding, made only in the best years, it is difficult to approach in its youth but obviously able to age in a protracted and complex way. The results of the vertical tasting referred to above were as follows:

1965 Faded, leathery/herbal nose; fruit not gone but drying out; uppish volatile acidity, the wine now into noble decrepitude.

1970 Leather and herbs, tea-leaf; some decent fruit on the palate; now on the downward slope, but still hanging on.

1976 Very acidic, with firm tannin; not much fruit left but a bit of sour cherry; some length; again, hanging on.

A wine of elegance and breeding, made only in the best years, the Riserva is difficult to approach in its youth but obviously able to age in a protracted and complex way

1981 This was the first Riserva of Castelli's reign, and also the first to benefit from destemming and malolactic fermentation. A wine of lively hue, with some tea-leaf on the nose; still quite full, with sour cherry fruit of fair concentration, and a sweet finish of good length. A big contrast with all of the previous wines.

1995 Good color, ruby with orange rim; cherry and tea-leaf on the nose; acid and tannin firm but concentrated and characterful; austere but of good length.

2004★ Remarkably deep hue; fresh cherry, sweet fruit on both nose and palate; acid and tannin firm but well covered; long, with lots of class.

2005 Dry tea-leaf on the nose; more elegant but less fruity than the 2004; quite classic, and a good reflection of the vintage.

Sangioveto

An IGT, aged 12 months in French barriques, this is a wine of concentration and power but with an underlying gracefulness that carries it through the years. The 2004 is classic, but will not be ready until 2012.

Left: The former monastic property, whose origins stretch back to the 11th century, is artfully portrayed on the estate's labels

Cultus Boni

This first came on the market in 2004, with the 2001 vintage. It is a more modern approach to Chianti Classico (but still sold as such), containing a small percentage of Merlot, as well as Colorino and Ciliegiolo, aged in barrique and aimed, successfully, at the international market.

Chianti Classico (*normale*)

A wine of fruit and fragrance, yet of firm backbone, as are all the wines of Badia, this is made to be drunk relatively young, though the 2004, from a great vintage, was awarded the coveted *tre bicchieri* in the *Gambero Rosso* guide, and clearly has an extra dimension.

Badia a Coltibuono
Total area: 800ha (1,977 acres)
Area under vine: 74ha (183 acres)
Average production: 333,000 bottles
53013 Gaiole in Chianti, Siena
Tel: +39 05 77 74 61 10
www.coltibuono.com

Castello di Brolio

Much credit must go to this unpretentious aristocrat wrenched in mid-career from the hedonistic existence of a Florence photographer to the unrelenting pressures of leadership of Chianti Classico's largest wine estate. This most historic of wine castles has been home to the Ricasoli family since 1141 and the center and pinnacle of Tuscan wine production from the mid-19th century, under the "Iron Baron" Bettino Ricasoli. He not only served as Italy's prime minister, but through his experiments he proposed the Chianti blend that was adopted for DOC purposes a century later. (It is important to note that the blend that Baron Ricasoli recommended consisted mainly of Sangiovese with some Canajuolo [sic] "to temper the hardness of the first, without taking from it any of its perfume"; plus "la Malvagia [sic], which may be

Much credit must go to this unpretentious aristocrat wrenched from the hedonistic existence of a Florence photographer to leadership of Chianti's largest wine estate

left out of wines destined for aging," since it tends to dilute the product of the first two grapes. In other words, contrary to the view most often put about, the baron did not advocate white grapes for the more important wines—only for those in a lighter and more early-drinking style.)

In the gloomy wine years of the 1970s and '80s, the *cantine* had been leased out to industrial producers such as Seagram's and Hardys, who had done their best to bring low the once-great reputation. Having retained ownership of the vineyards, the present Baron Bettino determined in the early 1990s to buy back the commercial rights as well and delegated his only child, the Iron Baron's great-great-great-grandson, to rescue the family name. As a result, Francesco says, "I have been living in a series of

labor sites for 15 years." The family motto is *Rien sans peine*: "nothing without hardship." It seems fitting.

And so began a period of massive investment, involving major works on the cellars but also, much more significantly, effort and expenditure in the field. Of the 250ha (618 acres) under vine, the Ricasolis, with the help of consultant Carlo Ferrini, have replanted 230ha (568 acres) since 1994. Nor have they done so in a slapdash manner; instead, they have studied, in collaboration with various universities, considerations such as clones (those widely available, as well as new ones developed via massal selection); soil analysis; and zoning, in the sense of marrying microclimate with soil and methods of working in the vineyard.

Despite its historic roots, the Brolio operation of today has a very modernistic feel. It is a business run on quality lines. Visiting parties, or individuals, are catered for—indeed, up to 35,000 people come through every year for a tour, a tasting, and/or a meal at the excellent restaurant Francesco recently established. Vinification methods are at the cutting edge of technology, with relatively small, open-top, conical, stainless-steel fermenters adaptable for semi-mechanical punching-down, while (almost) all of the wines are aged in barriques and tonneaux. A few old-style *botti* remain, but one senses that they are on their way out, like the long-serving, glass-lined concrete vats that were all destroyed to make way for the steel fermenters.

Above all, the blend for which Francesco's illustrious ancestor is so famous has been updated: Canaiolo and Malvasia are out; Cabernet and Merlot are in. In terms of quality, one cannot argue with the result. Any argument would be in terms of authenticity—but can one really argue with the man whose family put the Chianti blend on the map? If one can, the argument would center on the phrase: "without taking from it any of its perfume."

Right: Francesco Ricasoli, who renounced his career as a Florence photographer to resurrect his family's wine estate

FINEST WINES

Castello di Brolio Chianti Classico

The prize wine of Ricasoli, this is a blend of Sangiovese at 80% plus 20% Cabernet Sauvignon and Merlot. Needless to say, the 2004 is deep of color thanks to its Bordelais input. But while Sangiovese has lost something of its perfume to these powerful adjuncts, it does form the structure of the wine, the excellent, fruity acidity proclaiming this very much a Tuscan, if aromatically internationally oriented, wine. The main quality characteristic, however, resides not in the perfume but in the elegance of the wine, of which Francesco is justly proud.

Casalferro

The house Super-Tuscan is a blend of Sangiovese at two thirds and Merlot one third. The color is deep, and the nose is berry rather than cherry, with hints of pencil shavings. Acidity is low for Tuscany, and

there is in the 2003 a brooding, dark-chocolate, minty, espresso-coffee chewiness that no doubt pleases the pundits in international tastings.

Torricella

This Chardonnay is quite a surprise. Although it is part matured for a few months in oak, it manages to get the accent more on fruit than on wood. Fresh, clean, and varietal, it is among Tuscany's better whites. [2007★]

Above: Castello di Brolio, home to the Ricasoli family since the 12th century, towers over Chianti Classico's largest estate

Castello di Brolio

Total area: 1,200ha (2,965 acres)
Area under vine: 250ha (618 acres)
Average production: 2 million bottles
53013 Gaiole in Chianti, Siena
Tel: +39 05 77 73 01
www.ricasoli.it

San Giusto a Rentennano

Historically, this estate, and the Martini di Cigala family that runs it, have Ricasoli—and therefore aristocratic—connections, though they seem much more down to earth than your average baron, marquess, or count. At first impression, there seems to prevail a sense of hippy, laid-back cool, but this is an illusion. The organization of Luca (in charge of vineyards), brother Francesco (in charge of winemaking, with the help since 1999 of consultant enologist Attilio Pagli), and sister Elisabetta in support is sufficient to turn out some of the finest wines in Tuscany. Three of six other siblings share ownership, since they inherited it from their father Enrico in 1992, though they do not get directly involved.

Excellence in the vineyard is the foundation of their success. They have had organic certification since 2006—more for quality than ideology, though it does somehow add to the alternative atmosphere—and they have been using organic practices since 2001. Sangiovese, as one would expect, is the object of most of their attention: 88 percent of their vineyard area is planted to various clones, or massal selections, of the great Tuscan grape, with 3 percent reserved for Canaiolo, 3 percent for Malvasia and Trebbiano, and 6 percent for Merlot. In the case of Sangiovese and Canaiolo, much of their planting material has been of massal selection from vineyards more than 30 years old, which they send to the famous French nursery Guillaume for replication. The rest is from the latest clones, most recently those developed under the Chianti Classico 2000 project, poetically named CC1, 2, 3, 4, 5, and 6. Bunch-thinning, at the time of *invaiatura* (color change) is severe and can be up to 60 percent.

One curious feature of the winemaking process, revealed in conversation with the brothers, is that, despite their leaning toward authenticity in other areas (they criticize the use of French grapes in

Right: Luca, Elisabetta, and Francesco Martini di Cigala, three of the six siblings who together own San Giusto a Rentennano

At first impression, there seems to prevail a sense of hippy, laid-back cool, but this is an illusion, because the organization of Luca, Francesco, and Elisabetta is sufficient to turn out some of the finest wines in Tuscany

Tuscan classics, saying of the permitted 20 percent Cabernet/Merlot, "Who's to say it isn't 40 percent?"), they are quite prepared to resort in lesser years to practices such as concentration by evaporation and/or *salasso* (bleeding). In some matters they seem traditionalist—long maceration, increasing bottle aging, decreasing barrique influence; in others, modernist—use of new barriques, and so on. Not an easy one to pin down.

FINEST WINES

Percarlo IGT Toscana

One thing one can say without equivocation is that San Giusto can boast at least two wines of world-class quality. Top of the tree is Percarlo, named for a deceased friend, a 100% Sangiovese first released in 1986 (1983 vintage)—as near in style to top Brunello as it gets outside Montalcino, yet unique. Percarlo is a selection of the best and ripest bunches from various vineyards throughout the estate, aged 20–22 months in French barriques, bottled unfiltered. The 2004 and 2001, tasted in 2008, were shaping up to be excellent in a few years. A couple of years earlier, the family staged a vertical tasting of this phenomenon back to 1985, amounting to a demonstration that pure Sangiovese is capable of improving significantly with age, as the following notes show.

1999★ Fresh morello cherry on the nose; lots of ripe fruit on the palate, and firm but smooth tannins; balanced, with considerable length. Good for another ten years at least. High marks.

1998 Less concentrated than the 1999, already showing signs of aging. Some bitter tannins. Fine now, but not a distance runner.

1997 Bright, still fresh on the nose, cherry and spice. Explosive fruit on the palate, firm structure but good drinkability. Still time to go.

1996 Firm acidity, but good flavor and length. Very respectable for the vintage. Still time to go.

1995 Youthful, good sour cherry character; some evolution but the firm acidity and tannin will keep it going.

1994 A lesser wine from a weak vintage; on the way down but still drinking.

1993 An intriguing nose of fresh fruit and spices, still quite fresh though lacking concentration. Better than the '94 but not going anywhere.

1992 Remarkably deep and lively for a wine from such a terrible vintage, but the tannins are green and there is a hint of rot.

1991 Fresh strawberry and other soft red fruit on the nose, then sour cherry and spice on the palate. Hanging in there.

1990★ Surprisingly deep, vibrant color. Some evolution on the nose, but it still displays morello cherry. Rich, ripe, and balanced on the palate, with intense flavor and good acid-tannin balance. This is the best wine of the tasting, and still good for another ten years.

1989 Browning at the rim; medicinal on the nose, but sweet if decadent fruit in the mouth. Drink it with pleasure, but drink it now.

1988★ Concentrated, relatively youthful color. Herb and leather as well as fruit on the nose. A nice mix of vanilla and cherry fruit. Still going strong, this will make it to 30 years.

1987 Evolved color; an oldish palate, too, the acidity prevailing, but there is still some fruit; hanging on.

1986 Aging and thin, but not undrinkable.

1985★ Good color; a blast of tertiary and still some primary aromas on the nose, with leather, herbs, and spice. Balanced, concentrated, and complex, with a long, deliciously sweet finish. Perfect now, but could continue for a few years yet.

Vin San Giusto★
This Vin Santo is the other top wine of the estate: luscious and multidimensional, with a quasi-oily texture and wonderful acidity. This little miracle—almost a solid in liquid form—is aged in chestnut barrels of between 40 and 180 liters for six years and is capable of protracted laying down. Delicious!

Chianti Classico [V]
The basic Chianti, 95% Sangiovese plus Canaiolo, aged in *botti* and tonneaux, is one of the most drinkable and best balanced of its type.

Chianti Classico Riserva Le Baròncole
Although this, like the *normale*, is a blend of Sangiovese and Canaiolo, it is rather less successful

Above: The gently rolling landscape stretching toward Castelnuovo Berardenga near San Giusto

in its category, being a little too oaky for a fine Tuscan red.

La Ricolma
This 100% Merlot is less convincing still, having, in the vintage I tasted, some greenish tannins as well as an excess of oak; they intend to leave it longer in the vineyard to see if that helps. And to hell with the alcohol, which is already at 14%.

San Giusto a Rentennano
Total area: 160ha (395 acres)
Area under vine: 30ha (74 acres)
Average production: 85,000 bottles
Località San Giusto a Rentennano,
53013 Gaiole in Chianti, Siena
Tel: +39 05 77 74 71 21
www.fattoriasangiusto.it

Castello di Ama

Castello di Ama, in the central-southeastern uplands of Chianti Classico, where the limestone-rich hills are rocky and dry and Mediterranean *macchia* abounds, is one of the zone's historic estates. Its vineyards, among the highest of the denomination, at an average altitude of nearly 1,650ft (500m), were praised by Grand Duke Leopold Habsburg as long ago as 1773. Ama itself is a small, historic *borgo* that brings the word "picturesque" to mind. The bucolic and architectural charms of the village and surrounds are enhanced, every year since 2000, by an addition to the Castello di Ama art collection, works placed like surprise packages in cellar, garden, or villa.

The recent history involves a group of four Roman families who purchased the *borgo* in 1972. Head of the second-generation members of this clan is Lorenza Sebasti, wife of Marco Pallanti, who has been in charge of production since 1982. At this time, Ama had already begun making its famous *Selezioni di Vigneto* single-vineyard Chianti Classico wines, but it was Pallanti who advanced the concept, in many cases grafting Sangiovese, Merlot, or Malvasia Nera vines onto no-longer-required white varieties or Canaiolo. It was Pallanti, too, who brought the open-lyre system of vine-training to Tuscany. As the reestablishment of the vineyards progressed, Pallanti increased the plant density from 3,000 to around 5,300 plants per hectare, but he left a good quantity of old vines to lend complexity to the finished wines.

By the end of the 1980s there were four Chianti Classico crus, plus a basic wine of the denomination. But Pallanti's great ambition was to create a top-quality Chianti Classico, and with the 1996 vintage (released in 1998) they launched a new concept, which he describes as follows: "Before 1996 we made crus with our best material, and Chianti Classico was made with what was left. Since 1996, we make our Classico, and if there is enough top material left, also

the crus." Already, from 1990, they had eliminated two of the crus, leaving Bellavista (Sangiovese plus Malvasia Nera) and La Casuccia (Sangiovese plus Merlot). From now on, the reputation of the estate was to stand mainly on the merits of what Pallanti calls "Il Castello." Ama's owners pride themselves on being initiators of the reevaluation of the Chianti Classico denomination.

Despite this, and despite the fact that Pallanti later became president of the Chianti Classico *consorzio*, there is a certain ambivalence in Ama's attitude to the denomination, as evidenced by the fact that they continue to write the words "Chianti Classico" very small on the label, in gold against cream so that you almost have to seek out the DOCG, while Castello di Ama is written in bold capitals. Moreover, Pallanti seems happy to have Merlot in support of Sangiovese in both the Castello and La Casuccia, despite a growing opinion that the undeniably rather intrusive and certainly unrelated Bordeaux grapes should not be part of the DOCG blend. Couple this with the fact that all Ama's Chianti Classicos are barrique aged for 12 to 15 months, and that *salasso* (bleeding) is used to concentrate the wines in weaker vintages, and you end up with a distinctly mixed picture.

FINEST WINES

Castello di Ama Chianti Classico

"Today, all wine is good," says Marco Pallanti, "The difference is whether it has 'soul' or not." This is a statement with which I totally agree. For me, the Ama Chianti Classico does have soul, real Tuscan character, enhanced if anything by the relatively insignificant touch of Merlot (as well as Canaiolo and Malvasia Nera) and the hint of toast given by the barrique. It is a wine of poise and length that gives full satisfaction, as clearly demonstrated in the most recently tasted 2005★, but also in many earlier vintages. Pallanti rightly says that "Chianti Classico has always been a blended wine." The question is—and this has nothing to do with quality, only authenticity—should it be presented as Chianti Classico if it has non-Tuscan grapes in it?

Vigneto Bellavista
Of the two surviving Chianti Classico Riserva crus, the original, Vigneto Bellavista (90% Sangiovese, 10% Malvasia Nera) has been produced only five times since the mid-1990s. The 2004 is a wine of contrasts, its austerity offset by a rush of sweet fruit on the finish.

Vigneto La Casuccia
With 10% Merlot, this is the more international of the two crus. The Merlot here seems to have more effect on the whole than in the case of the Castello, but it retains the austerity of a high vineyard.

L'Apparita
Despite Pallanti's irritation at always being awarded high marks for his Super-Tuscan L'Apparita instead of for Castello, the plaudits continue to flow for this 100% Merlot, certainly one of the finest in Italy, and perhaps the tautest and most refined. First produced in 1985 from a section of the Bellavista vineyard at 1,610ft (490m), L'Apparita has become an icon of modern Italian wines.

Above: Marco Pallanti in the barrique cellar at Castello di Ama, home to one of many specially commissioned art installations

Castello di Ama
Total area: 250ha (618 acres)
Area under vine: 90ha (222 acres)
Average production: 300,000–350,00 bottles
Località Ama, 53013 Gaiole in Chianti, Siena
Tel: +39 05 77 74 60 31
www.castellodiama.it

Castello di Cacchiano

This imposing structure, parts of which date back to the 10th century, has been in the Ricasoli-Firidolfi family since the Middle Ages. Currently in charge is Giovanni Ricasoli-Firidolfi, who, as the elder son, took over from his mother, the formidable Elisabetta Balbi Valier, in 1998. Giovanni says that despite its arresting presence, the castle has always existed as a support for the even grander Castello di Brolio, and for years the fruit was not separately vinified. The vineyards are high, at an average altitude of more than 1,300ft (400m), and stony, so more inclined to give perfume and elegance than power and opulence. From the 1970s, when Cacchiano was established as a separate brand by Giovanni's father Alberto, the younger brother of Brolio's Baron Bettino Ricasoli, the wine was made by Tuscany's grand old man of wine, Giulio Gambelli, then by Federico Staderini. Since 2007, the consultant enologist has been Stefano Chioccioli.

Quality with tradition, not fashion nor following the market, has always been the philosophy of these aristocrats, who are in it for the long haul. They faithfully follow a replanting program that sees 2–3ha (5–7.5 acres) reconstituted every year, work overseen since 1992 by their head viticulturist Raffaello Biagi. Most new plantings, whether of Sangiovese, Canaiolo, or Malvasia Bianca (for Vin Santo), are from massal selection, taken from their own experimental vineyard, but they have also tried a few of the new clones. Tasting a cask sample, and referring to a row raging at the time about one Chianti producer's promotion of Puglian varieties, Giovanni asked, "If we can get this color and fruit from our grapes, why include the grapes of Puglia?" They have tried planting up to 9,260 vines per hectare, to *alberello*, but have fallen back to what they perceive as the best configuration, at 5,208 vines per hectare. Maceration time tends to be on the long side, up to 25 days, and aging takes place in a mix of large *botti* and barriques, the latter always playing a more minor role.

Giovanni complains, in the most genteel way, that he is at a disadvantage in the marketplace because he strictly forbids himself the additions and shortcuts that his neighbors undertake. "I pay for my purism both psychologically and financially," he says. But he is right: His wines are models of Tuscan purity.

FINEST WINES

Chianti Classico, Riserva and Riserva Millennio

The estate wine of Cacchiano, made in all but poor vintages, is a Chianti Classico, Giovanni being a staunch believer in promoting it rather than a Super-Tuscan as the top brand. In better years he may make a Riserva, and in top years like 1997 and 2007 he makes Riserva Millennio (referring to the family's thousand years of existence), describing the difference between them as that between "selected" grapes and "ultra-selected" grapes. He rarely makes them both. For all these wines the grape mix is 95% Sangiovese and 5% Canaiolo. The style is pure Tuscan, with floral/herby aromas and uncompromising sour cherry on the palate. Tannins are well handled, and you come away feeling you have drunk something of high breed and courageous character. The 2001 Riserva★ will be superb from 2011. The 1997 Millennio, the last wine made by Gambelli, is a jewel of old-style Tuscan viniculture, with dried fruits, herbs, and leather. "You need a particular market for these wines," says Giovanni, "one that seeks and understands the wines of once-upon-a-time." Fantastic!

Castello di Cacchiano IGT Toscana

This IGT, with a bit of Merlot, is well priced and very much in the house style—not at all "international." From 2006 there is also a 100% Merlot.

Vin Santo

The sweet wine, aged for seven years in *caratelli*, is complex, luscious, and one of the best around.

Castello di Cacchiano
Total area: 200ha (494 acres)
Area under vine: 31ha (77 acres)
Average production: 100,000–120,000 bottles
Località Monti in Chianti,
53010 Gaiole in Chianti, Siena
Tel: +39 05 77 74 70 18
www.castellodicacchiano.it

Rocca di Montegrossi

Marco Ricasoli-Firidolfi is the youngest of the vine-estate-owning triumvirate of Ricasolis, together with his brother Giovanni at Cacchiano and first cousin Francesco at Castello di Brolio. It was in 1994 that Marco "decided to split from the azienda of my mother (the late Elisabetta Balbi Valier) owing to a difference of opinion with my brother about the production of the wine."

His mother gave him the Vigneto San Marcellino, whose grapes were not vinified separately from others of the Cacchiano estate, and a cantina that he completely restructured and modernized in 1998. Since that time, in his words, "I have every year added a new vineyard around Vigneto San Marcellino, like a mosaic." Included in the planting material used for this purpose have been several of the Sangiovese clones developed under the Chianti Classico 2000 scheme, following the counsel of Dr Roberto Bandinelli of the University of Florence and also, since 2007, that of consultant Maria Guarini Mentre. Among the first to plant these clones, Marco says they are giving "excellent results."

FINEST WINES

Geremia

Marco, for all the professional advice he gets, including that of consultant enologist Attilio Pagli, remains very much his own man with his own clear ideas. One can taste his vision in the wines, which combine personality with territoriality. None of his wines illustrates this better than Geremia, a Super-Tuscan that in recent years has been made exclusively of Bordeaux grapes but that has a far more taut, more Tuscan feel to it than some of the internationalist blockbusters of the Maremma. Not that Geremia (named for an 8th-century ancestor) represents for him the heart of his production. That honor goes to Sangiovese, at the highest level in the form of the Chianti Classico Riserva San Marcellino.

Chianti Classico Riserva San Marcellino

An individual, pure Sangiovese wine of great class and aging potential, this is not produced in lesser years, when it goes into the *base* (pronounced "ba-zeh" and translated as "basic"). The excellent 2004★ is attractively scented and fruity on the nose, balanced and concentrated on the palate.

Chianti Classico [V]

The house Chianti Classico, fresh, vibrant, and highly drinkable, is the subject of a particular project of Marco's, who happens to be about the most passionate supporter in Tuscany of a grape that many others revile and uproot—namely Canaiolo (the blend until recently being about 90% Sangiovese with 10% Canaiolo, though elements of Colorino and Pugnitello began to creep in from 2007). Marco says: "Canaiolo for me is the best friend of Sangiovese because it gives everything and takes nothing from the character of Sangiovese." He went so far as to personally carry out a five-year massal selection of Canaiolo grapes, planting a vineyard from his selections in 2000, the first results of which are, he says, "very gratifying." As in his other reds, the *base* is not filtered.

While being a strong follower of the dictum that wine quality is made in the vineyard—for which purpose he has recently gone certifiably organic—Marco is very particular about what happens in the winery, where modern technology and technique meets old-fashioned attention to detail. Aging takes place in French oak, not necessarily small: 54hl for Chianti Classico; barrique and tonneaux for San Marcellino and Geremia.

Vin Santo ★

It is impossible to leave Rocca di Montegrossi without falling in love with the magnificent Vin Santo, from Malvasia (95%) and Canaiolo Nero (5%) grapes hung to dry for four or five months on movable rails, so humans can move between them removing berries with what Marco calls "vulgar rot." Aged six to seven years in 50–100-liter barrels of oak, mulberry, and cherry, sipping this is like drinking liquid raisins: pure nectar.

Rocca di Montegrossi
Total area: 100ha (247 acres)
Area under vine: 20ha (49 acres)
Average production: 70,000 bottles
Località Monti in Chianti,
53010 Gaiole in Chianti, Siena
Tel: +39 05 77 74 79 77
rocca_di_montegrossi@chianticlassico.com

Fontodi

So much has been written about this outstanding producer, by me and by others, that it hardly seems necessary to repeat the whole story. So perhaps we can move quickly on to the wines—and in particular to the 100 percent Sangiovese *chef d'oeuvre*, Flaccianello, of which Giovanni Manetti, with his eno-consultant for the past 30 years, Franco Bernabei, recently offered me and a colleague a vertical tasting of every year back to the beginning.

But first, here are a few details to fill you in. The Fontodi wine farm was purchased in 1968 by Florentine tile manufacturer Dino Manetti, father of Giovanni. Its position—smack in the geographical center of Chianti Classico, with south-facing vineyards rich in *galestro* (crumbling schistous rock), beautifully sited in Panzano's famous *conca d'oro* or "golden shell," at an altitude of 1,310–1,475ft (400–450m)—is pivotal, bestowing great light quality and daytime heat during the growing season, and cooler nighttime temperatures.

The vineyards are tended organically—there is even a small herd of Chianina beef cattle, whose manure is used as a fertilizer base, mixed with vine-cuttings compost. Some old vines, of the 1960s and '70s, are left, but most have been replaced at higher density with plants derived from massal selection, together with the best clones to emerge from the Chianti Classico 2000 project, in which Fontodi played a very active role.

The relatively recently rebuilt winery is beautifully equipped and works on the gravity principle, which eliminates the need for pumping. Everything is in place for the making of great wine—but of course no amount of terroir or technology will yield great wine without the right human beings in control. Remember Belfrage's law: The limit of a wine's quality is the limit of its maker's palate (think about it).

Right: Giovanni Manetti, the friendly face and generous host at his family's ideally situated estate in Panzano's "golden shell"

Everything is in place for the making of great wine—but of course
no amount of terroir or technology will yield great wine
without the right human beings in control

111

FINEST WINES

The significant wines here are three: **Chianti Classico**, **Chianti Classico Riserva Vigna del Sorbo**, and **Flaccianello IGT Toscana**. The first and third are pure Sangiovese; the second, ironically, a blend of Sangiovese (90%) and Cabernet Sauvignon. Ironically because one would think the blend would be the IGT, and the varietal the DOCG. But such is not the case. The Chianti Classico [V] is always a contender for the best of its type—even though it is by no means as expensive as some. It is remarkably consistent, even in lesser years, when the best Sangiovese goes into it instead of into the crus. But it is Flaccianello on which I wish to focus.

Flaccianello

This pure Sangiovese, aged in French barriques, is as near as one might get to an archetypal Chianti for our time, despite its IGT status. Until 2000 it was a single-vineyard wine, but by then they had enough mature replanted vines to grub up the old vineyard, and it has since been a selection of the best bunches from anywhere on the estate.

1981 This first vintage was suffering the effects of age, though there was still firm acidity and enough fruit to yield aromas of leather, spice, cherry liqueur, and prunes, plus something almost medicinal. Not bad for an off-year.

1982 First year of French barriques. Losing color, but fresh aromatically: dried fruits, mushroom, leather. Still some sweet cherry fruit on the palate. Improves with a breathe.

1983 Less aromatic on the nose, but fresher on the palate. Chunky, meaty, mushroomy, herbal, dried fruits among the descriptors. Good acid–tannin backbone. Drying out now.

1985 A great year. Deep color, cherries under alcohol, and plums/prunes on the palate. Still structured; at peak; by no means tired.

1986 Initial freshness becomes asperity. Losing fruit.

1987 More dilute, acidic, but fruit there too. Holding well for a lesser vintage.

1988 Ruby-garnet color. Splendid nose of truffles and *sottobosco*. Firm acidity, good tannin base, fresh fruit, but also tertiary aromas; balanced, graceful rather than forceful, long, and holding very well. Evidence that Sangiovese can make excellent wine.

1990 Deep colored and almost youthful, fresh cherry mingling with leather, graphite, coffee. Big and chewy. Giovanni Manetti's comment: "1988 is more English; 1990 is more American."

1991 Hard, chewy, lacking grace, but holding well.

1993 Similar: hard tannins, tough, the fruit is there behind but still needs to emerge.

1994 Classic, floral, tea-leaf aroma, cherry fruit, a little dilute but drinking nicely now.

1995 Classic Chianti style; firm structure and plenty of sour cherry fruit. At its peak.

1996 First year of punching down instead of pumping over. Deep color, licorice on the nose, sweet fruit, firm acid-tannin structure, balanced, but more correct than charming. Giovanni Manetti admitted: "From the mid–1990s, the effort has been to make wine that satisfies both the critics and the purists. It's a bit like trying to square the circle."

1997 A classic year. Tremendous fruit, and the structure to hold it in place, but the main impression is of sweetness and generosity. Almost Porty finish; hint of oak.

1998 Color quite deep. A hot year. Perhaps this is a little baked, with more power than finesse.

1999★ Magnificent! A youthful color, wafts of fruit and balsam on the nose, elegance and richness combined. Silky tannins, fennel and cherry, beautiful balance. The circle squared!

2000 Nothing cooked, but plenty of berry, cherry, and licorice aromas. Firm tannins, though the acid seems a touch low. Not quite the perfect balance of 1999, but still very good nevertheless.

2001 Deep color, attractive fresh cherry nose. Loads of succulent fruit and an almost Porty finish. Tannins still a bit aggressive, but very fine and very Sangiovese.

2004 Too young to taste (in 2008), but this appears to have all the constituents of a classic.

Fontodi

Total area: 138ha (341 acres)
Area under vine: 70ha (173 acres)
Average production: 300,000 bottles
Panzano in Chianti, Firenze
Tel: +39 05 58 52 005
www.fontodi.com

Il Molino di Grace

Frank Grace is a wealthy American businessman with a taste for perfection: in wine, in art, in architecture. It is therefore a compliment to the international standing of central Tuscany today that, following an exhaustive search through major vineyard areas of the world, he elected to put down roots in Chianti Classico, right in the center, south of Panzano, near to where the commune of Greve meets those of Castellina and Radda.

This was back in 1998, and Frank lost no time in calling on one of the select few star consultant enologists of Tuscany, Franco Bernabei. As a collector of modern art Frank wasted no time, either, in installing, in front of the traditionally stone-clad but functional winery, the sculpture (among others) that has become the symbol

Below: The picturesque surroundings of Il Molino di Grace, where the communes of Greve, Castellina, and Radda converge

FINEST WINES

Chianti Classico
The mainstay of production, this comes across as typical Sangiovese, with sour cherry notes mingled with *macchia* and something almost meaty, perhaps prematurely evolved. More interesting, indeed quirkier, today than in earlier editions.

Chianti Classico Riserva Il Margone
This represents a selection of the best 20% of the Riserva. It has more intensity of fruit and greater structure, so needs more time to mature, though like the *normale*, the tannins, of which there is no lack, are smooth.

Gratius
The apogee is represented by this single-vineyard IGT, which, like the above pair, is 100% Sangiovese from a single vineyard of 70-year-old vines at 1,300ft (400m) altitude. The 2004★ combines power with (no pun intended) grace, and scored high in a recent tasting as a worthy representative of the best of modern Tuscany. It should not be drunk until at least six years old.

of the estate, found on all its labels: *The Bearers* (*above*).

The first vintage, for Chianti Classico and Riserva, was 1999, appearing respectively in 2002 and 2003. At first the blend of all the Chianti Classico wines (of which there are four) contained significant amounts of Cabernet Sauvignon and Merlot, but to his credit Frank soon saw which way the wind was blowing, and elected to switch to 100 percent Sangiovese for all his serious wines.

Frank, clearly a man of energy, has expended a goodly portion of it promoting his wine, and he has been remarkably successful in that his relatively new winery—one of many, after all—is well represented in the guides and wine columns of the world. The next step is converting to organic viticulture, a process begun in 2008 for half the vineyards, with an eye to include all of them in time.

Frank Grace is a wealthy American with a taste for perfection. So it is a compliment to the international standing of Tuscany that he put down roots in Chianti Classico

Right: Frank Grace, the perfectionist owner who has successfully established and promoted his Chianti estate

Il Molino di Grace
Total area: 90ha (222 acres)
Area under vine: 44ha (109 acres)
Total production: 250,000 bottles
Località Il Volano-Lucarelli,
50020 Panzano in Chianti, Florence
Tel: +39 05 58 56 10 10
www.ilmolinodigrace.it

Agricola Querciabella

This business has been built up by the Milanese industrialist family of Castiglioni, beginning with the purchase of various properties of *mezzadri* (sharecroppers) in 1974 and continuing with the recent acquisition of a property in Radda in Chianti, shortly preceded by that of a farm in Tuscany's Maremma. The originator of these acquisitions was Giuseppe "Pepito" Castiglioni, who was followed by his son Sebastiano. The latter lived for a few years on the property at Ruffoli before moving north after his father's death, but he continues to take a committed interest in matters agricultural.

A major date in Querciabella's development was the hiring full time, in 1988, of one of Tuscany's premier enologists, Guido de Santi. Since that time, Querciabella has increasingly been seen as one of

Querciabella has increasingly been seen as one of the Chianti Classico estates at the highest quality level. It is to Sebastiano that the credit goes for this transformation

the Chianti Classico estates at the highest quality level. Another landmark date was the conversion, between 2000 and 2002, of the property into "one of the few estates in Europe to apply biodynamic agriculture to the totality of the vineyard."

It is to Sebastiano, a keen but not kooky biodynamist and vegetarian, that the credit goes for this transformation. "In Chianti, every producer lives in his own world. My world is biodynamic," he jokes. To ensure that his principles are followed strictly to the letter, he took on agronomist Dales d'Alessandro in 1998. D'Alessandro explains Castiglioni's thinking as follows: "With biodynamics, everything is upside down, or downside up,

Left: Sebastiano Castiglioni, the industrialist who is as comfortable with biodynamics as with the latest technology

depending on your point of view. You don't treat effects, you look for causes. The fundamental thing is that we work with the soil. The earth should be alive, not just a support. How can you speak of 'terroir' if the earth around the plant is dead? Once we have a living soil to a depth of 16–20in [40–50cm] we won't even need the homeopathic amounts of Bordeaux mix we use now." And again: "If you give minerals and water to the plant, it doesn't work to deepen its roots. The plant becomes like a child with his hamburger and TV." An interesting feature of Querciabella's biodynamism is that it is done purely for reasons of quality. There is no mention of it on the label.

As for new planting material, their need for which has increased dramatically with the purchase of estates in Radda and Maremma, d'Alessandro explained that they use material from both massal selection and recently developed clones. "We are looking for diversity, not just to increase the interest of our wine, but because in some years this combination of plant, root, and soil will work, and in other years it won't work but something else will. This is the nature of Sangiovese. It is possible for man to intervene to help the vine. We do this not with sprays and chemicals but with canopy management, as well as keeping the earth alive. Our vineyards are surrounded by woods—we never need insecticides; indeed, all our vines are tremendously healthy."

As one might imagine, there is plenty of money available to embellish the property, and it is indeed superb, with one of the most impressive *barricaie* (barrel cellars) in the land. Sebastiano is a great believer in aging in barrique, but happily de Santi seems to have mastered the knack of using the barrel as an instrument, rather than as a device for flavoring the wines.

Space has defeated me, but I would like to share one glorious experience with Sebastiano and friends at lunch alfresco, one sunny summer's day not long

ago. The wine list included: '82 Krug in magnum; '96 Pol Roger Blanc de Blancs; '90 Trimbach Riesling Clos Ste Hune; '89 Laville Haut-Brion Blanc; '90 de Vogüé Chambolle-Musigny Les Amoureuses; '97 Camartina; '95 Camartina; '94 Altamura Napa Valley Sangiovese; and, to finish, '89 Pétrus. The Camartinas, by the way, stood up extremely well to the competition.

Sebastiano assured us that he did not lunch like this every day. We left in a state of euphoria, enhanced by the fact that there were no breathalyzer-wielding carabinieri lurking on the road back to Greve.

FINEST WINES

Camartina

The flagship wine of Querciabella is a blend of Cabernet Sauvignon (increasing) and Sangiovese (decreasing), aged up to 20 months in barrique, new and of second passage. Sebastiano, a claret lover, is a great believer in Cabernet Sauvignon and slightly suspicious of Sangiovese, which he calls "a beast," though also "a challenge." Camartina ages well and, indeed, needs a good eight to ten years in bottle to achieve its potential. It is a wine of Bordeaux first-growth aristocracy and complexity but one that somehow manages to maintain an authentic Tuscan personality. This is brilliantly exemplified by the outstanding 1995, still remarkably youthful at over 10 years of age. Other top vintages include 1997, 1999★, 2001, and 2004.

Batàr

Querciabella's remarkable white wine, a blend of Chardonnay and Pinot Blanc, is one of Tuscany's few top-quality whites. Capable of improving in bottle for up to five or six years in a good vintage, it has lost its early overoakiness and is now a rival to Burgundy in style, though curiously it is sold in a Bordeaux bottle. The 2006★ is a class act.

Chianti Classico

Sangiovese with a touch of Cabernet Sauvignon (about 10% currently, down from 20%), this is smooth and svelte, one of the finest of its type, with an easy drinkability that masks its finesse and ageability. Sebastiano demonstrated his confidence in the wine by putting on a vertical that included remarkably lively versions of 2003 and 2002, problem vintages both, and brilliant wines from 2001 and 1999. The 1999 Riserva ('99 was the last Riserva year) was outstanding, as was the 1997.

Other wines include **Palafreno**, a fine Merlot/Sangiovese blend destined to become a pure Merlot under a different name, and **Mongrana**, the first of several wines to issue from the recently acquired estate in Maremma (not included below).

Above: Resident winemaker Guido de Santi in Querciabella's long barrel cellar, one of the most impressive in Italy

Agricola Querciabella
Total area (including Radda): 230ha (568 acres)
Area under vine (including Radda): 40ha (99 acres)
Average production: 270,000 bottles
Via di Barbiano 17, 50022 Greve in Chianti, Florence
Tel: +39 05 58 59 27 721
www.querciabella.com

Poggio Scalette

The most significant aspect of this estate is that it was founded by one of the elite of the Tuscan wine Renaissance—a man who, since the earliest days in the 1970s, acted as consultant enologist to owner-producers rather than making wine for himself. Not quite the poacher turned gamekeeper, but something along those lines.

Vittorio Fiore, Tuscan by adoption only (he was born to Italian parents in German-speaking Alto Adige), studied viticulture and enology at San Michele all'Adige in Trentino and Conegliano in the Veneto. In his 20s he moved around northern Italy taking various jobs, including that of director of the Association of Italian Enotechnicians, a post he held for eight years until 1978. Thereafter he decided to take up an offer to work in Tuscany, at Fattoria le Bocce. One year later, finding his services much sought after by the wealthy greenhorns who had by now begun buying up bargain Tuscan properties for tax purposes, he turned *libero professionista* (freelance consultant) and never looked back.

Poggio Scalette has perfect exposure; the kind of mean, rocky soil that gives the best wine; and a quality of light of which even Leonardo would—and probably did—approve

He did look forward, though, to the day when he would have his own property—to the time, indeed, when he would retire from consultancy and have the leisure to pour all his passion into his own product.

The chance came at the end of 1991, when he learned of an abandoned property on a hill above Greve, smack in the middle of the historic Chianti zone at between 1,150 and 1,640ft (350–500m) above sea level, with perfect exposure; the kind of mean, rocky soil that gives the best wine; and a quality of light of which even Leonardo would—and probably did—approve. Best of all, there was, mixed in with the olive trees, a wealth of old Sangiovese vines stretching back some 80 years or more.

Vittorio Fiore is a fortunate man—or at least a good father, of the sort that children wish to emulate, all four of his sons having chosen the way of wine. The eldest, Jurij (b. 1968), arrived at Poggio Scalette ("hill of little steps") from wine school in Beaune in 1993 and worked alongside his father to the point where, today, Jurij is pretty well running the show—with the benevolent paternal eye looking over his shoulder from time to time, of course.

With all his experience, Vittorio is also a mine of information, and I had a chance to pick his brains during an extremely bumpy ride around his estate with him and Jurij. The answer to the $64-million question—"Is Sangiovese a great grape?"—seems appropriate here. "There are two schools of thought on this," he replied. "One maintains that Sangiovese needs to be blended; the other, that Sangiovese can be great on its own. For me, Sangiovese is one of the greatest vines in the world, but it still requires much more study—we are now only two thirds of the way to understanding it. It is very sensitive to cold and to excessive rain, and it is very productive. The quantity has to be controlled at a maximum of 1.5kg [3.3lb] of fruit per plant. But when it is treated right, it is capable of giving wine of extremely high quality.

"Californians have asked me why they can't make great Sangiovese *in purezza*. I have told them they were treating Sangiovese as if it were Cabernet Sauvignon, trying to get up to 8kg [18lb] of fruit to the plant. Cabernet may give a decent wine at these production levels, but Sangiovese gives only *vinello* [plonk]."

FINEST WINES

Il Carbonaione (Alta Valle della Greve IGT)

The name of the estate is derived from the charcoal (*carbon*) deposits in the nearby woods. I tasted a range of Il Carbonaione—the only wine made at Poggio Scalette—back to the first vintage, 1992. The overall level was high, even though the 2002 and the 1992, being from the two poorest vintages of their respective decades, were at most respectable and, one suspected, somewhat refreshed. The color in all cases was deep and vibrant; the tannins were ripe, plentiful but reasonably soft; and the concentration was impressive, particularly considering the altitude of the vines, from which one would expect more elegance than power. In most cases there was an equilibrium of fruit and structure that augured well for the longer haul. As "best of the bunch" it is hard to choose between the 1999 and the 2001, with the 2004 only fractionally behind those two.

Sweet cherry fruit shines out on the palate, concentrated and seductive. A carpet of velvety tannins. An excellent example of the "new Sangiovese"

1992 Made entirely from old vines. Deep of color without excessive signs of age, but the nose is curiously flat. Good fruit-acid balance but the flavors are more earthy than fruity. Impressively alive for a 1992, but somewhat lacking in grace.

1993 The color is deep and reasonably youthful. Some lift on the nose—morello cherry. Concentrated and flavory with some finesse on the palate. The acid-fruit balance is typical of Sangiovese, and there are fine, ripe tannins. This has lasted well, showing no sign of breaking up—indeed it improves with air.

1995 This was picked during late October, in a year when late picking was essential. Deep-hued and impressively youthful. Typical cherry aromas of Sangiovese. Firm but ripe tannins on the palate, with a chunky structure and a wealth of cherry/berry fruit. Good life ahead.

1999 A star—deep of color and very young looking. Some oak on the nose, but fruit is there, too. Sweet cherry fruit shines out on the palate, concentrated and seductive. A carpet of velvety tannins. An excellent example of the "new Sangiovese"—but if it has a flaw, it's slightly too much oak.

2001★ Another star, though different from the 1999, the aromas tending more toward marzipan and spice than fruit. Round, ripe, full, concentrated, but elegant on the palate with firm but voluptuous tannins. A very long life ahead. This is perhaps marginally better than the 1999, lacking that obtrusive oaky note.

2002 The color is deep, the nose clean if a bit confected and oaky. Forward, immediate fruit on the palate, rather too supple, going on soupy. In a year reckoned to be disastrous for Sangiovese, this restores some confidence, even if it doesn't inspire.

Poggio Scalette
Area under vine: 15ha (37 acres)
Average production: 40,000–42,000 bottles
Via Barbiano 77,
50022 Greve in Chianti, Florence
Tel: +39 05 58 54 61 08
www.poggioscalette.it

Left: Vittorio Fiore, who after 20 years as a consultant was able to acquire his own perfectly situated vineyard above Greve

Tenute Folonari

The Folonaris are one of Italy's major wine families. Originally from Lombardy, they bought Ruffino in the early 20th century and made a fortune selling inexpensive branded wines when that was what the market demanded. In 2000, the family, consisting of six cousins and their families, went their separate ways, some retiring, one section retaining the Ruffino brand, another concentrating on specific estates under the name Ambrogio (father) and Giovanni (son—the eighth generation) Folonari Tenute. Currently the Tuscan *tenute* (estates) belonging to this group number seven: two in Chianti Classico (Nozzole and Cabreo, though the latter produces only IGT); one in Montalcino (La Fuga); one in Montepulciano (Torcalvano Gracciano); one in Bolgheri (Campo al Mare); one in Montecucco (Vigne a Porrona); and one in Rùfina (Conti Spalletti; *see Colognole*).

The essence of Giovanni's position is that he and his father are in wine as a business, not as a hobby or as some kind of pseudo-artistic pursuit

I decided to focus my inquiries on the best known, Nozzole. My visit did not get off to a particularly auspicious start: After having got lost a couple of times I finally found myself at the rather magnificent, if obviously uninhabited (other than by servants) villa, only to be informed that I was expected at the somewhat distant cellar. Anyway, after a measure of confusion, a tall, very good-looking young man, oozing charm and dynamism, turned up and announced himself as Giovanni. I was inclined to be suspicious, but Giovanni turned out to be very intelligent and perfectly frank in his presentation of the house philosophy, and although I did not necessarily agree with some of his views, I appreciated his no-nonsense approach.

The essence of Giovanni's position is that he is (or rather, they are) in wine as a business, not as a hobby or as some kind of pseudo-artistic pursuit. He believes strongly that the traditional style has had its day—it is not what the modern consumer is looking for. Consider the success of the New World against the decline of the Old World, he suggests. In business you have to accommodate yourself to the requirements of the market. On the other hand (and here our views tended to merge more), it is important to make wines that do not all taste the same, that reflect the terroir and climate from which they emerge, and that, in the final analysis, the consumer has to buy from you because he cannot find anything quite like them eleswhere.

Hence the concentration on estate wines of high quality. Hence, too, the maintenance of emphasis on Tuscany's principal ampelographical treasure, Sangiovese, as infuriating as it is (and impossible in places, such as Bolgheri—on which subject Giovanni has a running if friendly battle with Michele Satta), while carrying out high-profile work on international varieties like Cabernet, Merlot, Syrah, and Chardonnay. Hence, too, the extensive, but by no means exclusive (especially for Sangiovese) use of small French oak for maturation and, in the case of whites, for fermentation as well.

FINEST WINES

Il Pareto IGT
Among the many wines on offer here, top of the tree in terms of absolute quality is surely Il Pareto, the justly celebrated Cabernet Sauvignon from the Nozzole estate. Powerful, concentrated, and layered, with dark chocolate, berry fruit, raisins, and coffee grounds on the finish, this manages to remain smooth throughout. This is serious stuff, and certainly among Tuscany's few great Cabernet Sauvignons. [2004★]

Right: Ambrogio (the father) and Giovanni (the son), whose businesslike approach includes the production of terroir wines

Brunello di Montalcino La Fuga
By way of contrast with Il Pareto, I was struck by this on my most recent tasting, when I noted (during the "Brunellogate" scandal) of the 2003: "Looks like Sangiovese (not deep, beginning to orange); smells like Sangiovese (the noble decay of good Burgundy); tastes like Sangiovese (firm acidity, mellow, tannic but not tough); must be Sangiovese."

Cabreo
I have never been a great fan of these wines, because they strike me as rather too international. I still feel that way about the slick, Sangiovese (70%)/Cabernet Sauvignon red **Cabreo Il Borgo**, but at my most recent tasting of the white **Cabreo La Pietra** I felt that they had stepped back from the overoaked, overrich style and were beginning to get the more steely, minerally, less obviously oaky message from Burgundy. Not a great Chardonnay,

but one that you would be quite happy to drink.

Campo al Mare Bolgheri DOC
From the eponymous estate, this blend of Merlot (60%), both Cabernets, and Petit Verdot, is a typically ripe, smooth, Bordeaux-style wine. It makes up in drinkability what it lacks in complexity.

Above: Nozzole, one of the Folonari's seven Tuscan estates, and source of one of the region's great Cabernets, Il Pareto

Tenute Ambrogio e Giovanni Folonari
Total area: 385ha (951 acres)
Area under vine: 90ha (222 acres)
Average production (Nozzole): 400,000 bottles
Via di Nozzole 12, Località Passo dei Pecorai, 50022 Greve in Chianti, Florence
Tel: +39 05 58 59 811
www.tenutefolonari.com

Fattoria La Massa

Let me start this one with a statement of principle. I believe, and have maintained in several places, that it is a mistake to allow the grapes of Bordeaux, or the Rhône, or anywhere in France, into Chianti Classico (or Brunello, or Vino Nobile), which should, as a traditional wine, be an expression not only of the soil and the climate but also of the fruit of central Italy. That said, I will defend to the death (well, not quite) the right of anyone to grow and make quality wine with the grapes of other regions in a blend or varietally, as the fantasy takes them, as indeed the Californians do, and the Australians, and the South Africans et al. Only let them not usurp a traditional local name.

I therefore applaud the decision of Giampaolo Motta, the proprietor of La Massa, a splendid south-facing vineyard in Panzano's *conca d'oro*, to take his wines out of the DOCG system in order

Giampaolo Motta is not attempting to make Bordeaux-style wines in Chianti country; rather, he is making wines that share the attributes of the two regions

to give himself free rein as to how to make them. Giampaolo is unusual in that he came to Tuscany not from the north but from the south—Naples—and in that he has a particular passion for the wines of Bordeaux. Let it not be said he is attempting to make Bordeaux-style wines in Chianti country; rather, he is making wines that share the attributes of the two regions. And he is doing a fine job of it.

It was in 1992 that Giampaolo purchased this splendid property after working at various Tuscan sites. From the outset he was helped, even in the site selection, by Carlo Ferrini, another ex-*consorzio* agronomist/enologist who had taken the road of independent consultant. In the intervening years he has put a great deal of thought and a tremendous amount of work into his operation and believes that he reached a turning point with the 2006 vintage.

To detail all the changes he has wrought is not possible in the space available. Suffice it to say he has, without being officially organic, devised a very eco-friendly method of viticulture while paying particular attention, in association with the University of Bologna, to the particular soil and microclimate conditions of the various parts of his land. The vinification and aging, of course, are Bordeaux style.

FINEST WINES

Giorgio Primo

Giampaolo has restricted production to two wines. His pride and joy is Giorgio Primo, which began life in 1993 as a Chianti Classico but became IGT Toscana from 2002. Today the grape mix is 30% Sangiovese, 30% Merlot, 30% Cabernet Sauvignon, and 10% Petit Verdot—all unusually late-harvested, the Sangiovese in particular being left until the second half of October. The 2006★ is a deep-colored, full-bodied, mouth-filling wine, with a firm structure holding together a mass of fully ripe but elegant fruit. Some oak, from the 18-month aging period in French barrique, is evident, but the wine will doubtless harmonize in years to come and be magnificent for a long time.

La Massa IGT

This other wine was a Chianti Classico until 2003. He does not like to call it his "second wine," but given that it is of a similar grape mix (60% Sangiovese, 10% Cabernet Sauvignon, and 30% Merlot) from second-selection fruit (the grapes for both wines can come from anywhere on the estate), it is hard to think of it otherwise. Not so "second," however, that it cannot boast high quality in its own right.

Fattoria La Massa
Total area: 55ha (136 acres)
Area under vine: 27ha (67 acres)
Average production: 120,000 bottles
Via Case Sparse, 9,
50020 Panzano in Chianti, Florence
Tel: +39 05 58 52 72 2
info@fattorialamassa.com

Castello di Volpaia

This *castello* was originally a fortified village, "one of the best preserved villages in Tuscany," built in the 11th century as part of Florence's defenses against marauding Sienese. From about the middle of the 16th century, when the centuries-old struggle between Florence and Siena ended with the fall of Siena, and in the ensuing atmosphere of peace, more and more farms (*poderi*) were established beyond the walls of fortified towns like Volpaia.

In the 1950s, as we have seen, the system of *mezzadria* (sharecropping) was terminated and many properties came on the market—*case coloniche*, castles and villas, whole villages, even, often with hundreds of hectares of land and a population sometimes in three figures, too. It was a golden moment for bargain hunters—and do we not all wish we had had the foresight to snap up some

Volpaia is one of the leaders of the Tuscan wine rinascimento, and much work has gone into making this one of the showpiece estates of modern Tuscany

derelict property that today is worth millions? Most of us did not, fools or paupers (or as yet unborn) that we were, but among those who did was one Raffaello Stianti, whose daughter Giovanella is still in overall charge, aided by resident agronomist/enologist Lorenzo Regoli, high-flying consultant enologist Riccardo Cotarella, and, since 2006, her son Nicolò Mascheroni Stianti.

Volpaia is, and has remained, one of the leaders of the Tuscan wine *rinascimento*, and much work has gone into making this one of the showpiece estates of modern Tuscany.

Perhaps the most important thing to grasp about Volpaia wines is the peculiarity of their style, due to their rather special terroir. They derive from

vineyards enjoying excellent southeast-around-to-southwest-facing exposures, and they benefit, in this age of climate change, from a relatively high altitude of 1,470–2,130ft (450–650m). They also luxuriate in the tender care of people determined to produce the highest quality of which they are capable—people who have experimented with plant density (arriving at an ideal of about 5,500 plants per hectare), different pruning methods (they have concluded that Guyot is preferable to cordon, despite the greater labor involved), and seeding between rows to avoid erosion on their steep slopes; with rootstock (110R turns out to be the best for their predominant soil). These are people, indeed, who have made major efforts to improve their plant stock, using first field grafting and later massal selection, as well as approved clones, and who have followed organic principles in their vineyards for many years, officially since 2000.

And yet despite all this, the wines incline, in an age that at least until recently has preferred power to finesse, toward elegance rather than concentration and depth. This is partly due to the altitude, but mainly to the fact that Volpaia's soils are not on the whole typical of those of Chianti Classico, in that they are low in clay and chalk, and high in sand, as well as in that sandy rock called *macigno del Chianti*, especially in the upper vineyards. These soils tend to permeability and are poor in nitrogen but rich in microelements.

There is some argument as to whether Riccardo Cotarella is the right man to oversee these discreet and atypical wines. My own opinion is that fruit definition has improved since he came on the scene, but possibly at the expense of a touch of that ethereal quality that one always associated with the wines of Volpaia and that remains, by the very nature of their terroir, their calling card.

Right: Giovanella Stianti whose far-sighted father bought Castello di Volpaia, with her husband Carlo Mascheroni

FINEST WINES

Chianti Classico Riserva Coltassala

This single-vineyard wine is Volpaia's flagship. Its first vintage was 1980, and since the beginning it has consisted of 95% Sangiovese and 5% Mammolo, a supporting grape that features frequently in Montepulciano, though much less in Chianti Classico. Chianti Classico Riserva, in fact, is what it has been since 1998, as a result of a bold decision to validate that denomination, which at the time was fetching much lower prices than the Super-Tuscans, to which category (Vino da Tavola, then IGT) Coltassala had belonged previously. This is a wine of breeding that can stand up to 15 years' aging in a good vintage like 1995, 1997, or 2001. The 2005, fine-boned and perfumed, is a worthy representative from a less-than-brilliant vintage.

Chianti Classico Riserva

Almost as good as Coltassala—indeed, in some vintages like 2005★ even better, partly because it gets less new oak (80% Slavonian *botte*, 20% new barrique)—is this Chianti Classico Riserva from selected grapes of the best vineyards. It is a wine of great refinement and excellent balance.

Chianti Classico

The bread-and-butter wine (90% Sangiovese, 10% Merlot and Syrah) is always one of the most refined and graceful wines of its class, as in 2006 [V].

Balifico

A Super-Tuscan IGT, this single-vineyard wine has not changed its two thirds Sangiovese, one third Cabernet Sauvignon makeup since its 1987 inception. The subtle and elegant 2005 promises well.

Vin Santo

Aged at least five years in *caratelli*, beautifully balanced and redolent of candied and tropical fruits, this is certainly one of the stars of the genre.

Above left and right: Grapes for Vin Santo; a *botte* for Chianti
Left: the winery nestles amid its favorably situated vineyards

Castello di Volpaia

Total area: 368ha (909 acres)
Area under vine: 46ha (114 acres)
Average production: 250,000 bottles
Località Volpaia, 53017 Radda in Chianti, Siena
Tel: +39 05 77 73 80 66
www.volpaia.com

Montevertine

Montevertine is now well into its second generation in the person of Martino Manetti, though the first lives on, in more ways than one. The late Sergio Manetti (who passed away in 2000) was undoubtedly one of the most iconoclastic, yet most innovative, influences in the history of modern Chianti Classico, even though he put the denomination behind him as long as a quarter-century ago. He did not have clout in the economic or political sense, but he had a voice and, by God, he let it thunder, verbally and in print. And, of course, he had one of the iconic wines of the Tuscan so-called renaissance: Le Pergole Torte.

The Montevertine story begins in 1967, three years before Martino's birth, when Sergio, an industrialist from Poggibonsi, bought the property in Radda in Chianti at auction, the only person to bid. The property may have been, in Martino's words, "medieval"—no water, gas, or electricity—but Sergio only intended it as a place in the country, not as a source of wine, except for himself and his friends. In 1968, he planted the Le Pergole Torte vineyard (though the wine of that name did not appear for another decade), and he brought in his old friend, the now-famous enologist and master taster Giulio Gambelli, to help. (Martino affirms: "Giulio has always been our consultant, our friend, our *padreterno* [god].") By the mid-1970s, Sergio had installed a cantina in what had been the stables and had planted more vineyards (both under Gambelli's direction), including the Sodaccio vineyard, which was later to give its name to a wine almost as famous as Le Pergole Torte. His friends said he was mad to invest money in agriculture at a time of economic hardship, and indeed the first years were difficult, needing a hard head and plenty of what Martino admiringly calls *coraggio*.

It was in 1975 that Sergio first felt the need to make a wine that was special, and he made an experimental cuvée of pure Sangiovese from the Le Pergole Torte vineyard. 1976 was not suitable, but in 1977 he had another go, making enough wine to fill five barriques that his US agent, Neil Empson, had acquired from Domaine de la Romanée-Conti.

"Essentially, we have altered almost nothing about Le Pergole Torte since it first came out," says Martino. "Yes, there have been changes in the cantina, in respect of some vinification equipment. But we still use glass-lined concrete for fermentation without temperature control; maceration time is still a minimum of three weeks; and we still age six months in barrique and 18 months in large *botti*, though some of the *botti* today are no longer of Slavonian oak but of Allier. We do not filter at bottling. Until 1999 we used only grapes from the original vineyards; 2000 is the first vintage in which the new vineyards entered the equation."

Any consideration of Montevertine must include mention of Sergio Manetti's epic battle with the Consorzio Vino Chianti Classico. In 1981, attempting to do the reputation of his zone a favor by allowing his undoubtedly very superior cru to be included in the denomination, he offered Le Pergole Torte to the tasting commission as a Chianti Classico Riserva. (Until then, knowing it to contravene the letter, as distinct from the spirit, of the law, which required that Chianti Classico be a blended wine, he had labeled it as Vino da Tavola.) The samples were rejected, in the immortal words of the document that the Manettis still defiantly display on the wall of the cantina, as "not suitable for bottling." The next year, an irate Sergio took all of his wines out of the DOC and recategorized them as Vino da Tavola (now IGT), a policy that his son perpetuates, maintaining that he would not consider reentering a system controlled by big producers who "make wines for journalists, not for consumers. I do not," he insists, "want a wine to blow my mind. I want a wine of elegance, perfume, and good persistence in the mouth, that marries well with the food on my plate." Which is what Le Pergole Torte continues, triumphantly, to be—and much more.

Right: Martino Manetti, with his daughter Gloria and a photograph of his iconoclastic and influential father, Sergio

FINEST WINES

The Montevertine range of wines numbers three. At the top is **Le Pergole Torte**, made only in good years. In the middle, representing Chianti Classico, as it were, is the wine called **Montevertine**. The basic, everyday brew is called **Pian del Ciampolo**. There used to be a fourth, **Il Sodaccio**, like Montevertine and Pian del Ciampolo, a blend of Sangiovese and small amounts of Canaiolo and/or Colorino. But the Il Sodaccio plot, decimated by esca, was taken out in the late 1990s, and although the vineyard was later replanted, Martino will not revive the name.

Le Pergole Torte
A couple of years ago, Martino laid on a tasting of old vintages of Le Pergole Torte back to 1979. The general theme was elegance and purity of fruit, and if the tasting was not quite sufficient to prove single-handedly that Sangiovese is a great grape, it came very close, demonstrating that it is, at the very least, a variety of unique personality. In a good year, in the right hands, it is capable of excellence, preferably when the traditional approach is taken—that is, where the winemaker has not gone for excessive concentration in terms of color, fruit, tannin, or extract generally but has, in Martino's own words, "done everything he can to *non rovinare* [not ruin] the wine and, beyond that, as little as possible."

1990 Riserva★ (in magnum). Of the three vats of 1990, one was distinctly better than the others.

Sergio Manetti decided to call it Riserva—quite illegally, because it was only a Vino da Tavola. To rub it in he attached a neck label where the Consorzio's Gallo Nero would normally be. It showed a man with a black moustache (a *baffo nero*). Nose of fresh cherries and Mediterranean macchia. Starts subtly, but fruit explodes mid-palate and grows from there. "This really is great Sangiovese," I noted.

1999 Bright, diaphanous. Strawberry/raspberry nose, a floral hint. Good fruit-acid balance, ripe tannins, soft berry fruit, a touch softer than 2001. Attractive, sweet, good length, great elegance. Apparently, much of this was consumed at the Quirinale, palace of the Italian President in Rome.

2001 Bright, medium-deep color. Fine, understated nose, clean and pure—floral, herbal, cherry fruit. Mouth-watering acidity, notes of sour cherry, no noticeable oak. Stony, mineral, a bit austere but great purity and promise.

Above: A proud but simple sign proclaims the name of one of Tuscany's most special single vineyards, Le Pergole Torte

Montevertine
Total area: 35ha (86 acres)
Area under vine: 15ha (37 acres), one third rented
Average production: 60,000–70,000 bottles
Via di Barbiano 17,
53017 Radda in Chianti, Siena
Tel: +39 05 77 73 80 09
www.montevertine.it

Fattoria Poggiopiano

There is not a whole lot to say about this operation, except that they make good wine. The Bartoli family are ordinary Florentines—dentists, shoe merchants—who bought a rather rundown house in San Casciano, not far from the Antinori winery there, in 1992 and have turned it into a beautiful family residence-cum-cantina, with a view to die for from their terrace over the southern Florentine hills.

When they started, they had 7ha (17 acres) of vineyard and not much experience in the ways of wine, but they invited in as enological consultant one of the young up-and-comers, Luca d'Attoma, who seems to have the secret of how to make Chianti Classico sappy and succulent (too often one comes across Chiantis you can admire but are not so sure you want to drink). This is without

The most celebrated of Poggiopiano's wines is Rosso di Sera, a multiple tre bicchieri winner that can contain up to 15% Colorino as well as Sangiovese

any use in their top three wines of French grapes, though they are enthusiastic converts to the aging of wine in French barriques. D'Attoma left in 2006 and was replaced by another high-flying wine consultant, Attilio Pagli, together with his assistant Valentino Ciarla. With the added help of viticultural consultant Stefano Dini from 2008, there is no reason why they should not go from strength to strength.

One weapon they seem to have used to good effect is Colorino, which occupies 8 percent of their vineyard space and gives depth and structure to the wines—in particular to their much-lauded Super-Tuscan Rosso di Sera. The vines were old when they arrived, and since then they have replanted using massal-selection material multiplied by the French nursery Guillaume. But the sheer fruitiness

of their wines apparently comes from Sangiovese, some old vineyards of which came with the property, while new plantings—at 5,000–10,000 plants per hectare—have come mainly from clones approved under the Chianti Classico 2000 project, such as R23 and R24.

FINEST WINES

Rosso di Sera
The most celebrated of Poggiopiano's wines is Rosso di Sera, a multiple *tre bicchieri* winner that can contain up to 15% Colorino as well as Sangiovese. It could be a Chianti Classico, but for commercial reasons they prefer to class it as IGT Toscana. Aged for 15–18 months in barrique, it is a wine of depth, complexity, and elegance, capable of aging at least 15 years. [2004★]

Chianti Classico [V]
More important commercially, indeed remarkable for its drinkability and value, is the straight Chianti Classico, almost entirely Sangiovese with a trace of Canaiolo. It, too, is aged in barrique, but mainly used, as opposed to Rosso di Sera's mainly new.

Tradizione
A recent addition to the range is Tradizione, placed between the two above in terms of quality and price, and classed as a Chianti Classico cru as distinct from Riserva. From a vineyard planted at 9,000 vines per hectare, called Vigna Stretta, it has a sumptuousness that one does not particularly associate with "tradition."

M'ama non M'ama
At the basic level there is this unoaked IGT, which translates not as "Mummy doesn't love me," but as "She loves me, she loves me not." A simple quaffing wine at an interesting price.

Fattoria Poggiopiano
Total area: 29ha (72 acres)
Area under vine: 22ha (54 acres)
Average production: 160,000 bottles
Via di Pisignano 26,
50026 San Casciano in Val di Pesa, Florence
Tel: +39 05 58 22 96 29
www.fattoriapoggiopiano.it

East and West of Florence

These are not official wine zones; rather, they are a geographical convenience for the purposes of dividing this book.

East of Florence

We can divide this into three: Florence itself; Rùfina, some 19 miles (30km) east and slightly north of the city up the valley of the Sieve River, which flows into the Arno at Pontassieve; and the Arno Valley, or Val d'Arno, which from Pontassieve loops south toward Arezzo before climbing up into the Apennine ridge.

The city of Florence itself has insufficient space for commercial viticultural activities, though there are, even today, patches of vines here and there. The importance of Florence for us is that it is where two of the biggest and most important animals in the circus—Antinori and Frescobaldi—have their headquarters, their operations being spread around the region and beyond to such an extent that it is necessary to seek them out in their center.

Rùfina—a medium-sized, typically Tuscan town, functional rather than aesthetic architecturally, though surrounded by beautiful hills aspiring to be mountains—is quantitatively the smallest, if qualitatively by far the most important, of the Chianti subzones, apart from Classico itself. (It should not be confused, as it always is, with Ruffino, another of the big beasts, which happens by pure coincidence to have its headquarters within the Rùfina area.) Rùfina is linked with another denominated wine zone, Pomino, whose vineyards tend to be higher in altitude than those of Rùfina. Pomino is one of the four denominated quality zones in Grand Duke Cosimo III's *bando* of 1716.

The *disciplinare* for Chianti Rùfina (or any of the other Chianti subzones for that matter) is slightly different from those of Chianti Classico but basically very similar. The main difference is in the minimum requirement for Sangiovese—75 quintals

per hectare, as against 80 for Classico—and in the continuing permission to include up to 10 percent white grapes, which virtually no one does today. The *disciplinare* for Pomino Rosso is more international, Sangiovese being required at a minimum of only 50 percent, with Pinot Nero or Merlot making up to 50 percent of the balance.

Down in the Arno Valley, the folks feel more free to interpret the rules as they see fit—or even to dispense with rules altogether.

West of Florence

We may again divide this into three: Carmignano; Lucca/Montecarlo; and inland Pisa. Carmignano is more or less at the center of a triangle formed by Florence, Pistoia to the west and north, and Empoli to the west and south, where Monte Albano and associated hills begin to rise out of the plain. There is a Chianti Montalbano, but it lacks prestige, and producers will use almost any denomination rather than the DOCG. Carmignano was another of the four quality zones denominated by Cosimo III, but it had almost slipped into a terminal coma when Count Ugo Contini Bonacossi revived it (*see Capezzana*).

Lucca is a superbly preserved walled city of modest wine credentials, in the form of Colline Lucchesi DOC (red and white, but better red) and Montecarlo DOC, the latter benefiting from a name that, unlike that of its neighbor, everyone can pronounce and instantly recognize, if for the wrong reason. People might gamble here with white-wine production from an eclectic lineup of grape varieties, but there are no roulette tables.

The wines of Pisa are a mixed bag, including Chianti Colline Pisane, of a prestige level similar to that of Montalbano, and Montescudaio, similar again. From a practical point of view, it is useful to distinguish between those of an inland style, such as Ghizzano and Sangervasio, and those of a more coastal style, like Castello del Terriccio and Caiarossa, which are covered under Maremma.

Left: The Basilica di Santa Maria del Fiore in Florence
Over: The rugged beauty of Rùfina, a great Chianti subzone

Marchesi Antinori

S̲o much has been spoken and written respecting this giant of modern Italian quality wine production that to run through it all again would seem repetitive. So I will try to minimize the generalities and stick to the particulars of the four wines that have been selected for this book, out of the many that the house of Antinori produces in Tuscany, Italy, and the rest of the world.

Even the minimum does, however, require brief historical notes concerning the Antinori family itself: their involvement as early as 1285 in the guild of silkmakers, an industry that remained important in the Florentine economy until well into the 20th century; their initiation into the world of wine in 1385, when Giovanni di Pierso Antinori joined the winemakers' guild (l'Arte dei Vinattieri); their purchase in 1506, by Nicolò Antinori, of the imposing downtown-Florence palazzo that carries the family name and remains its headquarters to this day; their involvement, through Alessandro Antinori in the 16th century, in the selling of Florentine estate wines in Europe and North Africa; their reorganization in 1898 as a serious wine producer and merchant under the title Fattoria dei Marchesi Lodovico e Piero Antinori. For 26 generations the family Antinori has been involved in the Tuscan wine trade—arguably never more successfully than under the leadership of today's paterfamilias, Piero Antinori, who, most would agree, has done more than any other individual to raise the standard of Italy in the wine markets of the world. He is followed in his turn by three very able and committed daughters, Albiera, Allegra, and Alessia, who, in their turn, are working on the following generation.

In recent years, the house of Antinori has put much energy into the establishment of wine-production centers around Italy and beyond, and indeed in Tuscany alone they now own properties in Chianti Classico, Montalcino, Montepulciano,

Right: Marchesi Piero Antinori at the Palazzo Antinori in Florence, which has remained in his family since 1506

For 26 generations, the family Antinori has been involved in the Tuscan wine trade—arguably never more successfully than under the leadership of today's paterfamilias, Piero Antinori

Cortona, southern Maremma, Bolgheri, Colli Fiorentini, and probably half a dozen other places acquired since I started writing this book. We will focus on four wines from three separate estates—the iconic wines of Marchesi Antinori.

FINEST WINES

Tignanello

Pride of place must go to Tignanello, the wine that first broke the mold in Tuscan wine production. From the Tenuta Tignanello—as the Santa Cristina estate has been renamed—this wine was first produced in 1970 as a Chianti Classico Riserva, complete with Canaiolo and white grapes but aged in French barriques. It became a Vino da Tavola in 1971, when the white grapes were dropped and it was first dosed with Cabernet, settling into the current blend of 85% Sangiovese, 10% Cabernet Sauvignon, and 5% Cabernet Franc, though it was not made again until 1975. In other words, it is a wine very much influenced by the Bordeaux style but retaining, as the Antinoris have always proudly maintained, a

Tuscan soul. Since 2001, a replanting program has been under way, using massal-selected material and various clones developed by themselves and others in recent years, and of course increasing density to a maximum of 5,400 plants per hectare. The program will continue gradually, keeping a balance between young and old, until 50ha (124 acres) are replanted. Because of their altitude (about 1,310ft [400m]), to ensure full ripening, especially of the Sangiovese, they have come up with a technique of crushing the *albarese* rocks and spreading the debris between rows to increase reflected heat and reduce weed intrusion.

I have tasted many vintages of Tignanello and must confess I have never been quite convinced by it in terms of Tuscan authenticity, though I appreciate how it would be attractive to the international palate. The 2001 that I tasted for this exercise was of a deep, indeed opaque, aspect—startlingly so for a wine that is mainly Sangiovese—demonstrating how far a little Cabernet can go. The aromas were not what I expect from Sangiovese, though there was plenty of brambly fruit there, and on the palate it was thick and concentrated, dark chocolate and coffee grounds, almost more a food than a beverage. Weighty and concentrated were the descriptors that came to mind—a wine brilliantly constructed for the accumulation of points in the Parker era. It will be interesting to look at it again in a few years to check the evolution, but I would not drink this now. Sorry, because I did try hard to like it. But hey, it is a runaway commercial success, even at its lofty price, so what does my opinion matter?

Solaia

Also made at Tenuta Tignanello, Solaia was first produced in 1978 as a 100% Cabernet (80% Cabernet Sauvignon, 20% Cabernet Franc), and remained so in 1979. Since then it has contained 20% Sangiovese, except in the difficult 2002 vintage, when it was again 100% Cabernet. If 85% of Sangiovese can get lost in a blend containing only 15% Cabernet, there would not appear to be much hope for a mere 20%, but actually it seemed to me that there was a certain balance in the 2001★ that I tasted that I could not find in the Tignanello of the same vintage. Herbal, minty, cinnamon, and clove aromas wafted from the glass. There was a pleasantly zippy acidity and an interesting battle going on between the tannins and the fruit, the latter just beginning to prevail. A wine of personality and structure, it is clearly capable of aging well. I look forward to retasting it in subsequent years.

Guado al Tasso

This wine comes from the estate of the same name in Bolgheri. It was first made in 1990, and the current *uvaggio* is 50% Cabernet Sauvignon, 40% Merlot, and 10% Syrah, with slight variations. Antinori used to market Sassicaia, the wine of Piero Antinori's cousin, and when they lost that they were inspired to make a similar Bordeaux-style wine in the northern Maremma. It ticks many of the right boxes—cassis and blackberry fruit, some mint, some licorice, pepper, tobacco, graphite. It is fresh and enticing of aroma and satisfying on the palate but ultimately lacking the subtlety of Sassicaia or the opulence of Ornellaia.

Cervaro della Sala

This leading white wine comes from the Antinori estate in Umbria called Castello della Sala, an impressive medieval castle in the Orvieto zone. Conceived as the white version of Solaia, with a bit of local variety (in this case, Grechetto) dominated

by a French variety (Chardonnay, at 80% until 2004, 85% since then), Cervaro ranks as one of Italy's half-dozen top-quality white wines south of Veneto and Friuli. The wine, barrique-fermented and held six months on the fine lees, is delicious—floral and elegant, with complex aromas and a layered palate—but the token Grechetto is as lost here as the Sangiovese is in Solaia. On the evidence of a vertical tasting held a few years ago going back to the earliest vintages (the first was 1985), Cervaro from a good vintage like 2006 may age well for up to 15 or so years. [2006★]

Left: A family tree hanging proudly in the Palazzo Antinori
Above: A chair bearing the family crest, still in use today

Marchesi Antinori

Area under vine (Tuscany, Umbria, Piemonte, Puglia): 1,764ha (4,359 acres)
Average production (worldwide): 20 million bottles
Via di Pisignano 26,
50026 San Casciano in Val di Pesa, Florence
Tel: +39 05 52 35 95
www.antinori.it

Marchesi de' Frescobaldi

What was said about Antinori may, to some extent, be said about Frescobaldi: They boast a long and proud history as agriculturists and viticulturists; they were involved from the beginning in the driving upmarket—the "renaissance"—of Tuscan wine; during the boom time of Italian wine, in the late 20th/early 21st century, they have invested widely throughout their native Tuscany and, in one instance, beyond (Conte Attems in Friuli), acquiring a portfolio of estates of the highest prestige, while directing enormous effort and resources into the improvement of vineyards and winemaking facilities alike.

Frescobaldi, never knowingly over-PRed, can see their great rival Antinori's six centuries plus as wine merchants and raise it, claiming 700 years and more than 30 generations in the wine game, as "attested by multitudinous historical sources." In the 16th century, they were supplying wine to the English court, to say nothing of their contribution to Tuscan culture of a host of "illustrious authors, explorers, musicians, financiers, politicians and statesmen." In the 19th century, a strategic marriage brought together the Frescobaldis with the degli Albizi family of Florence, and they like to credit distant uncle Vittorio degli Albizi with, among other things, introducing "international grape varieties, including Pinot Bianco, Pinot Nero, Chardonnay, Cabernet Sauvignon, and Merlot" to Tuscan viticulture, via the family *tenute* of Castello di Nipozzano (Rùfina) and especially Castello di Pomino (above Rùfina).

Today, Frescobaldi, for all the length and breadth of its interests, remains largely a family affair, run by brothers Vittorio, Leonardo, and Ferdinando, plus, as the older generation winds down, more and more Frescobaldis of the younger generation, represented, for example, by Lamberto (head of production) and Tiziana (PR). Non-family members

Right: (*left to right*) Lamberto, Vittorio, and Leonardo Frescobaldi, whose family has been in wine for 700 years

The Frescobaldis boast a long and proud history as agriculturists and viticulturists and were involved from the beginning in the driving upmarket—the "renaissance"—of Tuscan wine

in key positions include Nicolò d'Afflitto, overall enological consulant (the various estates also have their own resident enologists) and Giovanni Geddes, managing director, headhunted a decade ago from (you guessed it) Antinori.

The present portfolio of Gruppo Frescobaldi and its subsidiary Tenute di Toscana, which controls Ornellaia, Castel Giocondo, and Luce della Vite, is complex, and I would not bore you with the details even if I understood them. We will concentrate here on the top wines of the five most important estates.

FINEST WINES

Castello di Pomino Benefizio Pomino Bianco Riserva
This white wine comes from 100% Chardonnay grapes grown in a 9ha (22-acre) vineyard at an average altitude of 2,297ft (700m) in the zone of Pomino, high above the Sieve Valley to the northeast of Florence. The Frescobaldis dominate the zone vineyard-wise, as the Apennine Mountains do altitude-wise, their 108ha (267 acres) under vine constituting over 90% of the delimited area. Pomino has been recognized as a prime grape-growing zone of Tuscany since the 1716 decree of Grand Duke Cosimo III effectively denominated four Tuscan zones as being of special worth. This is where Vittorio degli Albizi concentrated his work on international varieties, and not surprisingly at this altitude, it is the whites, and Pinot Nero, that have particularly thrived—though with climate change, the more substantial reds may yet have their day. Benefizio, first produced in 1973, has established itself as one of the few classic white wines of Tuscany, and now that they have learned to restrain the oak and emphasize the minerality (from the 2007 vintage), the wine has gained immeasurably in finesse and subtle complexity.

Castello di Nipozzano Montesodi Chianti Rùfina Riserva
This single-vineyard Sangiovese of very low yield comes from the Nipozzano estate, with 240ha (593 acres) under vine, above Pontassieve in the Rùfina zone. It was first produced in 1974 and has remained a DOC(G) wine throughout, despite having more the characteristics of a Super-Tuscan, with its (erstwhile) illicit varietal content and its barrique

aging—today 18 months in new barrels. In a year like 2004★ it is generally regarded as the highest expression of Chianti Rùfina—perhaps together with Selvapiana's Bucerchiale. Today it is into its second incarnation, since over the past 15 years the entire Montesodi vineyard has been replanted at medium-high density with quality clones. The young wine is tight and unyielding when first opened, but it opens to reveal a brambly, sour-cherry aroma with hints of lead pencil. The fruit on the palate is concentrated, and while the tannins are multiple and the acidity brisk, the fruit prevails. A very modern expression of a classic wine, it ages remarkably well, as attested by a recently tasted 1974, which still boasted a lively color and some cherry fruit on both nose and palate along with some interesting tertiary flavors.

Castel Giocondo Brunello di Montalcino
Castel Giocondo is the second-largest estate in Montalcino after Banfi, with a total 815ha (2,014 acres), of which 235ha (581 acres) are under vine, and more than 150ha (371 acres) are registered to Brunello. On the southwest slope of the zone, it was purchased by Frescobaldi in 1989. Major wines from this estate include a **Brunello Riserva Ripe al Convento**, first produced in 1986 and made in very good years only; and a 100% Merlot called **Lamaione**, from a 12ha (30-acre) vineyard of that name, which is often included among the best of its type from Merlot-mad Tuscany. The mainstay of production, however, is the basic **Brunello**, the 2004 vintage of which is a classic of its type, with aromas of wild cherry and a lively acid backbone enhanced by plentiful if ripe tannins. Endowed with plenty of flavor and nuance, this wine should drink well through the second decade of the present century. Its classic style, it should be noted, is in stark contrast to the preceding vintage, 2003 having been an exceptionally hot year that has left its own strong stamp on the wines.

Luce della Vite
This azienda (whose name means "light of the vine") was established at Montalcino in the mid-1990s by Marchesi de' Frescobaldi and Robert Mondavi, though Frescobaldi has subsequently bought out the Americans. The plan was, and remains, to combine the high-quality Sangiovese of Montalcino with Merlot, with the usual extended aging in new barrique (in this case, 24 months) that is almost taken for granted in a Super-Tuscan. A second wine, **Lucente**, which adds a bit of Cabernet to the mix, is also made, and recently

a **Brunello** has been added. **Luce della Vite** itself is a sumptuously packaged, very expensive wine of deep, almost opaque color, redolent ripe berry fruit on the nose, and a positively luxurious mouthfeel, the tannins being dense but silky. The oak (90% new barrique for 24 months) is cleverly judged, lending subtle balsam and eucalyptus notes, while the firm acid line running through the wine is a tribute to the low-yield Sangiovese employed. As in 2006, the whole tastes very modern and very expensive—and it is.

Ornellaia

This is the principal wine of the eponymous estate at Bolgheri, with 97ha (240 acres) under vine, that began life in the mid-1980s as an Antinori property, specifically that of Piero's brother Lodovico. It is said that Lodovico, having raised it to the level of Sassicaia's main rival in Bolgheri, sorely regrets selling it to the Frescobaldi-Mondavi consortium, which in turn sold the Mondavi shares to Frescobaldi-controlled Tenute di Toscana; and well he might, since under winemaker Axel Heinz, who came on board in 2005, the property has gone from strength to strength. Ornellaia (the wine) is a blend of Cabernet Sauvignon (60%), Merlot, Cabernet Franc, and (since 2003) Petit Verdot. The 2005, flagged (on the back label) as the 20th-

anniversary edition, is better than its vintage suggests (2005 was in general better on the coast than it was inland, especially for early ripeners), redolent of ripe blackcurrant fruit and aromas of classy oak, with beautifully managed tannins and a concentrated palate that finishes rich and sweet. Very seductive and polished, it is more up-front and less Bordelais than Sassicaia but should age well over 20 years, though the 2004★ has the edge over it for sheer intensity of aroma and flavor. The seductive character is multiplied in **Masseto**, 100% Merlot, which is more iconic in a way than Ornellaia itself. A massive wine in terms of color, aroma, flavor, concentration, and alcohol, it contends with no more than two or three others as the best Merlot in Italy.

Above: Axel Heinz, winemaker of Ornellaia and Masseto, which he has taken to new heights since his arrival in 2005

Marchesi de' Frescobaldi
Total area (Tuscany): 4,000+ha (9,884+ acres)
Area under vine (Tuscany): 1,000+ha (2,471+acres)
Average production: 10 million bottles
Via S. Spirito 11, 50125 Florence
Tel: +39 05 52 71 41
www.frescobaldi.it

Fattoria Selvapiana

This is *the* icon estate of Rùfina—if you discount Frescobaldi, whose reach extends much farther than its home zone—and the one whose old bottles are most often produced to demonstrate that the Chiantis of Rùfina are indeed, as the myth maintains, the longest lasting of them all. An occasion in Florence in the mid-1990s is often cited, when the top names of Tuscany (Antinori, Frescobaldi, Biondi-Santi, and so on) put together a tasting of old wines. Everyone agreed that the 1947 Selvapiana stole the show.

Selvapiana is the property of Francesco Giuntini Antinori, one of the great gentlemen of Tuscan wine. He is also one of the great anomalies. Whoever heard of a "gentleman" coming out with *parolaccie* (curse words) in four languages, and relishing (good-naturedly) the discomfiture of the recipients, who never know quite what to make of it? A teetotaler, he has the reputation of having one of the finest noses in the business. An Antinori, he does not use the name out of consideration for his famous relatives who do. An aristocrat of ancient breed (he is the fifth generation since banker Michele Giuntini acquired the property in 1827)—of a type, indeed, that always passes possessions to the family, even if, like him, they had the wisdom to remain unmarried—he has adopted Federico and Silvia Masseti, the children of his long-serving *fattore*, and it is they, not his sister's progeny, who today run the establishment and who will inherit it all.

There are times when Francesco playfully chides Federico for spending all his money—as on the *modernissimo* new cellar constructed in the early 2000s, but it was generally agreed that they could not carry on making, aging, and storing all the wine in the depths of the centuries-old villa that sits high above the road from Pontassieve to Rùfina. A new cellar was needed not to technologize the wine, but to give the grapes the best chance of being

Right: Francesco Giuntini Antinori (*left*), the fifth-generation owner of Selvapiana, with estate manager Federico Masseti

Selvapiana is the property of Francesco Giuntini Antinori, one of the great gentlemen of Tuscan wine. He is also one of the great anomalies. A teetotaler, he has one of the finest noses in the business

translated into quality wine, for Selvapiana has long stood above all for excellence in the vineyard. A replanting program was initiated way back in 1988, both with new clones and with the fruits of a massal selection from their finest vineyard, Bucerchiale. That said, there are one or two points on which they differ from other high-quality producers. One is the fact that, most unusually, they no longer carry out bunch-thinning but aim to restrict yields with ruthless pruning (they have halved the length of the fruiting arm to 16–20 inches [40–50cm]), minimal fertilization (they are, in any case, certified organic and considering going biodynamic), and attentive canopy management. In the vinification, they—with the agreement of Franco Bernabei, their consultant enologist since 1978—allow the temperature to rise to 90°F (32°C) (most try to keep it below 86°F [30°C]). And while they use barriques for their top cru, Bucerchiale, only 10 percent are new.

FINEST WINES

Bucerchiale
A pure Sangiovese that Selvapiana has kept as a Chianti Rùfina Riserva since it was first made in 1979 (though that was strictly illegal until the law changed in the 1990s), this is a single-vineyard wine of great breed and structure. When it gets the fruit right and has had time to mellow (as in 1990 or 1997), it can be among the most complete and satisfying wines of Tuscany. [2004★]

Chianti Rùfina
Until 1997 there was a regular Riserva, but this is now included in the Chianti Rùfina. Sangiovese with a tiny touch of Canaiolo, it is more approachable in youth, yet still quite structured. These are wines for purists.

Fornace IGT
This combines Cabernet Sauvignon and Merlot with 20% Sangiovese and is obviously aimed more at the international market.

Vin Santo
Traditionally made, fermented and aged five years in small *caratelli*, this is one of the best of its genre.

Petrognano Pomino Rosso
Selvapiana has also been entrusted with the vineyards, and therefore the wine production, of the Pomino property of Petrognano, Pomino being a viticultural zone attached to Rùfina at a somewhat higher altitude, where Frescobaldi is practically the only other producer. Current production includes a Pomino Rosso and a Pomino Bianco is planned.

Above: Some of the many ancient bottles at Selvapiana
Right: Part of the centuries-old villa, where traditions are strong

Fattoria Selvapiana
Total area: 250ha (618 acres)
Area under vine: 70ha (173 acres)
Average production: 200,000 bottles
Località Selvapiana, 50068 Rùfina, Florence
Tel: +39 05 58 36 98 48
www.selvapiana.it

Galiga e Vetrice

here are various reasons why I am including
this producer among the august of Tuscany,
though they are not to be found in any of
the major guides. In the first place, they are my
landlord—since I would like to stay, this is a pretty
good reason, don't you think? I have been doing
business with them for donkey's years—another
good reason, since I would like to continue. They
are friends, and they make the most marvelous roast
potatoes, and I would like to eat them many more
times. Also, their olive oil is fabulous; I have visited
their estate every November since 1996 with my
friend, oil connoisseur Mannie Berk, and we agree
that there is probably no finer oil on the planet.

Meet the Grati family, Tuscan vintners since
the 19th century and *viticoltori* for five generations
(there is currently a sixth in the shape of two very
pretty little girls called Carlotta and Costanza).
Great-grandfather Grato Grati is a phenomenon
of the Tuscan wine world in his insistence on the
old way of doing things. An octogenarian, he has
today effectively passed the baton to his heirs—son
Gianfranco, who runs the winery and the business
(and whose wife Nicoletta cooks those legendary
potatoes); grandson-in-law Luca Rossi, who
manages the vineyards; granddaughter Cristiana
and grandson Gualberto, who help in the winery.
But by and large, they still do things Grato's way.

Gualberto is himself a reason for including
Galiga e Vetrice in this book, since he is shaping
up to be one of the most important viticultural
archivists in Tuscany. He spent many years
studying at the University of Milan, famous for its
ampelographical and viticultural research work,
and today he collaborates with academics of the
faculty of horticulture and arboriculture at Florence
University, and the faculty of archeology at Siena
University, seeking out original vine material in the
vineyards of Rùfina and surrounds. This is a critical

Right: Three generations of the Grati family: great-grandfather
Grato, his son Gianfranco, and grandson Gualberto

Their Vin Santo is one of the best in Tuscany, and they are among the last
to age their Chianti Rùfina Riservas in large containers like botti
for indeterminate periods—20 years or more

time for this research, as historic vineyards are replaced by modern clones. Soon there will be little or nothing left of the old ampelographical Tuscany, so it's now or never, and people on the production side, as distinct from the academic side, are needed.

FINEST WINES

Chianti Rùfina Villa di Vetrice [V]
This basic Chianti Rùfina, from Sangiovese, Canaiolo, and Colorino, is honest, artisanal, and of a style that threatened to die out in the 1990s, but today is making a come-back. It is also incredibly well priced—no mean consideration, after all.

Chianti Rùfina Riserva Nicolas Belfrage MW Selection and Riserva del Signor Grato (or simply Grato Grati)
I blushingly play a modest role in the blending and/or selection of these tasty wines. (Do I need a better reason than that for including them?) The Grati are among the very last, if not *the* last, to age their Chianti Rùfina riservas in large containers like *botti* or glass-lined cement for indeterminate

periods—20 years or more (there is, as I write, a considerable volume remaining of 1988 Riserva★, still very much alive and kicking, lying in tank). Such wines are now practically museum-pieces.

Vin Santo del Chianti Rùfina Villa di Vetrice
This, the *pièce de résistance*, is made from Sangiovese, Trebbiano, and Malvasia, and aged 10–15 years on the *madre* in *caratelli*. The current vintage on sale, the 1992★, is undoubtedly one of the best in Tuscany—certainly among the top five of the traditional style.

And, if you have to kill to get hold of a bottle of Olio Extra Vergine di Oliva Villa di Vetrice, do it.

Above: Adhering to traditional ways, the Grati may be the only producers still to hold their riservas in wood for many years

Fattoria di Galiga e Vetrice
Total area: 560ha (1,384 acres)
Area under vine: 140ha (346 acres)
Average production: 700,000 bottles
Via Trieste, 30, 50068 Rùfina, Florence
Tel: +39 05 58 39 70 08
www.grati.it

Ruffino

This is the other wine-active side of the Folonari family, to which reference is made in the profile on Tenute Ambrogio e Giovanni Folonari (under Greve in the Chianti Classico section). The Ruffino operation was purchased by the Folonari family of Brescia in 1913, and they built up a huge, worldwide business. This part of the family—brothers Paolo and Marco Folonari and their sons—got the historic brand name attached to the commercial/industrial side of the company when the split occurred in 1999, but like their cousins they have taken the road of acquiring quality estates, of which they currently own the same number in Tuscany—seven. These are Gretole, Montemasso, and Santedame in Chianti Classico; Poggio Casciano in Colli Fiorentini; La Solatia in Colli Senesi; Greppone Mazzi in Montalcino; and Lodola Nuova in Montepulciano.

That would be far too much to cover adequately here, so we will focus on the viticultural side of their activities, on which subject they sponsored a three-day symposium in 2006, under the direction of their chief agronomist for the past eight years, Maurizio Bogoni. Bogoni explained that two thirds of Ruffino's viticultural area was planted to Sangiovese, so it was important for them to get the grape right. Given Sangiovese's defects—a tendency toward high yields; large, tight clusters in older clones and biotypes; irregularity of phenolic ripening; a thin skin that implies vulnerability to rot in damp late-season conditions; and a general variability and unpredictability that can drive a grower mad—there was plenty of work to do. Projects they were involved in, he told the audience, included *zonazione* ("zoning"), with a view to achieving compatibility between grape/clone and soil/microclimate; mixing the clones planted in a given vineyard to compensate for unforeseen and inexplicable failures; matching rootstocks to a given soil's "weakness" or "strength"; achieving a planting density neither too low for balanced production

per plant nor too high in terms of maintenance cost (recently planted vineyards have 5,000–6,700 plants per hectare); and determining the right training method, in order to achieve uniformity of bunch distribution, balanced productivity, and ease of mechanical and manual operations (this for them was cordon spur, which according to others does not deliver the highest quality).

On the subject of mixing clones, Ruffino, according to Bogoni, uses about 15 different types of Sangiovese in its vineyards. The important consideration, according to Professor Attilio Scienza, one of several star academic turns at the Ruffino symposium ("We are not seeking a super-clone, we are seeking a selection of clones") was to achieve consistency of production. This was the advantage, according to Bogoni, of having a large number of vineyards from which to select. "We select vineyard by vineyard," he said, "not clone by clone. The most important factor is not the grape; it's the site." One can appreciate the logic of such a view coming from a big player for whom consistency is crucial. A small producer would be more likely to talk up the importance of differences from vineyard to vineyard and year to year.

FINEST WINES

Chianti Classico Riserva Ducale Oro

Leaving aside the millions of bottles of Chianti Ruffino, the most important product from a quality point of view is probably the Riserva Ducale Oro, an evolution of the Chianti Stravecchio first produced in 1927. Today Oro is made from grapes selected at three Chianti Classico properties and is a blend of 85% Sangiovese with 15% Colorino, Merlot, and Cabernet Sauvignon. Prior to 1999 it was a Tuscan blend of 75% Sangiovese plus Canaiolo, Malvasia Nera, and Colorino, and until the early 1980s it even contained white grapes, as Chianti did. Oro today is aged five months in barrique, with 28 months in large *botte*. A tasting back to 1955 revealed that the wine is eminently capable of aging well (it is recorked every 20 years or so)—the 1955 is hanging on respectably, while the 1964 has plenty of noble maturity. Good marks also went to the 1973 and especially to the 1985★, about which I wrote that it was "fleshy and balanced, with plenty of fruit, mineral, savory, and herby flavors; evolved, but the acidity and tannins will keep it going." Younger vintages included the 1990, more youthful and concentrated, with some impressive fresh and dried fruit and tea-leaf aromas, and perhaps a slightly too solid structure, which makes it marginally less enjoyable than the 1985, but which will keep it for longer. The 1995, with its attractive herby, spicy, mushroomy nose and sweet fruit on the palate, is concentrated and complex. 1999 marked the year that French grapes first went into the blend, since when (2001, 2003, and 2004) the wine has been more chunky, more concentrated, more international, and, for me, less interesting.

Romitorio di Santedame Toscana IGT
This is a unique blend of 60% Colorino and 40% Merlot—a wine of great personality, wherein the austerity of the Italian grape is mellowed by the juicy, fleshy Merlot. Probably now Ruffino's best, most characterful wine, though I thought it had more terroir character before Merlot replaced the Sangiovese. [2004★]

Brunello di Montalcino Greppone Mazzi
This Brunello is made partly from old vines and partly from more recently planted vineyards. It is aged 36 months in large oak, and has the sturdiness and elegance of fine, traditionally made Brunello.

Vino Nobile di Montepulciano Lodola Nuova
A blend of 90% Sangiovese and 10% Merlot, this wine is also aged in large oak, but for only two rather than three years. The sour cherry of Sangiovese runs right through the wine's heart, while Merlot provides a soft and juicy backdrop, perhaps lacking just a touch in intensity.

Right: Adolfo Folonari against a backdrop of case ends from the company's best-known wine, its Chianti Classico Riserva

Ruffino
Area under vine: 700ha (1,730 acres)
Average production: 14.5 million bottles
Via Aretina 42, 50065 Pontassieve, Florence
Tel: +39 05 58 36 05
www.ruffino.it

The Ruffino operation was purchased by the Folonari family of Brescia in 1913, and they built up a huge, worldwide business

Colognole

It was in 1892 that Conte Venceslao Spalletti, of Emilia, purchased land in the Chianti zones of Rùfina and Montalbano, respectively 20 miles (30km) east and west of Florence. By 1912, his sons Giambattista and Cesare were engaged in wine and olive-oil production, building a cantina in the town of Rùfina in the 1930s.

By the 1950s and '60s, the Spalletti brand was synonymous with high-quality Tuscan wine, especially reds for laying down. The grandfather of Cesare and Mario Coda Nunziante—sons of Contessa Gabriella Spalletti, who between them run Colognole today—had already at that time established a healthy international trade. But alas he died in 1966, and his son, brother of Contessa Gabriella, sold his share to the giant Cinzano, which immediately proceeded to drive the brand downmarket (it is, however, making a comeback today, as part of the Tenute Ambrogio e Giovanni Folonari range). To complete a very potted version of a long story, Contessa Gabriella reestablished the family wine business in 1990 as Azienda Agricola Colognole.

Colognole is in fact divided into three parts. One is in Rùfina, on the banks of the River Sieve, at an altitude of around 1,000ft (300m); there are around 90ha (222 acres) in total, the vineyards among which are currently rented out. A second part is on the higher slopes of Monte Giovi, the mountain that looms almost 3,280ft (1,000m) above Rùfina; there are no vineyards among the 230ha (568 acres), but Cesare Coda Nunziante likes to joke that these high slopes, at an altitude of 2,300–2,950ft (700–900m), will come in handy when climate change really starts to bite. Indeed, the University of Florence is already carrying out a white wine experiment with a crossing they call Sauvignon di Rufina. The third part, which is really the first, is the original "Colognole" estate, extending over 380ha (939 acres) in total, on the lower, mainly south-facing slopes of Monte Giovi, at 920–1,700ft (280–520m).

It is in the last of the three that the 15-year replanting program got going in earnest from 1995, and with this now complete they are turning their attention to the renewal, mainly with the latest clones of Sangiovese plus a minor amount of their own massal-selection Colorino, of the 25ha (62 acres) of vineyard first planted in Rùfina at their Poggio Reale estate in the '70s and early '80s.

Meanwhile, the wines, with the help of consultant enologist Andrea Giovannini, have been going from strength to strength. And to prove that Rùfina's excellent reputation for long-lived wines is well founded, they are capable of pulling from the cellars of their magnificent, 17th-century villa a bottle such as the superb 1967 Spalletti Chianti Poggio Reale, which remains lively, harmonious, and unguessably youthful.

FINEST WINES

Chianti Rùfina [V]
Fresh, precise, and remarkably good value, this straight Chianti Rùfina is particularly successful. Made from Sangiovese with a dollop of Colorino, it is aged exclusively in Slavonian oak *botti*.

Chianti Rùfina Riserva del Don
This wine is named for that best of the best that would be given to a southern feudal lord (Contessa Gabriella's husband came from Naples) as his yearly tribute. It is made from a selection of grapes from the best sites in the various vineyards and aged in *botti* and French tonneaux. A deeper and more concentrated wine than the *normale*, it manages nevertheless to retain all the signature Rùfina elegance. The 2004 ★ vintage is particularly successful for both wines.

Colognole
Total area: 700ha (1,730 acres)
Area under vine: 27ha (67 acres)
Average production: 100,000–120,000 bottles
Via del Palagio 15,
50068 Colognole Rùfina, Florence
Tel: +39 05 58 31 98 70
www.colognole.it

Il Carnasciale

To visit this beautiful property, perched fortuitously on the ridge of the Chianti mountains, looking down into two valleys, is almost to forget that one is in Tuscany. The owner, Bettina Rogosky, is from Berlin, though she lived for a while in New York. Her son Moritz is a fashion designer who lives in Paris. The winemaker, Peter Schilling, is from Germany; the enological consultant, Vittorio Fiore, is from Trentino-Alto Adige; and the sole grape variety used is... Well, its parents, Cabernet Franc and Merlot (it apparently being a crossing of these two), are of course Bordelais, but it was discovered (in the 1950s) in Veneto's Colli Euganei by a Romagnan agronomist, who still consults for Il Carnasciale, called Remigio Bordini. Dr Bordini has kept his "Caberlot" under wraps ever since, and nowhere in the world is it grown other than in this tiny vineyard (a magnum of Il Caberlot to anyone who disproves this assertion).

It is passion all round at this jewel of a property. One feels it in their love of the place and of the wine which, despite its air of exclusivity, has been a great market success

Bettina herself is a magnetic woman *d'un certain age* (she seems at least ten years younger than she is) who might, with her passion to hug each and every one of the 3,400 vines in the nearest of her three vineyards, be thought slightly dotty, if you did not also have the impression that she knows *exactly* what she is doing. Indeed, it is passion all round at this jewel of a property. One feels it in their love of the place and of the wine which, despite its air of exclusivity, has been a great market success (it is sold solely in magnum, and until recently was reserved entirely for a select few *enoteche* and restaurants, such as Cibreo in Florence and the three Michelin-star l'Ambroisie in Paris).

They did not start yesterday. When Bettina and Wolf Rogosky returned to Europe from the USA in the mid-1980s (he died in 1996), they looked around for a place to grow grapes. Via the wines of Vecchie Terre di Montefili, they found Vittorio Fiore (*see Poggio Scalette*), who introduced them to Bordini and found them this spot, advising them—way ahead of the time when high density and low production per plant became sacred according to the fine winemaker's gospel—to plant at up to 10,000 vines per hectare. They adopted the *alberello* method, tied up to a supporting stake, with a mere five bunches per plant.

More recent developments have included Peter Schilling's arrival in 2002 ("I decided to come here after I tasted the 1996"), and the planting of two new vineyards at lower altitudes. More important still has been the introduction of a second wine, which is exactly that. Made in the same way, it is only at the level of the finished wine that the tasting panel—Bettina, Moritz, Fiore, and Bordini—decides which batches shall be first and which shall be second. The latter wine, called Carnasciale, gets the dubious distinction of going into normal 75cl bottles.

FINEST WINES

Let's say I was impressed beyond expectations. The **Carnasciale** we tasted was velvety smooth, with succulent but rather easy berry fruit flavors. The **Il Caberlot** was much more structured, savory as well as fruity, with some astringency, not immediately pleasurable, but set to improve over time, as the 1996—Peter's choice—amply demonstrated. Impressive, but the personal jury remains out as to whether this is great wine or merely very good. [2006★]

Azienda Vinicola Podere Il Carnasciale
Total area: 27ha (67 acres)
Area under vine: 2ha (5 acres)
Average production: 2,500 magnums
Località San Leonino, 82
52020 Mercatale Valdarno, Arezzo
Tel: +39 05 59 91 11 42
www.caberlot.eu

Tenuta di Capezzana

In the 1980s and '90s I had frequent occasion to visit this large and dynamic estate, where there always seems to be something going on—a tasting or a group visit, a course or a celebration—almost invariably involving a sumptuous meal at what must be one of the finest gastronomic centers of this gastronomically inclined province. Florence is not far away to the east, and Pistoia is even closer to the west, so visitors abound (they encourage tour parties, which make for a commercially interesting sideline). The amazing Medici villa of Poggio a Caiano is just down the road. It is, all in all, a very civilized place to be.

A number of features distinguish Capezzana, winewise. It is an intensely family affair, with several of the seven children and umpteen grandchildren and in-laws of family heads Ugo

Conte Ugo, an amazingly spry octogenarian, stands with Piero Antinori, Giulio Gambelli, Giacomo Tachis, and one or two others as the authors of the Tuscan wine rinascimento

and Lisa Contini Bonacossi involved in various ways. Benedetta is the winemaker, helped by consultant enologist Stefano Chioccioli since 1998. Filippo is responsible for the vineyards, aided by nephews Gaddo and Ugo, and is helped in his turn by Chioccioli as consultant agronomist. Beatrice is in charge of sales and marketing, with the assistance of niece Serena, who doubles as president of the Consorzio di Carmignano. Vittorio—brother of Benedetta, Filippo, and Beatrice, and father of Serena, Gaddo, and Ugo—disappeared from the scene for several years, but he is back in an as-yet-undefined role. At the apex of the extended family pyramid is the venerable Conte Ugo (they are all counts and countesses, but they make little of it), an amazingly spry octogenarian who

stands with Piero Antinori, Giulio Gambelli, Giacomo Tachis, and one or two others as an author of the Tuscan wine *rinascimento*.

Since Ugo began working at Capezzana in 1945, amazing changes have taken place there. He reintroduced Cabernet Sauvignon to the Carmignano *uvaggio* (they claim Cabernet has been here "since the time of the Medici"), clandestinely bringing in cuttings that he happened to find on the ground at a place called Château Lafite. Today, Carmignano—a denomination for all practical purposes reinvented by Ugo in his capacity as a representative on the national DOC committee—is the only DOC(G) that requires the blending of Cabernet Sauvignon or Franc (a minimum 10 percent, though they go nearer the maximum 20 percent, plus 10 percent Merlot in some vintages). All Cabernet plantings are made from their own massal-selected material, among the finest in Tuscany. Ugo's principal contribution, however, was providing the wise and reasonable leadership in which this family machine could work efficiently, with a minimum of the squabbles and petty jealousies that would be likely to characterize such an operation elsewhere.

When I was a frequent visitor and enthusiastic diner at Capezzana, the wines were consistently good but, to use the word of one British buyer, "underwhelming." In the past ten years, under Chioccioli's supervision, and since the family came together cohesively, things have been turned right around. Half of the area has been replanted at much higher density (6,200–9,600 plants per hectare as compared with 4,000 in the old vineyards); the cantina, parts of which date back to the 16th century, has been overhauled, reequipped, and modernized; and wine production has been rationalized, with Carmignano Riserva eliminated in order to focus on the major wine, Carmignano, as well as to improve quality in the bread-and-butter line Barco Reale.

Right: Ugo and Lisa Contini Bonacossi, who have inspired many of their children and grandchildren to work with them

FINEST WINES

Carmignano DOCG

This flagship wine has been made on the estate since 1925, and old vintages from the 1930s remain in the cellars of the villa, even though they are now pretty well past it. It was not until Ugo decided to bolster the Sangiovese of this relatively low-lying zone (only some 650ft [200m] above sea level) with Cabernet that it developed the sturdiness to age well. Those who knock the blending of Sangiovese and Cabernet per se should refer to this wine before and after. Today's blend—20% Cabernet Sauvignon to give color and structure, and 80% Sangiovese—is an excellent example of how well these two grapes can coexist in a harmonious whole without losing Tuscan typicity. The oak element—12 months in French tonneaux—is well handled and unobtrusive. Of recent years, the 2001 and 2004★ are particularly successful, and the 2002 and 2005 very respectable for their respective vintages.

Barco Reale del Carmignano

A DOC since 1994, this blend of 70% Sangiovese, 15% Cabernet Sauvignon, 5% Cabernet Franc, and 10% Canaiolo is the house quaffing wine. These days it fulfills its role admirably: a superior drink, without the layers of flavor and textures, or the terroir, of Carmignano. The 2006 [V] is a good example.

Ghiaie della Furba

This is one of the original Super-Tuscans (IGT Toscana), dating back to 1979. It started life as a blend of one third Cabernet Sauvignon, one third Cabernet Franc, and one third Merlot but is today 50% Cabernet Sauvignon, 30% Merlot, and 20% Syrah. Aged 14 months in French barriques, it is inescapably Gallic in style but very well made. I rated the 2003 only slightly lower than the 2005 Carmignano, which seems to me to have more quintessential character.

Vin Santo

Capezzana is famous for its sweet wine (first vintage 1959), today classed as DOC Carmignano, which spends a good five years in *caratelli*. It is certainly one of the finest of its type, with a lovely balance between dried fruit and caramel.

Above: Tenuta di Capezzana, where there are still dramatic Renaissance sculptures from Florence in its heyday

Tenuta di Capezzana
Total area: 675ha (1,668 acres)
Area under vine: 104ha (257 acres)
Average production: 600,000 bottles
Via Capezzana 100, 59015 Carmignano, Prato
Tel: +39 05 58 70 60 05
www.capezzana.it

Tenuta di Valgiano

The Tenuta di Valgiano property, 6 miles (10km) northeast of the medieval walled city of Lucca, goes back to the 15th century or earlier. For most of the past 200 years it was in the hands of the Sani family, from whom it was purchased in 1993 by current owner Moreno Petrini, who lives there with his wife Laura di Collobiano, in charge of the commercial side.

At the beginning they engaged in wine production with mild enthusiasm, but bit by bit became convinced, mainly thanks to the quality of the wine that issued from the fruit of the oldest vineyard, that that they were sitting on, not just a vineyard like hundreds of others, but a terroir capable of bringing forth wine of a very special character. Contemporaneously, and with the invaluable help of winemaker and fellow *appassionato* Saverio Petrilli, there developed the desire to treat the land with as much respect as possible, and so they began to adopt organic (from 1997), and later biodynamic (from 2002) methods.

Today they have established Valgiano as a working farm, with production of oil and honey, eggs and ham, and fresh vegetables from the *orto*. They like to think of themselves as traditionalists, though from a radical point of view that is only partially true. They believe in Sangiovese as a grape for blending rather than for varietal use, which is undeniably the traditional approach, but the accompanying vines are Syrah and Merlot, not Canaiolo, Colorino, or Ciliegiolo. Aging takes place in cement and oak, but the oak tends to be small and French, not large and Slavonian. Certainly they eschew the use of any type of additive or any forcing of the wine, or any adjustments in terms of acidity, aroma, or texture. Their aim is to produce wines of purity and elegance, wines that reflect the land with which they have been entrusted and the weather conditions that Nature gives them from year to year.

The engaging Moreno has carried his enthusiasm one step further, being a founder of the Associazione dei Grandi Cru della Costa Toscana. This is a group of some hundred producers along the Tyrrhenian coastal strip that takes responsibility for promotion and general cooperation and collaboration between members. Its most high-profile activity is the annual press tasting that takes place in spring in the splendid and not-to-be-missed town of Lucca.

FINEST WINES

Tenuta di Valgiano Rosso

This is selected from the 10ha (25 acres) of top-quality vineyard surrounding the house, and consists of Sangiovese at around two thirds plus Syrah and Merlot. Initial crushing is by foot, and alcohol and malolactic fermentation is in oak. The wine is aged in oak for about a year with a further 6 months in cement. I tasted the '06, '05, and '04 and found them all rich and full of sappy, plummy fruit with notes of licorice and blackberry, any tendency to jamminess cut by a firm tannic backbone. The '04 and '06 will last 20 years. The '05, from a weaker, rainier vintage, has good aromas on the nose but less fullness and roundness on the palate.

Palistorti Rosso

Also a DOC Colline Lucchesi, this is from soils and vines of lower age or quality than that of Tenuta. Otherwise the grape mix and aging are similar. The 2006 is juicy and plummy like its senior, but with less structure it is aimed at earlier drinking.

Tenuta di Valgiano Bianco

This is Chardonnay and Sauvignon with a splash of Vermentino (the Palistorti white, like its senior, is DOC Colline Lucchesi with more Vermentino plus a bit of Trebbiano and Malvasia). Both are clean and fresh, the Tenuta having more pungency, length, and creaminess of texture. The Tenuta in particular is highly creditable for a Tuscan white.

Tenuta di Valgiano
Total area: 60ha (148 acres)
Area under vine: 25ha (62 acres)
Average production: 70,000 bottles
Via di Valgiano 7, 55010 Valgiano, Lucca
Tel: +39 05 83 40 22 71
www.valgiano.it

Tenuta di Ghizzano

Ginevra Venerosi Pesciolini is one of Italy's most dynamic and dedicated *donne del vino* (women of wine). Taking over from her father Pierfrancesco when he was indisposed for health reasons, Ginevra has built this historic property into one of the jewels of Tuscany, through intelligence, hard work, good contacts, inspiration, and not a little luck. The luck comes from being born to an estate that her family (which they trace back at least as far as the age of Charlemagne in the 9th century) has owned since 1370. This is an estate that was always involved in agriculture, including viniculture, up to but not beyond a

Ginevra Venerosi Pesciolini is one of Italy's most dynamic and dedicated women of wine, and she has built this historic property into one of the jewels of Tuscany

certain basic quality level; an estate near enough to the Tyrrhenian to enjoy the mitigating effects of the sea air and light, so important for the Bordeaux varieties, but far enough inland (toward Florence) and at an altitude sufficient (up to 650ft [200m]) to grow serious Sangiovese.

Ginevra's contacts include the rich and powerful of Tuscan society (they are counts but do not flaunt the fact)—people in a position to help with promotion and distribution, as well as with top winemakers such as Carlo Ferrini, her enological guru since 1998. The inspiration is represented by an organic, recently biodynamic, approach to viticulture, which allows her to make a product of great purity, an approach aided by the fact that, having 360ha (890 acres) in total, there are very few neighbors whose allopathic treatments might float menacingly in her direction on a wayward breeze.

The estate's first wine to be bottled was Veneroso, named for ancestor Veneroso Venerosi.

In the years since then, the estate, in Ginevra's words, has been "profoundly revolutionized" in respect of viticulture. Some 85 percent of the current 18ha (44 acres) of vineyard have been replanted using massal-selection material at densities that have increased from the original 2,500 vines per hectare, through 4,500 in 1989, to 6,600 in the vineyards most recently converted. The aim is to get up to 20ha (49 acres). It has been hard work, especially since they still have 25ha (62 acres) of olive grove and 150ha (371 acres) of grain. But they have been faithful to the knowledge that there will always be a market for those who produce "very little but very well," as Ginevra puts it.

FINEST WINES

Veneroso
The geographical position of Tenuta di Ghizzano is suitable for both international and native varieties. They are not in a classic zone, such as Chianti Classico or Montalcino, and there is thus no reason why they, like their friends a bit farther east in Carmignano, should not make the most of this felicitous situation. Veneroso achieves this brilliantly, combining the sumptuousness of warm-climate Cabernet Sauvignon (40%) with the elegance and restraint of low-cropped Sangiovese (60%). This is a delicious, intensely Tuscan wine, serious and capable of good aging. [2004★]

Nambrot
Named for their ancestor of Carolingian times, this wine started life as a varietal Merlot but today includes Petit Verdot (20%) and Cabernet Franc (10%). Aged, like Veneroso, in oak of various sizes for up to 18 months, a vintage like the 2005 keeps the emphasis firmly on fruit (small black berry fruit) and displays something of the graphite and balsam of quality claret.

> **Tenuta di Ghizzano**
> Total area: 360ha (890 acres)
> Area under vine: 18ha (44 acres)
> Average production: 80,000 bottles
> Via della Chiesa 1,
> 56030 Ghizzano di Peccioli, Pisa
> Tel: +39 05 87 63 00 96
> www.tenutadighizzano.com

Sangervasio

Like many others in late 20th-century Tuscany, the Sangervasio wine farm developed out of a much more diverse agricultural reality, a reality with deep historic roots. The founding of the village of Sangervasio can be dated back to 754 AD, and its castle was erected toward the end of the first millennium by the powerful Gherardesca clan, which wielded phenomenal power and owned vast areas of land in coastal and near-coastal Tuscany from the early Middle Ages right through to the 20th century. Since 1960—that is, since around the time of the ending of *mezzadria*—it has been the property of the Tommasini, a family of industrialists from the nearby town of Pontedera. Until the early 1990s, it remained a diversified agricultural operation, in the manner of so many of its peers, growing grain as well as making oil and wine of a basic commercial standard. It was the decision of the current generation, and notably of Luca Tommasini, to go in for quality wine production. It was a decision that has led to a long and still fruitful collaboration with enological consultant Luca d'Attoma; to the extension of organic methods in a biodynamic direction, something they find relatively easy, their vineyards not being contiguous with any chemically-controlled fields; and to an increasing recognition of the excellence and value of their products on the international wine scene.

Luca Tommasini likes to think of his estate—400ha (988 acres), all in one piece in the hills of the Val d'Era—as being a very special enclave, enjoying as it does an arboristically mixed culture that includes oaks (*lecci* and *cerri*) as well as olives, cypresses, and umbrella pines. Like its neighbor Ghizzano, Sangervasio is near enough to the sea to benefit from sea breezes, keeping the atmosphere clear and guaranteeing maximum photosynthesis-enhancing light, yet is sufficiently upland to ensure flavor-favoring cool evenings and nights.

Among the grape varieties, pride of place has been given to Sangiovese, but the Tommasini are realistic enough to cater to the current demand for the fruitier, mellower characteristics of the international varieties from this zone, mainly Merlot and Cabernet. One peculiarity of the estate's planting policy is having two vineyards at 12,000 plants per hectare, one for Sangiovese and one for Merlot. Most of the other recent vineyards are planted to selected clones at around 6,000 plants per hectare.

FINEST WINES

A Sirio IGT Toscana
Top of the Sangervasio wine-tree is this blend of 95% Sangiovese with 5% Cabernet, from a vineyard planted at 12,000 vines per hectare, dedicated to the grandfather of Luca and his siblings Laura and Claudio. A wine of complexity and character, it is aged 18 months in barrique and 18 months in bottle.

I Renai IGT Toscana
A 100% Merlot wine, this has never quite convinced me in the same way as A Sirio, having a certain toughness about it, which is precisely what Tuscan coastal Merlot at its best so successfully avoids. It is aged like A Sirio, and similarly sold unfiltered. Perhaps it just needs more time.

Sangervasio Rosso IGT Toscana [V]
A more immediately accessible wine, made from the best grapes that fail to make the cut for the two crus, so Sangiovese 70%, Merlot 20%, and Cabernet 10%. It is hard to beat for everyday drinking.

Vin Santo Recinaio ★
Probably the best Sangervasio wine in absolute terms is its fabulous Vin Santo Recinaio, made from 80% Trebbiano and 20% San Colombano, aged 6–8 years in *caratelli* under the eaves of the winery. Drinking it is like imbibing liquid fudge or caramel, except that it has a beautiful acidity to keep it from waxing sticky.

Azienda Agricola Sangervasio
Total area: 400ha (988 acres)
Area under vine: 22ha (54 acres)
Average production: 100,000 bottles
Località San Gervasio, Palaia, Pisa
Tel: +39 05 87 48 33 60
www.sangervasio.com

Tuscan Coast

Tuscany's "Maremma" has, from almost total obscurity in a wine sense, become ultra-fashionable over the past 30 years or so—partly because it is (or was) an area of trendy Tuscany where an azienda could be picked up for a relative song, compared with Chianti Classico or Montalcino; partly because the winters are milder near the sea; and partly, if not mainly, because its wines became known and appreciated, at medium to high prices, the world over. It is a phenomenon that might be referred to as the Sassicaia effect, whose center was really in the northern sector in the zone of Bolgheri, on that strip of coastland that is trying today to market itself as the Costa degli Etruschi.

Northern Maremma

For the sake of convenience, we will again divide the area into three sections. First, the near-coastal parts of the province of Pisa that really owe more, in terms of wine styles, to Bolgheri than to the "west of Florence." This is a zone where Bordeaux varieties—the Cabernets, Merlot, and Petit Verdot—thrive, unlike Sangiovese, which struggles in the somewhat too high median temperature to achieve finesse. Also, as in Bolgheri, there is increasing success with the Rhône grapes, notably Syrah.

Then there is Bolgheri itself, which is really the commune of Castagneto Carducci, of which the arty little village of Bolgheri is administratively a *frazione*. The headquarters of Sassicaia, or rather the Tenuta San Guido, is on the cypress-lined avenue leading to the village from the Via Aurelia. Angelo Gaja, too, has taken up the Bordeaux challenge here, at his Ca' Marcanda, a kind of architectural *opera d'arte* more notable for its visual aesthetics than for the personality of its cold if perfect wines, in which, somehow, one can taste the fact that the owner lives a long way away. Other famous names associated with Bolgheri and its surrounds include Antinori and, more recently, Frescobaldi, Folonari, and—all the way from California—Delia Viader.

A few miles south of Castagneto, in the zone called Val di Cornia, is the town of Suvereto, with conditions similar to those in Bolgheri and a similar leaning toward cultivation of the Bordeaux varieties among the steadily growing wine fraternity gathering in the vicinity. When, in the mid-1990s, the gold rush to acquire vineyard land in Bolgheri began to approach its peak and prices started rising dramatically, it was largely to Suvereto that the seekers of liquid gold turned their attention. Whereas 20 years ago you would find scarcely a mention of this zone in the wine guides (not that there were anything like as many of them in those days either), today there would be more than 20 entries and rising.

Southern Maremma

Since we are into tripartite divisions of zones—strictly unofficially, let it be repeated, solely for the purposes of this book—why not also divide this zone into three? This, the southern section of the Maremma, is the Maremma proper, the coastal area and inland hills relating to the Tyrrhenian stretch of the province of Grosseto.

Leaving aside the beaches and the resorts, this is a zone of rocky hills and crags, of forests and infuriatingly winding roads, of eerie castles and lost gems of medieval architecture, such as the extraordinary walled town of Pitigliano. This is darkest Tuscany, where you can easily get as lost as in a jungle before emerging on to something totally modern like an *autostrada*, giving you the feeling that, during your sojourn there, you had been caught up in some kind of time warp.

And is this where Sangiovese was conceived? Certainly, one important, rarely mentioned grape here is Ciliegiolo, now scientifically designated as a "parent" of the great Tuscan. But the larger question will probably never be answered.

Right: The gateway to the village of Bolgheri, at the center of the coastal strip to which many famous names have flocked

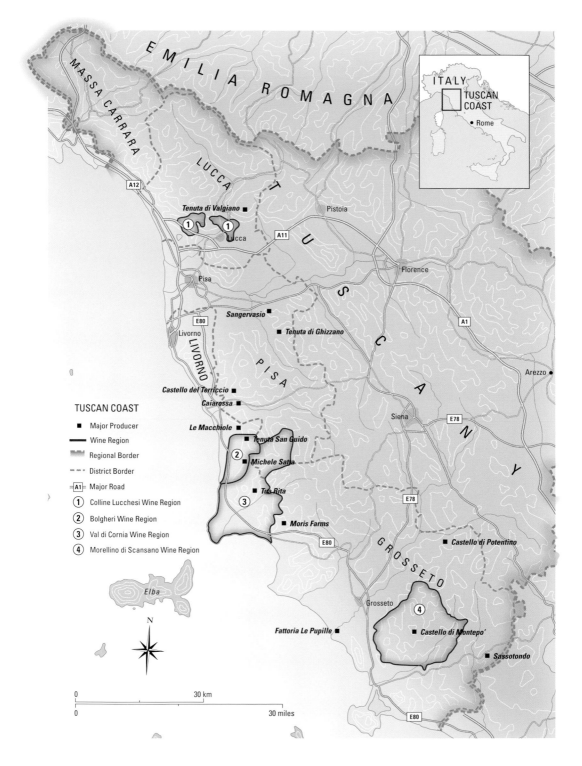

Above: Beyond Bolgheri rises the hill with part of the famous Sassicaia vineyard and its ruined *castiglioncello* at the summit

Of our three divisions, by far the largest and most important is Scansano, where the DOCG Morellino di Scansano holds sway. Morellino is the local name for Sangiovese, though like Prugnolo Gentile, Brunello, and Sangioveto, there is little to distinguish it from other Sangioveses, clonal derivatives mostly developed in recent years, except where producers have attempted massal selection from old, even pre-phylloxera, stock tucked away in the depths of their, or more likely small neighbors', vineyards or *orti*. Current regulations would have Morellino at a minimum of 85 percent of any blend, the remaining 15 percent being devoted to a number of alternatives according to the producer. These may include the Bordeaux varieties, which would seem to have little to do with the wine style of the zone, but increasingly often consists of Alicante or Grenache. The option also exists for a pure Sangiovese. In any case, DOC Morellino di Scansano is often downgraded by producers here, convinced they can make more profit by going IGT and adding a few dollops of Cabernet or Merlot.

The other two subzones of this extended area are Montecucco and what can only be described as "other Maremma." Pitigliano, at the extreme south of the province of Grosseto, on the Lazio border, officially stands for a white wine based on Trebbiano, but there are producers in the area who make much more interesting Ciliegiolo. As for Montecucco—a zone stretching west and south of Montalcino and including part of the lower slopes of Monte Amiata—it makes an eclectic mix of reds and whites from a diversity of grapes. As in the Scansano area, Montecucco, whose DOC dates back only to 1998, has been flooded in recent years by vineyard seekers—including some big names— unable to find or afford a property in the more classic zones of inland Tuscany.

Tenuta San Guido (Sassicaia)

All of the producers profiled in this book, plus quite a few others, were sent a questionnaire to fill out concerning their reality, their history, their production. A very few declined, or could not be bothered, to do so, and Tenuta San Guido, known to most people as Sassicaia (which is the wine name, not the estate name) was among them—presumably because they feel they do not need the publicity. Having no new material to go on, and considering that an entry on San Guido is absolutely necessary for a book with the present title, I have pinched part of a piece I wrote a couple of years back for *The World of Fine Wine* magazine, based on an interview and tasting at the estate (one of many, before and since; on this occasion specifically to taste the great 1985 after 20 years). And since the author and publisher are the same as are responsible for this book, I trust there will be no lawsuits. I mean, if you cannot plagiarize yourself, who can you plagiarize?

The originator of Sassicaia, Marchese Mario Incisa della Rocchetta, father of current owner Nicolò, was a *piemontese* vine grower who in 1943 moved to the Tuscan estate that his Gherardesca wife (sister of Piero Antinori's mother) had inherited. The story has often been related, so I will keep it short. Mario, like many Italian aristocrats of the age, was a claret buff and was determined to demonstrate that Italy was also capable of making high-quality wine. He noted that the soils on his estate were similar in their gravelly, mid-density composition to those of Bordeaux (Sassicaia means "stony place") and that, as in Bordeaux, the proximity of the sea made for cooler summers and warmer winters than in inland areas, while providing greater differences between day- and nighttime temperatures—all factors conducive to elegance in wine. At first, winemaking was just a hobby, additional to the

Right: Marchese Nicolò Incisa della Rocchetta, who, at his San Guido estate, can indulge his passion for both horses and wine

Sassicaia's preeminence among the wines of Bolgheri, indeed of Italy,
has been recognized by the granting of a unique DOC:
Bolgheri Sassicaia. It remains a mighty icon

real commercial activities of olive-oil and flower-bulb production. He sourced some Cabernet cuttings from a colleague of the noble Salviati family near Pisa, and he followed the traditional French production model, restricting yields to around 40–45hl/ha, fermenting in open-top wood *tini* for at least 20 days and aging in small oak barrels for three years.

In those days, the wine produced was not offered commercially but was consumed by friends and family or sold privately, in barrel or in certain years in bottle, to acquaintances. But the reputation grew, especially of the aged wine, and in 1970 Nicolò managed to persuade his father to call in the professionals in the form of the Antinori cousins and—especially—the Antinori winemaker Dr Giacomo Tachis (who, incidentally, has stayed with Sassicaia even though he left Antinori in the 1990s).

It was Tachis—still the chief enological consultant for Sassicaia—who set the parameters for the future wine. These parameters remain pretty well as established: the blend at around 85% Cabernet Sauvignon, 15% Cabernet Franc; yields restricted to around 30hl/ha, very low for Italy 40 years ago; aging in French barriques (as distinct from the Slavonian barriques favored by Mario), one third new each year, for about 24 months.

Not a lot has changed. Sassicaia's preeminence among the wines of Bolgheri, indeed of Italy, has been recognized by the granting of a unique DOC: Bolgheri Sassicaia. Sebastiano Rosa, the stepson of Nicolò, has come in to help run the show. A couple of new wines have been introduced, in particular the Merlot/Cabernet/Sangiovese blend Guidalberto, but while attracting favorable comment, Guidalberto has not set the world on fire like its senior partner. Sassicaia remains a mighty icon, a wine whose credibility has helped raise that of Italian wines generally. The motto here might be: If it isn't broken, don't fix it.

FINEST WINES

Sassicaia

I noted at a vertical tasting of Sassicaia in the 1980s that it took about seven years for the wine's real character to come through, so I am not sure how fair it is to score it before it has reached that age. There was, however, no such problem with the 1985★ that I went to the vineyard to taste a couple of years ago, when it really was sensational.

For once I found myself in agreement with Robert Parker, who made it his first ever 100-point Italian wine and commented that it was "one of the greatest wines I have ever tasted, from anywhere." The wine, I noted, was remarkably youthful in color and in substance. The classic blackcurrant aroma of Cabernet Sauvignon is there, together with the equally classic lead pencil of Cabernet aged in French oak, plus a wealth of herbs, spices, and leather. There is a remarkable liveliness to the palate, quantities of rich, sweet fruit, and dense but smooth tannins. A wine of great elegance but even greater youthfulness, of which I noted, with some exaggeration, "it seems as though it was made yesterday" and "the freshness is incredible—you'd never get that (it pains me to say) with a 20-year-old Sangiovese. Deserves the perfect score."

Having enthused so fully about the 1985 phenomenon, I can only briefly note that subsequent exceptional vintages have included the 1998, the 2001, and the 2004, all of which have displayed the elegance that is Sassicaia's calling card, together with a profusion of primary or tertiary aromas, depending on the amount of bottle age.

Right: Dr Giacomo Tachis, the distinguished consultant who first set the parameters for Sassicaia and still oversees it today

Tenuta San Guido (Sassicaia)
Total area: 2,500ha (6,177 acres)
Area under vine: 90ha (222 acres)
Average production: 430,000 bottles
Località Le Capanne, 27
57022 Bolgheri, Livorno
Tel: +39 05 65 76 20 03
www.sassicaia.com

Castello del Terriccio

enuta del Terriccio—now Castello del Terriccio, named for a ruined castle constructed in medieval times to defend against marauding Saracens—is a large and ancient estate on the border between the provinces of Pisa and Livorno, some 12 miles (20km) north of Bolgheri and stretching from the Tyrrhenian coast for several miles inland to the Pisan hills, to an altitude of 1,000ft (300m). In 1922, it was purchased from the Princes Poniatowski by the grandfather of current owner Gian Annibale Rossi di Medelana e Serafini Ferri. Dr Rossi himself took over in 1975, when it was much more of a classic farm than it is today, growing vegetables, grain, and medicinal herbs, and rearing cattle and horses. Olives and grapes were present, too, but at a functional level of quality. Today, the grapes, along with the horses bred for

show jumping, constitute the property's principal production, at quality levels to challenge all Italy.

This was not an immediate transition. It was not until the end of the 1980s that Dr Rossi decided to concentrate his agricultural efforts on wine grapes, and then only after an unfortunate horse-riding accident that left him in a wheelchair. Dr Rossi had always been an admirer of Bordeaux, as well as being a good friend of the Marchesi Incisa della Rocchetta of Sassicaia fame. He concluded that the smart money in this part of the world was not on traditional Tuscan varieties but on those of Bordeaux and France generally, for whose wines one could also command a substantially higher price than for those of the local Sangiovese-based Montescudaio DOC.

An essential piece of the puzzle was put in place by the hiring of Tuscany's consultant enologist best known for international-style wines—Carlo Ferrini. The horse-loving Dr Rossi is particularly fond of Ferrini's judgment on their first red wine, Lupicaia of the 1993 vintage: "This is an excellent horse, Dr Rossi. If we succeed in training it well, it will surely become a first-class jumper." Since then, Terriccio's vineyard area has increased to 65ha (161 acres), with a target of 100ha (247 acres). Some 10 percent of that vineyard space is dedicated to white grapes —French, of course—which Dr Rossi considers sufficiently important to enlist a separate consultant enologist (currently Giovanni Passoni of Friuli).

2001

IMBOTTIGLIATO DAL PRODUTTORE
G.A. ROSSI DI MEDELANA
CASTELLINA MARITTIMA (PI) - ITALIA

FINEST WINES

Lupicaia
This is Terriccio's flagship wine, currently a blend of 85% Cabernet Sauvignon, 10% Merlot, and 5% Petit Verdot, of which the Cabernet comes from a single vineyard. Winemaking methods are "updated tradition," involving maceration for up to four weeks, malolactic (like alcoholic fermentation) in steel, and aging in barrique and tonneau for 14–18 months.

Right: Dr Gian Annibale Rossi di Medelana e Serafini Ferri at the estate he has increasingly devoted to high-quality wine

The wine when young is quite fruity and mature enough to be drunk, unlike a top claret of similar age, but is also capable of changing and improving in bottle, as the magnificent 1997★ demonstrates. Aromas, apart from the inevitable blackcurrants, include loganberries, morello cherries, truffles, and an almost balsamic element conferred no doubt by the eucalyptus trees imported from Australia and growing in proximity to the vineyard. The texture is like a velvet carpet in the mouth.

Tassinaia

A sort of second wine to Lupicaia, this can, from positive vintages, be very nearly as good. Composed of equal amounts of Cabernet Sauvignon, Merlot, and Sangiovese, it is the first two varieties that dominate aromatically, though the Sangiovese undoubtedly informs the mouthfeel, especially in terms of acidity. Not quite so full and lush as Lupicaia, nor are the flavors quite so intense, but Tassinaia is doubtless capable of aging well over a period of ten years.

Castello del Terriccio

A Rhône-style wine, being dominated (at 50%) by Syrah, with notes of pepper and *peperoncino*, spice and garrigue. The fruit is not so developed, though, and the structure seems to dominate. Perhaps it needs more time.

Con Vento

The white wines include this convincing Sauvignon Blanc called Con Vento, with surprisingly persistent gooseberry fruit on both nose and palate, and bright, citric acidity to balance.

Rondinaia

A barrique-aged Chardonnay that is perfectly decent but nothing to get too excited about in the context of Chardonnays of the world.

Right: Terriccio's consultant Carlo Ferrini, one of the enologists who has helped establish a more international style

Castello del Terriccio
Total area: 1,867ha (4,613 acres)
Area under vine: 65ha (161 acres)
Average production: 300,000 bottles
Località Terriccio,
56040 Castellina Marittima, Pisa
Tel: +39 05 06 99 709
www.terriccio.it

Le Macchiole

It seems a long time ago, and no time at all, that Eugenio Campolmi passed away at the ridiculously young age of 40. Eugenio was a pioneer of Bolgheri, one of the first, after Incisa della Rocchetta, of course, to recognize the enormous potential for quality in the clay-rich but structured soils (with alluvial deposits and calcareous fragments) of the gentle slopes lying beneath the Bolgheri hills, some 3 miles (5km) inland from the Tyrrhenian Sea. Eugenio understood that the nearer you get to the hills, into the area subsequently dubbed the "El Dorado of Italian viticulture," the better, and it was this insight that, in 1983, drove him to the enormous effort of replanting his vineyards farther inland from their original position.

Eugenio was different from the owners of certain other rather grand properties of the so-called Costa degli Etruschi, in that he did not give himself aristocratic airs or subsist on inflated ego but was instead down to earth, plain speaking, full of humor, yet serious of purpose. He understood that the kind of high quality he sought came at a price—that of tiny yields and meticulous attention at every stage of the growing season. He understood that great wine can come only from great fruit, and that the only grapes likely to come great in this part of Tuscany were not Italian but French.

When I first started visiting Le Macchiole, in the mid-1990s, he was making basically three wines: Paleo Rosso, from a blend of Cabernet Sauvignon and Sangiovese at 10 percent; Paleo Bianco, from Sauvignon and Chardonnay; and Macchiole, from a blend of what was left. He was also experimenting with a few small barrels of a pure Merlot and even fewer of a pure Syrah, subsequently called Messorio and Scrio respectively.

This being an experimental stage, things were changing. First, Cabernet Franc was added to Paleo Rosso, and Sangiovese was reduced and

Right: Massimo Merli, who, together with his sister Cinzia, is realizing the vision of her late husband Eugenio Campolmi

The late Eugenio Campolmi understood that great wine can come only from great fruit, and that the only grapes likely to come great in this part of Tuscany were not Italian but French

subsequently dropped. Then Eugenio became convinced that Cabernet Franc was more suited to Bolgheri conditions than Cabernet Sauvignon was, and gradually he increased the Franc until, from 2001, it became 100 percent varietal. By this time, Messorio and Scrio had increased in volume (though they are, as ever, strictly on allocation, with people all over the world begging for more), so that now the top three wines were all pure expressions of their grape variety.

Today, Eugenio's work is being carried forward by his widow, Cinzia Merli, with the aid of her brother Massimo in the vineyards and of consultant enologist Luca d'Attoma (an old friend of Eugenio, at Le Macchiole since 1991). The cantina, a rough-and-ready building when I first saw it, with none of the pretensions to great architecture displayed by other cellars in the neighborhood, has been rebuilt in a practical rather than artistic manner. If Eugenio is looking down from the great vineyard in the sky, I am sure he is quite satisfied.

FINEST WINES

Paleo Rosso

This flagship wine is deep and youthful of color but not opaque, with a persistent, elegant aroma of cedar and berry, spicy fruit on the palate, great concentration, and plentiful, plummy, soft tannins. No excess of oak aromas despite 15 months in barrique, 10% of which are half-size (112 liters). Not typically Tuscan at all, yet not French either—far too ripe and juicy for a Cab Franc *in purezza*, and certainly showing no green pepper. Since the 2001★ appeared in 2004, it has been hailed as the greatest Cab Franc in Italy, if not the world.

Messorio

Certainly up there with Italy's top Merlots, this is a mouth-filler—an explosion of fruit threatening to go off in every direction but held together by a ripe, though firm, tannicity. Quite alcoholic at around 14%, but it carries it well. Very sensual wine.

Scrio

Somewhere between the Australian and Rhône styles of Syrah, combining the plumpness and fruit of the former with the structure and restraint of the latter.

Other wines are **Bolgheri DOC [V]**, ex-Macchiole, which is a blend of Merlot, Cabernet, and Sangiovese; and **Paleo Bianco**, a very distinctive white from Sauvignon (70%) and Chardonnay.

Above: Respect has always been paramount at Le Macchiole, and this sign demands silence while the wine rests

Le Macchiole
Area under vine: 22ha (54 acres)
Average production: 100,000 bottles
Via Bolgherese 189, 57020 Bolgheri, Livorno
Tel: +39 05 65 76 60 92
www.lemacchiole.it

Tua Rita

When I first visited this estate in the mid-1990s, it was a secret known to a very few. In truth, I had never heard of the Val di Cornia nor of Suvereto, and I was persuaded to visit only at the insistence of a wine-journalist friend who lived not far away. The first thing that struck me about Tua Rita (named for Rita Tua, who owns it with her husband Virgilio Bisti) was how very small it was—a real garage winery, with a cellar attached to the house, stuffed as full as its very limited space would allow with fermentation equipment and barrels. The tasting table doubled up as an office desk, and the *degustazione* was done on the hoof. As

The years have rolled by, and inevitably Tua Rita has turned from a well-kept secret into a world-famous winery. Indeed, it is now probably Suvereto's most famous

I recall, there was a wine that was mainly Sangiovese, another, quite striking, of the Bordeaux-blend style, and one barrique (perhaps two, but not more) of a quite spectacular Merlot (I do not think it even had a name at the time). The American buyer I was with immediately tried to corner the entire production, without asking the price, and I seem to recall he got about half.

The years have rolled by, and inevitably (in hindsight, that wonderful thing) Tua Rita has turned from a well-kept secret into a world-famous winery, no longer quite garage or boutique size now that they have expanded their vineyard area to around 20ha (49 acres). Indeed, it is now probably Suvereto's most famous winery, though that contention would be more in dispute here than in Bolgheri, where all bend the knee to Sassicaia. They have dispensed with their first consultant enologist, Luca d'Attoma, and from 1998 have taken on a second in the form of Stefano Chioccioli. Stefano Frascolla, Rita and

Virgilio's son-in-law, has come in to run the business side; they have constructed a large, purpose-built winery; and production has risen more than tenfold.

But the wine I tasted on that occasion some dozen years ago lingers on as one of my most memorable tasting experiences. It is a view, it seems, in which I am not alone, since Redigaffi, on the basis of a couple of 100-point ratings by American pundits, has become a cult wine selling on strict allocation at very high prices. What the folks at Tua Rita might be worried about, however, is not whether or not Redigaffi is considered one of the top five, or top three, or top in absolute terms among Italian Merlots, but rather whether its phenomenal success might risk putting their other excellent wines in the shade.

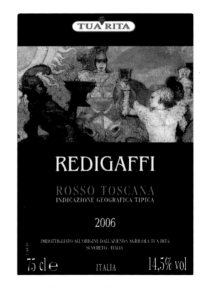

FINEST WINES

Redigaffi IGT Toscana
Obviously we have to start with Redigaffi: 100% Merlot, 25hl/ha, vineyards planted at up to 8,000 plants per hectare, dry extract 40g/l (very high), alcohol around 15%, aged up to 18 months in new

barriques, unfiltered. Redigaffi in good years like 2001★ is a big, opulent, no-holds-barred wine, as charged with color, flavor, alcohol, and sweet ripe tannins as is possible for a table wine. The aromas are red berry and blackberry and would be almost jammy were it not for the wealth of silky tannins and the roast-coffee and dark-chocolate aromas on the finish.

Giusto di Notri IGT Toscana
A blend of Cabernet Sauvignon at 50%, Cabernet Franc at 15%, Merlot at 30%, and Petit Verdot at 5%, this otherwise shares many of Redigaffi's characteristics but with a slightly lower extract. Deep of color, rich and concentrated, but more restrained and less hedonistically opulent than Redigaffi. Ripe, blackcurrant-liqueur fruit sits well with the tobacco and vanilla aromas from the 70% new oak.

Syrah IGT Toscana
Like Redigaffi, 25hl/ha, nearly 15% alcohol, and high (6.6g/l) acidity. A blockbuster style, more akin to Australian Shiraz than the likes of Côte Rôtie.

Rosso dei Notri IGT Toscana
This wine is from Stefano Frascolla's own estate and consists of Sangiovese at 60% plus Merlot, Syrah, and Cabernet Sauvignon. The most approachable wine of the group, though still quite chunky, ripe, and smooth.

Redigaffi in good years like 2001 is a big, opulent, no-holds-barred wine, as charged with color, flavor, alcohol, and sweet ripe tannins as is possible for a table wine

Right: Rita Tua, who, together with her husband Virgilio Bisti, has grown her initially small estate into a leading producer

Tua Rita
Total area: 35ha (86 acres)
Area under vine: 22ha (54 acres)
Average production: 130,000 bottles
Località Notri 81,
Suvereto, Livorno
Tel: +39 05 65 82 92 37
www.tuarita.it

Caiarossa

aiarossa is *in* Italy—a secluded spot inland from the Tuscan coast and the town of Cecina, in rolling hills at more than 500ft (150m) near the picturesque village of Riparbella. But it is not entirely *of* Italy, the owner since 2004, Eric Jelgersma, being Dutch (he also has a stake in châteaux Giscours and du Tertre in Margaux), and the winemaker/vineyard manager since 2006 being a young Frenchman, Dominique Génot. One might expect them, therefore, to be prejudiced in favor of Bordeaux styles and against the Tuscan; but while they do indeed make use of French grapes and methods in their principal wine, the second wine is almost entirely Sangiovese—and one of the best I have tasted in terms of value. I was impressed, in fact, by Génot's positive attitude toward Sangiovese, in particular by the fact that he, almost alone among winemakers in Tuscany, considers Sangiovese to be not "difficult"—at least not in the vineyard—but rather a grape of "great potential."

Almost alone among winemakers in Tuscany, Génot considers Sangiovese to be not "difficult"—at least not in the vineyard—but rather a grape of "great potential"

Perhaps that is because of the amazing lengths to which they go to get their zoning right—that is, to match soils with varieties and rootstocks, so that every variety is planted where it has optimum chances of thriving, the whole being backed by multitank vinification. It is Génot who carries out this work, with the advice of consultant agronomist Andrea Paoletti, and one has to say that if these people can get Sangiovese so right (near the coast, too, where Sangiovese is "not supposed to do well"), it bodes well for the future in Tuscany, provided producers are willing to put as much work into zoning as these people.

Another of the bees in their bonnet is biodynamics, though Génot, who has worked in Napa and New Zealand, as well as with the biodynamic Alsace producer Zind Humbrecht, is not fanatical about it, presenting his methods in a quality rather than an ideological context.

FINEST WINES

Caiarossa
The lead wine is a blend of up to eight varieties, with the preponderance going to Merlot, the two Cabernets (Génot is a particular fan of Cabernet Franc here), Sangiovese at 20-25%, plus Petit Verdot, Alicante, Syrah, and Mourvèdre, the last three in tiny quantities. All parcels undergo double *triage* and are vinified separately (with a long maceration of 20-30 days). *Assemblage* happens only at the end of the lengthy aging process (10-18 months, according to the variety). The 2004★ is svelte and smooth, with rich but silky tannins, has ripe, intense fruit, and carries its elevated alcohol and oak (25% new) well. The wine is too lush to resemble Bordeaux and is instead an excellent example of a coastal Tuscan, French-based red.

Pergolaia [V]
A highly successful expression of its principal grape, Sangiovese (95%), this retains its essential Tuscan-ness, despite the inclusion at 5% of Merlot and Cabernet, achieving integrity and typicity at a remarkably reasonable price.

Caiarossa Bianco
A Viognier/Chardonnay blend of good fruit intensity, viscosity, and weight. The 2005★ is better and more characterful than most Tuscan whites.

Right: Dominique Génot, who may see Sangiovese's potential rather than its problems precisely because he is not Tuscan

Caiarossa
Total area: 40ha (99 acres)
Area under vine: 16ha (40 acres), double by 2010
Average production: 50,000 bottles
Località Serra all'Olio 59,
56046 Riparbella, Pisa
Tel: +39 05 86 69 90 16
www.caiarossa.it

Michele Satta

Many big names have relocated to fashionable Bolgheri over the past few years, but Michele Satta was not one of them. Instead, Michele arrived from Lombardy back in 1974, when vineyards had 2,000 plants per hectare, each carrying more kilos of fruit than Michele has children (six, including five daughters), vines grew higgledy-piggledy, all mixed together, and wine was a minor agricultural product, sold in bulk. The golden age, whose sun shines so brightly upon Bolgheri today, was not even a glint in the eye.

Michele started off as a fieldhand but went solo in 1983 with rented vineyards, one of the first (with Piermario Meletti of Grattamacco and Eugenio Campolmi of Le Macchiole) to do so. He built a cantina and started buying land from 1988, bringing

Michele arrived from Lombardy back in 1974, when the golden age, whose sun shines so brightly upon Bolgheri today, was not even a glint in the eye

in consultant enologist Attilio Pagli, with whom he still works. He started refining with oak, small and large, from 1990, and in 1991 he planted his first vineyard to Cabernet, Merlot, Syrah, and Sangiovese. His predilection is for Sangiovese and Syrah, with a surprising fondness, too, for Teroldego.

"The features of our wine reality are lots of heat, excellent luminosity, but unfortunately very little water. Merlot does not work in Bolgheri's conditions: It ripens too quickly, all sugar and unripe polyphenols. For the same reason—no water, plus the fact that our topsoil is sandy and porous—it is important to plant not on the hillside, which causes water stress," says Michele.

He is probably best known for his Sangiovese, Cavaliere, since 2003 no longer from rented

vineyards but from his own plantings, taken by massal selection from the old fields. "Everyone sneers at Sangiovese on the coast, but they haven't really tried it. With Sangiovese you need lots of patience. We're still learning."

FINEST WINES

Cavaliere Toscana IGT

This 100% Sangiovese effectively gives the lie to the doomsayers. Aromas are typical for the variety, more morello than sour cherry, with ripe but not overripe fruit and enough acid/tannin structure in the 2004★ to stave off jamminess. It closes on a slightly bitter note, which balances the sweetness of the fruit. Good length and persistence. An old bottle, from 1996, with Burgundian noble decadence, shows it can age well, too. Wood aging for recent vintages is in 35hl *botti*, so mercifully there are no oak aromas.

I Castagni Bolgheri Superiore DOC

From a single vineyard purchased in 1997, this blend is 70% Cabernet Sauvignon, 20% Syrah, and 10% Teroldego. The nose is cassis, but the palate is too ripe and round to resemble Bordeaux, the "burned rubber" of Syrah coming through on the finish. A gutsy rather than subtle wine.

Piastraia Bolgheri Rosso DOC

The blend here is 25% each of Sangiovese, Merlot, Syrah, and Cabernet. Deep-hued and redolent of plummy, blackberry fruit, it has better acid lift than I Castagni, with Sangiovese doing its job.

Of the two whites, my definite preference is for the bright, sparky Vermentino/Sauvignon blend **Costa di Giulia**, over the 100% Viognier **Giovin Re** (an anagram of Viognier), the latter being somewhat overweight and oaky for my taste.

Right: Michele Satta, an early pioneer in Bolgheri, whose Cavaliere showed that Sangiovese could do well on the coast

Michele Satta
Area under vine: 30ha (74 acres), half owned
Average production: 170,000 bottles
Località Casone Ugolino 23,
57022 Castagneto Carducci, Livorno
Tel: +39 05 65 77 30 41
www.michelesatta.com

Castello di Montepò

T he Castello di Montepò is a mightily impressive structure that must have struck the fear of God into the hearts of besiegers of the 11th and subsequent centuries. Perched high on its rocky spur in the commune of Scansano, of Morellino fame, it has in recent times stood more as a wine "château" than as a wartime redoubt—indeed, more as a symbol of the ambitions of the human soul than as a bulwark against physical force.

If Jacopo Biondi Santi, in his website and elsewhere, speaks proudly of his ancestors of more ancient lineage, descending "in an unbroken male line" to the early 14th century and therefore almost as far back in history as the castle itself, there does seem, in his failure to include in the praise perhaps the most illustrious of them all, to be an element of the classic father/son rivalry. Admittedly, Franco Biondi Santi, of the Greppo estate in Montalcino, is a hard act to follow, and some of us know all too well what problems may be nurtured in the breast of the ambitious man bent on establishing his own identity and his own place in the world by having a famous father. But perhaps it is that very need to be his own man that pushed Jacopo to take on the challenge of Montepò, "with no contribution from my father or my father-in-law," as he puts it.

It was in the late 1990s that Jacopo purchased Montepò from the Greene family, currently of Castello di Potentino (*qv*). Previously, from the early '90s, there had been some sort of rift (the details of which no one was ever quite sure) with Franco over his winemaking style, which Jacopo, in accordance with the general opinion of the fine-wine community at the time, once described as "too hard" and "fossilized." Already in the early to mid-1990s he had started producing his more "contemporary" wines, with grapes of vineyards

Right: Jacopo Biondi Santi, whose home is now Montepò, where he has successfully been plowing his own furrow

Jacopo Biondi Santi feels that wine should be approachable within a reasonable period of time. But he thinks his top wine, Schidione, would be able to last 100 years

rented in various corners of Tuscany. Montepò, then, was more than a base of his own, more than a statement of independence, but a sort of viticultural home for his wines, where in a single estate he could tend his vines and make his wines according to his lights. ("I am essentially a viticulturist," he once commented, though since 2003 he has dispensed with enological consultants and tackled all operations together with Luca Martelli.)

A massive planting program was initiated, the area under vine having now expanded fivefold in a decade, with an ultimate goal of 100ha (247 acres), the majority Sangiovese element comprising entirely of the Biondi Santi clone BBS11. This, paradoxically, must be some kind of endorsement of what his father is doing, since very few producers in Tuscany today would risk all on a single clone of Sangiovese.

Rightly or wrongly, the contention for which Franco Biondi Santi is most famed is that his 100 percent Sangiovese wines, from top years, are capable of aging 100 years. As a rebel, you would not expect Jacopo to agree with this, and for the most part he would not—feeling that wine, while retaining classicity, should be approachable within a reasonable period of time. Interestingly, though, during my most recent visit, Jacopo did let drop that he thought his top wine, Schidione, from an exceptional year, would be able to last 100 years. Alas, I will not be there to test it—as I was in 1995 to confirm that Jacopo's great-grandfather's 1891 Brunello had just about made the trip.

FINEST WINES

Schidione IGT Toscana
This blend of Sangiovese BBS11 at 40%, Cabernet Sauvignon at 40%, and Merlot at 20% is barrique aged for up to 24 months. A dense, compact wine with lots of berry/cherry fruit and mocha/dark-chocolate character, with very firm acidity but ripe tannins, it improves if opened 24–48 hours before drinking, as my tasting of the 2000★ showed.

Sassoalloro IGT Toscana
A 100% Sangiovese BBS11, with less barrique aging, this is certainly much more immediate than a classic Greppo wine: some complexity, good integrity, typical Sangiovese acidity, but as in the 2005, relatively soft tannins.

Montepaone IGT Toscana
100% Cabernet Sauvignon. French of aroma, but Tuscan of structure; good, but up to and including

Above: The apparently impregnable Castello di Montepò, whose custodians are now engaged in more peaceful pursuits

the 2000 vintage, this is not among Tuscany's top Cabernets—yet.

Safiro IGT Toscana

This strikes me as a reasonable attempt at making Sauvignon Blanc in Tuscany—mineral and reasonably subtle compared with most New World versions. But I can't help wondering whether Sauvignon is really the right grape for Tuscany, and whether Maremma is really the right place.

Castello di Montepò

Total area: 500ha (1,236 acres)
Area under vine: 50ha (124 acres)
Total production: 300,000 bottles
Castello di Montepò, 58050 Scansano, Grosseto
Tel: +39 05 77 84 82 38
www.biondisantimontepo.com

Castello di Potentino

There are so many angles to the story of this place that it is hard to know where to begin. Castello di Potentino is a very imposing, slightly eerie-looking and almost other-worldly, 11th-century castle (but with Etruscan foundations). It stands near the town of Seggiano, famed for its oil, on the slopes of southern Tuscany's Monte Amiata, the massive magic mountain that looms over Montalcino to the south. The building, though inhabited in past centuries by various important families and groups, was in a state of serious neglect when Englishwoman Charlotte Horton and her mother Sally Greene arrived in 2000, having sold their previous wine castle, Castello di Montepò, to Jacopo Biondi Santi, son of Franco. Charlotte's aim was to make "real wine" ("Everyone talks about *vin de terroir*, but we make it")—wine made as naturally as possible and reflecting to the maximum the character of the enchanted *locus* (her word) that she had adopted. Grapes were planted from the best clones available, and from 2003, more so with the 2004 vintage, wines were made with the fruit of the estate, the consultant enologist Marco Stefanini lending a hand ("He's been with us some time because he doesn't want to do things to wine").

Charlotte has poured much effort into the restoration of the castle, trying to make it appear "as if we had not done it." The place is usually alive with guests, who are quickly turned into workers during the day, celebrants at night.

However, Charlotte is interested in more than just the castle. She has a keen interest in the arts and in culture generally, organizing various "non-barbaric events" using the castle as a focal point. Her great passion, though, apart from her vines (which she tends herself), her wines, and her oil from 100-year-old *olivastra seggiano* olive trees, is delving into the archeology of

Right: Englishwoman Charlotte Horton, who has dug back into Potentino's past, as well as helping secure its future

Charlotte's aim was to make "real wine" ("Everyone talks about vin de terroir, but we make it") —wine made as naturally as possible and reflecting to the maximum the character of the enchanted locus that she had adopted

early Tuscan winemaking. Some years ago she discovered on her land an ancient winemaking vat dug out of the volcanic stone of the mountain. Since then, several others have been unearthed by or near the stream (presumably once a navigable river) called Vivo, which passes through her property. The origin and age of these vessels, which could be Etruscan or post-Etruscan but are certainly many centuries old, is currently the subject of an ongoing debate.

Charlotte's great passion, apart from her vines (which she tends herself), her wines, and her oil from 100-year-old olive trees, is delving into early Tuscan winemaking

FINEST WINES

Charlotte has made a rough and ready, if "real," wine in the "Etruscan" vats, with crushing by foot, of course. But for commercial purposes she produces two other wines: **Montecucco DOC Sacromonte** (holy mountain), her "wine for drinking," a 100% Sangiovese; and **IGT Piropo** (referring to a fiery ruby hue), which she describes as her *vino filosofico*, a blend of Sangiovese, Pinot Nero, and Alicante. Both are wines of *spalla* (backbone), yet with a complexity of aroma and flavor that justifies her claim to originality. No attempt is made to "improve" color; natural yeasts are employed; no press wine is added; vinification and aging takes place in 50hl vats of French oak (16 months for Sacromonte, 24 months for Piropo). "What about organic methods?" she was asked. "We place the emphasis on wine," she replied, "not on ideology."

Left: Old olive trees surround more recently planted vines, but the history of winemaking here stretches back centuries

Castello di Potentino
Total area: 22ha (54 acres)
Area under vine: 4ha (10 acres)
Average production: 20,000 bottles
58038 Seggiano, Grosseto
Tel: +39 05 64 95 00 14
www.potentino.com

Fattoria Le Pupille

Elisabetta Geppetti is a woman of unusual energy, determination, and vision. She was only 20 when, in 1985, she first took the reins at her family's 2ha (5-acre) estate near Pereta in the Scansano zone. It was a time when Tuscan wines were at a low ebb—those of Scansano almost off the map—and women winemakers were almost non-existent. Already the estate benefited from the consultancy of Giacomo Tachis, chief winemaker at Antinori and Sassicaia, and with his advice, Elisabetta set about pulling her beloved native land up by its enological bootstraps. The original wine was, of course, Morellino di Scansano, which, with her respect for tradition, remains the mainstay of production. Her tastes also include an international aspect, manifested in the Maremma's first Super-Tuscan, the Cabernet-based Saffredi, planted in

Elisabetta Geppetti is a woman of unusual energy, determination, and vision, who set about pulling her beloved native land up by its enological bootstraps

1985 and first released in 1989. There followed other innovations, though Elisabetta was careful to keep the international grapes separate from her Sangiovese-based wines (except for Pelofino), despite the option contained in the Morellino *disciplinare* of including them at up to 15 percent. Probably the most important addition to the range, post-Saffredi, has been the single-vineyard Morellino di Scansano called Poggio Valente, from the original vineyard at Pereta, whose old vines (mainly Sangiovese) are boosted by younger ones, partly from new clones and partly from massal-selected material.

Somehow, as if she did not have enough work on her hands, bearing and raising her vinous children amid the constant upgrading of vineyards, the

building of a modern winery at Istia d'Ombrone (functional since 2001), and the jetting worldwide to promote her estate and her area (she was even chair—the first—of the Morellino di Scansano Consorzio in the 1990s), Elisabetta has found time to produce five children of the human variety. She has had help: Following Dr Tachis's withdrawal in 1994, she enlisted the aid of Riccardo Cotarella and subsequently, from 2000, Christian le Sommer, formerly of Yquem and Latour and currently consultant to Lafite Rothschild for its international operations. More important from a daily-running point of view, she has been supported in vineyard and winery since 2001 by Sergio Bucci, who graciously elucidated operations when I visited.

FINEST WINES

Morellino di Scansano [V]
The basic Morellino di Scansano is made from Sangiovese (88%), Malvasia Nera, and Alicante (Grenache, but with differences arising from long presence in the area), without wood aging, and is intended to be consumed within three years of production. Elisabetta believes in a fresh, fruity wine, easy of access—the kind of everyday style that Morellino di Scansano had always been associated with in the past, but better, as the 2007 clearly demonstrates.

Morellino di Scansano Riserva Poggio Valente
This cru wine—97% Sangiovese, the remainder Malvasia Nera—is made in a much more serious way than Il Poggio, with prolonged skin contact and 15 months' barrique aging (40% new). The wood is well handled, fruit character predominating. The wine can have quite a tannic kick in youth, depending on the vintage, but coming from a vineyard at an altitude of around 820ft (250m), there is none of the easy jamminess associated with coastal Sangiovese. Accordingly, it has good aging potential, and the most recently tasted 2005 should reward patience and time.

Saffredi IGT Maremma Toscana
Now made from Cabernet Sauvignon and Merlot at 45% each, plus a touch of Alicante and Syrah,

this is a modern-day classic of the Super-Tuscan category. Aged 18–20 months in mainly new barriques, it comes from a vineyard in the same zone, and with the same characteristics, as that of Poggio Valente. It should be noted that Cabernet, if not the other Bordeaux varieties, is quite traditional in this part of the world, rejoicing in local parlance in the sobriquet "Bordò". The wine is big in structure, concentration, and alcohol, but thanks to a good acid and tannin backbone it manages an element of elegance. The 2001★ is capable of aging a good 20 years.

Pelofino

A recent addition to the range, this is the only case of a native/international blend (Sangiovese plus Cabernet Sauvignon, Cabernet Franc, and Syrah). Very rich in color and in body, the wine has creamy, smooth tannins and fresh acidity. It is very much a New World style, and you would not guess, in a blind tasting, that Sangiovese was present... so you might be tempted to wonder why it is there. Destined for early consumption.

Above: the visionary Elisabetta Geppetti, who has helped put Scansano on the map since succeeding to her family winery

Fattoria Le Pupille
Total area: 400ha (544 acres)
Area under vine: 65ha (178 acres)
Average production: 450,000 bottles
Piagge del Maiano 92A,
Località Istia d'Ombrone, 58100 Grosseto
Tel: +39 05 64 40 95 17
www.elisabettageppetti.com

Moris Farms

At separate locations in the province of Grosseto, this is really two estates owned by the Moris family, who have been practicing agriculture here for generations (though the primacy of viticulture is relatively recent) and who, by the way, are not of British but of Spanish origin, if rather distantly. So, no: Moris with one "r" is not a typo.

The original farm, Fattoria Poggetti, is near the medieval town of Massa Marittima and boasts its own boar enclosure; a view of Elba and Corsica on a clear day; 3,600 cypress trees, planted from 1937 by grandfather Gualtier Moris; and some 37ha (91 acres) of vineyard, about two thirds Sangiovese (almost all replanted with clones since 1990), but with a healthy representation (15 percent) of Cabernet Sauvignon, which they claim was in their vineyards from unspecified times past. They also have around 10 percent Syrah, which they say works well in the clay-based soils of Massa but less well in the sand-dominated terrain of Podere Le Mozzine, purchased with remarkable foresight (or good luck, or both) by Gualtier in Morellino di Scansano in 1971.

For the past 30 years, the farms have been run not by a Moris but by a husband of a Moris, Adolfo Parentini, aided and abetted since 1988 by consultant enologist Attilio Pagli, since 1996 by viticulturist Andrea Paoletti, and more recently, on the sales side, by his son Giulio. For the past 20 years or so, Moris Farms has been recognized, with Fattoria Le Pupille, as one of the founders of quality production in the Maremma, with judicious use of the "improving" grapes of France and the technology of barrique management. They are canny enough to recognize that the lighter wines of Le Mozzine should get less or no barriquing compared with the sturdier, more tannic products of Monteregio.

Straddling the "before" and "after" stages of southern Tuscan wine development, they make the point that the transition from the quantity to the quality mind-set was not easy. As recently as the early 1990s they had difficulty persuading pickers to undertake bunch-thinning in July and to take two or more passes through the vineyard at vintage time. Today, modern practices are in place, and there is even harvesting by machine (around 80 percent)—something yet to catch on in traditional Tuscany.

FINEST WINES

Avvoltore IGT Toscana
This top cru (from Poggetti) is named for a hill that is named for a falcon-type game-bird. The first vintage was 1988, making it, with Saffredi, the first Maremma Super-Tuscan. The *uvaggio* is 75% Sangiovese, 20% Cabernet, and 5% Syrah (25% Cabernet until 1995). It spends 12 months in barrique—a wine of complexity and character, rich but rounded, a Tuscan modern classic. [2004★]

Morellino di Scansano
The mainstay of production (from Le Mozzine) is 90% Sangiovese plus "others." This light, fruity, easy-drinking wine sees no oak. In better years there may be a riserva, aged a minimum of two years.

Monteregio di Massa Marittima DOC
A wine of greater substance than the Morellino, but also of much lower sales. Sangiovese 90% plus Cabernet. Acceptable but not particularly exciting.

Scalabreto Passito Rosso VDT
As a Vino da Tavola it is allowed no mention of vintage, variety, or provenance, but between us it's a blend of Syrah and Montepulciano picked late in November and December. Now this is exciting: a vibrant pink, intense sweetness cut by firm acidity.

Moris Farms are also experimenting with a grape native to the hills north of Massa Marittima called Gorgottesco—one to watch.

Moris Farms
Total area: 476ha (1,176 acres)
Area under vine: 70ha (173 acres)
Average production: 400,000 bottles
Fattoria Poggetti, Località Cura Nuova
58024 Massa Marittima, Grosseto
Tel: +39 05 66 91 91 35
www.morisfarms.it

Sassotondo

It was at a tasting featuring the top wines of the Tuscan coast, a few years back, that San Lorenzo, the flagship wine of this estate, stood out for me, among the Sassicaias and Ornellaias, as being the wine on display with the most character. Following it up with a visit to the property, hidden away in the backwoods of southern Maremma near the fairytale walled medieval town of Pitigliano, I discovered what it was that made these wines special.

There is, first of all, the grape variety Ciliegiolo, which has probably been part of Tuscan horticulture since the Garden of Eden and that DNA research has established is a "parent" of Sangiovese (*see Chapter 3*). It is a difficult grape to tame, having tight bunches, large berries, and a propensity to overproduce. But handled correctly, Ciliegiolo can bring forth amazing nectar, as the owners of Sassotondo—almost alone so far—have shown.

Probably part of Tuscan horticulture since the Garden of Eden, Ciliegiolo can bring forth amazing nectar, as the owners of Sassotondo have shown

Second, there is the owning couple—Carla Benini and Edoardo Ventimiglia—passionate producers who, in 1998, gave up a good life in Rome for a relatively lonely struggle with nature in the southern Maremma, where they had bought a property in 1990. Taking on consultant Attilio Pagli, one of the best in the business, was a positive step. Establishing an organic, probably soon to graduate to biodynamic, viticultural system was another important step. Using only massal selection from the old San Lorenzo vineyard for replanting was yet another.

Third, there is the local soil—strongly and ubiquitously tufaceous, therefore high in potassium and magnesium, somewhat saline, giving wines of deep color, high extract, and rich sapidity, with spicy/peppery notes. Even the restructured cantina is dug out of tufa, in which one may find evidence of previous civilizations (neolithic, Etruscan, Roman, medieval) such as tunnels, caves, tombs, and wells. The *sassotondo* from which the estate takes its name is a large, round stone in the middle of a field.

FINEST WINES

San Lorenzo
100% Ciliegiolo, from a single vineyard with old vines, this is a big wine but not without elegance. Aged for 24 months in French barriques, 75% new, it pits firm acids and tannins against opulent fruit in a contest that, from a good vintage, is going to take several years to resolve, as the 2001★, powerful yet elegant and still youthful, fully demonstrated.

Ciliegiolo [V]
This young red, aged only in steel and sold within the first year, can be a monster, at 13.5–15% alcohol, with rich, deep fruit, peppery and fiery—a winter warmer, Jumilla-style. Modestly priced, this is among the best value for money wines in Italy.

Franze
A DOC Sovana (which must be at least 50% Sangiovese), this is in fact a pure Sangiovese that, while interesting as an example of good Maremma Sangiovese, struggles alongside its Ciliegiolo partners.

Numero Sei
The sole white is made from Sauvignon Blanc and Greco, the latter being partially macerated (for four days) and barrique aged. An oxidative style, with citrus peel and ripe apricots on the nose, suggesting sweetness, it shocks with its austerity and dryness on the palate. An oddball—perhaps for those who love the white wines of cult Friuli producer Josko Gravner.

Sassotondo
Total area: 72ha (178 acres)
Area under vine: 11ha (27 acres)
Average production: 40,000 bottles
Azienda Agricola Carla Benini,
Pian di Conati 52, 58010 Sovana, Grosseto
Tel: +39 05 64 61 42 18
www.sassotondo.it

Montalcino

Montalcino, with its wine Brunello, has been one of the great success stories of modern-day Italian wine—no doubt the greatest in central Italy (which is why it gets so many entries in a book on the finest wines). In the circumstances, you might expect it to have a long enological history, like Chianti Classico and Montepulciano, but in fact, as a name and as a vinous reality, Brunello di Montalcino goes back only as far as the latter half of the 19th century.

The history of the town, a fortified citadel on top of a high hill, visible from below for many miles around, is much longer. Excavations in the area have uncovered Etruscan and Roman remnants. Its famous abbey, Sant'Antimo, was, according to a document of AD814, the recipient of land *sub monte Lucini* (below Montalcino). The town, which developed into something very close to its present architectural self between the 13th and 17th centuries, was made a *città* ("city") by Pope Pius II (a local lad of the Piccolomini brood) in 1462. During this time it found itself caught in the wars between Florence and Siena, mainly on the Sienese side, but for the past 400 years or so it has had a relatively quiet time of it, getting on with its daily business which is, almost exclusively, agriculture.

Vines, of course, played their part but were only one of a number of crops. Prior to the mid-19th century, the red wines of Montalcino were called Vermiglio, and there is some evidence that they were appreciated for their quality, with King William III of England allegedly a fan. The wine, like that of other parts of Tuscany, such as Chianti (in fact, Montalcino today finds itself in the Chianti Colli Senesi production zone), tended to be a blend of varieties—Sangiovese and Canaiolo, Colorino, Tenerone, Gorgottesco, Trebbiano, and Malvasia. A Montalcino specialty that found wide favor was the sweet Moscadello.

It was a local pharmacist, Clemente Santi, who in the early part of the 19th century, at his Greppo estate, started experimenting with vines and vinification styles with the aim of making wines of more elevated quality. The work was carried forward by his grandson, Ferruccio Biondi Santi, who isolated a clone of Sangiovese Grosso that he hoped would prove to be the inspiration behind the dreamed-of 100-year wine. In reference to its brownish hue at vintage time, it was dubbed "Brunello." By the time the great vintages of 1888 and 1891 rolled around, Ferruccio was ready to lay down a good few bottles for his progeny to display in defense of his thesis.

Ferruccio was succeeded by his son Tancredi, an inspired enologist who, among other things, brought the handful of producers of Brunello together as a cooperative when phylloxera threatened to wipe them all out. There was a bit of a surge in the 1920s and '30s, but the war flattened business again, and even after 1967, when Brunello became a DOC, there were very few producers of the wine.

Expansion, faction, and legislation

It was not until the 1980s that Brunello began taking off, in the sense that money began pouring in from outside, vineyards were snapped up, and buildings were restored or built in the architectural manner of the zone (with so many wide vistas and beautiful buildings, Montalcino is to be visited for the aesthetics alone, never mind the wine). Today, planting in the Montalcino DOCG zone has reached saturation point, with 1,900ha (4,695 acres) of the total 3,000ha (7,413 acres) under vine qualifying for Brunello. The wine is featured on the lists of all the great restaurants of the world, and at high prices. Indeed, all seemed perfectly heavenly—until 2008, with its financial crises and scandals, and suddenly the commercial weather took a turn for the worse.

Since major expansion began (the number of bottlers rising from 12 in 1967 to 74 in 1987 and 208 in 2008), there have been two factions in Montalcino:

Right: Montalcino, now the most prestigious wine town in Tuscany, offers beautiful views over the surrounding hills

- ■ Major Producer
- ▬ Montalcino Wine Region
- ⊶ Railway
- SR2 Major Road

ITALY

● MONTALCINO
● Rome

Buonconvento

SR2

Torrenieri

SR2

San
Quirico
d'Orcia

Valdicava ■

Siro Pacenti ■

Salvioni (La Cerbaiola) ■
Montalcino

■ Fuligni

MONTALCINO

■ Il Colle

Pian dell'Orino ■
Le Potazzine ■   ■ Cerbaiona
Biondi-Santi ■

Brunelli ■
■ Salicutti

Tavernelle

Case Basse ■   Poggio
Antico ■

Mastrojanni ■

Camigliano ■
Camigliano ■

Castelnuovo
dell' Abate

Argiano ■   Il Poggione ■   Lisini ■   Ciacci
Piccolomini   ■ Poggio
di Sotto

Sesti ■

Agostina Pieri ■

Castello Banfi ■   ■ Col d'Orcia

SP64

N

0 _____ 3 km
0 _____ 3 miles

those who would remain true to the original concept of Brunello as a single-varietal, long-aged wine for laying down—if not for 100 years, then at least for five or ten; and those who would internationalize the vinification and speed up the commercialization. Both have had their triumphs. The modernists have succeeded in reducing the minimum aging period in oak from four years to two, which has enabled them to use more barrique to get a mellower, more silky palate plus (though they would not admit it) a few added aromas beloved of the less sophisticated wine-drinking public—vanilla, woodsmoke, coffee, and dark chocolate—that would not be there without the charred barrique. The traditionalists have managed to keep the total aging period at four years, the majority of which for them will be passed in large oak *botti*, and if the modernists want to hold the wine for two years in bottle, good luck to them. The traditionalists have also managed to retain Brunello's and Rosso's 100 percent Sangiovese varietal makeup—something that infuriates the modernists, who see nothing wrong in continuing the late 20th-century *nouvelle tradition* of blending in "ameliorative" grapes to soften and round out the sometimes difficult or deficient Sangiovese. Indeed, the modernists argue that the Bordeaux varieties were prevalent in Montalcino in the 19th century, and point out that in the first draft of the Brunello DOC *disciplinare*, drawn up in 1966, allowance was made for 10–15 percent inclusion of other black grapes in the blend; this was, after all, and still is, a Chianti zone (Colli Senesi). I heard a rumor that this proposal was shot down by the most prestigious man on the scene at the time—Pierluigi Talenti of the Franceschi estate Il Poggione—who, being the major source of quality Sangiovese for others, was loath to lose business to other varieties.

The modernists claim that blending is justified by the fact that it is what the public wants. True enough, for the majority of the public. The traditionalists response is: Bother the public,

we're here to make wine as art; it's expensive and exclusive, and it is essential that it remain unique and not come to taste like the wine of other parts of Tuscany, or indeed of other parts of the world. Even assuming that the modernists were right (which I do not believe they are), their position is strictly illegal, it being a criminal offense knowingly to blend varieties other than Sangiovese in Brunello.

Brunellopoli and beyond

Brunellogate—or *Brunellopoli* to the Italians—was a scandal that broke early in 2008, whereby many wineries were investigated and the 2003 Brunellos of four major ones blocked by the authorities on the suspicion they had been blended. At the time of writing, nothing has been proved, and the wineries in question—following a lot of declassification and not a little politicking—were more or less quickly back in business. But the inquiries continue, and there could be further repercussions, not least because the technology for detecting unauthorized varieties in a wine by color is getting better all the time. And while the 2003s alone were implicated, at the time of the investigation, the wines of 2004, '05, '06, and '07 were all made—if not blended. The drama continues.

Montalcino is known mainly, of course, for Brunello, but it does produce other wines, including Rosso di Montalcino, which currently must also be 100 percent Sangiovese but its aging period is much shorter (at least one year, which need not be in oak, though it usually is). Some producers who oppose blending for Brunello are not against it for Rosso. If you really want to blend, however, you can resort to DOC Sant'Antimo, which allows a variety of grapes and blends, most of which are pretty uninteresting. You are more likely to get a good wine under the IGT Toscano.

Finally, certain producers have revived the old sweet wine of Montalcino—Moscadello—which can be made like Moscato d'Asti, light and frothing, or may be made from dried grapes.

Biondi-Santi (Tenuta Greppo)

Franco Biondi Santi's Greppo is the iconic estate of Montalcino, and the man himself, now well into his 80s, is a legend in his own lifetime. He gets little help, in the matter of wine production, from his son Jacopo, who is dubious about his father's dyed-in-the-wool traditionalism and, in any case, has his hands full at his own Maremma estate of Castello di Montepò. Thus Franco is obliged to carry on effectively as his own agronomist and winemaker, in the manner, as he puts it, of a "continuer, not an initiator." "Even as an old man I have to live on the run," he complains. "I would like to retire, but I can't find the time."

The impressive Greppo estate, not far south of the town of Montalcino, with vineyards at an altitude of 1,247–1,640ft (380–500m), may not be large by modern-day Montalcino standards, but it gives every appearance of being as perfectly run as a Bordeaux premier cru château. In his role of "continuer," Franco has faithfully followed his father Tancredi's system since he took over in 1969. The clones used for planting the vineyards, when replacement is required, come from Biondi-Santi's own massal-selected material; indeed, the principal one is today generally available under the title BBS11. The grapes for the Brunello Riserva—the wine he maintains is capable in top vintages of lasting 100 years—must be from vineyards of a minimum age of 25 years, and those for the Brunello Annata must be at least ten years old. No herbicides or insecticides are used, in order not to compromise the natural yeasts. Fermentation of riserva wines takes place in oak *tini*, maceration is for a surprisingly short 15 days, and temperature control is achieved by *rimontaggio* rather than electronically or mechanically. No additives other than SO_2 are employed. And aging, of course, takes place over a minimum of three years in large Slavonian oak *botti*, some of them being very old themselves.

"Mine is a wine for patient people," comments Franco. By which he means that the bottles (of

Riserva, at least) should be laid down in a suitable place for a few decades before opening (this may require recorking from time to time, and Franco makes quite a ceremony of this, inviting journalists as witnesses and using one bottle of a given wine to top up others that have ullage). This applies also, he insists, to the drinking of it—from a bottle opened 24 hours earlier, sipping reflectively, not rushing.

The wines are distributed by Biondi Santi Spa (Inc.), run by Jacopo's inlaws, the Tagliabue family, who also have their own Villa Poggio Salvi label.

FINEST WINES

Biondi-Santi Brunello di Montalcino Riserva
I have been involved in a couple of vertical tastings of this famous wine, in 1994 and in 2006. Given the importance of these wines in a Tuscan fine-wine context, I think it appropriate to give some detailed notes.

2004 Too young to judge at the time of tasting (from wood), though Franco thinks it will rival the greatest.

1999 The nose is still closed, but the palate has a certain ripeness and richness of fruit, with signature, firm acidity. Needs time.

1995 Fresh nose, with herbal and mushroom notes; hint of cinnamon. Full, tight palate, structured but good underlying fruit; good life ahead.

1985 Color still fairly youthful. Pure nose, floral, herbal. Very structured, with compact fruit, as well as great freshness, intensity, and elegance. Still evolving positively.

1975★ The deepest color yet. Sour cherry, tea leaf, and elder flower on the nose; some leather and mushroom, too. Classic, gamy, Sangiovese: elegant, complex, and intense on the palate. Michael Broadbent MW described it as "superb by any first-growth standards."

1964 There is some discrepancy between my two

Right: Franco Biondi Santi, who has continued to run his iconic estate on traditional lines for the past 40 years

notes on this generally very good vintage. In 1994, I noted: "Tremendous structure, very concentrated, lively fruit; very youthful, needs time." Twelve years later I liked it less, because I felt it had not moved on as I had hoped, still being very hard. Agreed that it will last 100 years, though.

1955 Some people's favorite ("a classic by any yardstick," according to Michael Broadbent), though I noted in 1994 that it was already quite evolved, with compact, elegant fruit, mainly dried, hints of tar, and a balanced, sweet finish. Later I noted that it was "oldish" both in color and on the palate, with some rather harsh tannins: "Not convinced it will make 100 years—on a downward course."

1945 The first time I tasted it I found it old on the nose, tarry, minerally, and losing its fruit. Twelve years later it showed much better.

1925 Tawny color, tar and mushroom. "Lingering and elegant—a fascinating wine."

1891 In 1994 I gave this top marks—indeed the perfect score—with the following note: "Tawny color, but rosy tints. Tar and mushrooms on the nose. Acid firm, tannins gone. Lovely, sweet, almost youthful fruit on the palate, and a long, lingering finish; very impressive and convincing. Would that humans could be as lively as this at the age of 103!" Other tasters agreed on its exceptional quality, specifically Anthony Dias Blue, who gave it 96 (his top mark), and Gabbrielli and Cernilli of *Gambero Rosso,* who scored it 95 (their second-highest mark after 97 for the 1955).

The other Riserva vintages that scored highly in the 1994 tasting were 1988, 1982, and 1971.

Right: The beautiful driveway at Tenuta Greppo, the original Brunello di Montalcino estate, still impeccably run today

Biondi-Santi (Tenuta Greppo)
Total area: 150ha (370 acres)
Area under vine: 22ha (54 acres)
Average production: 60,000–70,000 bottles
Tenuta Greppo,
53024 Montalcino, Siena
Tel: +39 05 77 84 80 87
www.biondisanti.it

Camigliano

In their unobtrusive way, the wines of Camigliano—one of the earliest producers of Brunello di Montalcino, tucked away in one of the remotest corners of the Montalcino territory, southwest of the town and overlooking the multiple vineyards of Banfi—have become among the most respected and sought after for a number of reasons.

First, unlike many of the producers that have sprung up here like mushrooms in recent decades, Camigliano has a history. It is one of a chain of castles (which include Banfi's Poggio alle Mura) that served as watchtowers in medieval times, based in a medieval *borgo* (hamlet) whose roots go back to Etruscan times. As one passes through its ancient arches and along its stone byways, one

Unlike many of the producers that have sprung up in Montalcino like mushrooms in recent decades, Camigliano has a history. One gets a feeling almost of timelessness

gets a feeling almost of timelessness. There is little movement or sound in the town, and yet you realize that it is not abandoned, there being, within its walls and deep in its cellars, a major winery at work here and a population of some 30 souls in the *case coloniche*, with the washing hung out to dry and the old ladies standing around having a desultory chat. There is even a restaurant, though we are seemingly in the middle of nowhere.

Camigliano is large, with more than 500ha (1,235 acres) of property, nearly 100ha (247 acres) of vineyard, and large areas of olive grove. Not Montalcino's largest, certainly, but one of them.

It was in 1957 that the Milanese Walter Ghezzi, father of current proprietor Gualtiero, bought this sprawling estate, fresh from the thrall of *mezzadria* (sharecropping); at the time the houses lacked electric lighting. Montalcino, which was to become

the richest commune in Tuscany in the 1990s, was then one of the poorest in all Italy. Wine played an incredibly minor part in the local economy, and what Walter found was stables for the raising of Chianina beef cattle, facilites for pigs and turkeys, and some organic vegetable gardens.

The first vintage of Brunello was 1964. But it was not until the 1980s that Gualtiero, with his wife Laura, took over from his father and began a program of planting and replanting vineyards (current density about 5,500 plants per hectare), and later restructuring the *borgo* and the cantina.

The other most important change of note was the taking on of consultant enologist Lorenzo Landi in 2001. Landi had made his mark as enologist of the various properties of Saiagricola (see Fattoria del Cerro), for whom he still consults, as well as acting as a *libero professionista*. The hallmark of his wines is seriousness combined with drinkability, which is what most characterizes the production of Camigliano today.

FINEST WINES

Brunello di Montalcino
Another word to describe Camigliano's wines is reliable. The flagship Brunello is quality Sangiovese all the way. Since 1999, and especially in the excellent 2001 and 2004★ vintages, it has cherry, leather, and herb aromas, and exactly the sort of brooding structure, without wood flavoring, that you would expect in a bona fide Brunello aged entirely in large oak *botti* in the traditional manner. Although it can be drunk with enjoyment in most vintages upon release, it also repays laying down for 15–20 years.

Gualto
A recent addition to the range, this is a Brunello of special selection that the Ghezzis produce only in good vintages; it is not a Riserva but released a year later than the Brunello *normale*. The superb 2001 and 2004 vintages have greater concentration and

Right: Gualtiero Ghezzi who, together with his wife Laura, has established Camigliano as one of Brunello's finest estates

depth than their *normale* counterparts, and there is a nod to modernity in the form of a limited amount of barrique aging. But the wine stays closer to the traditional Tuscan norm than to the international.

Rosso di Montalcino

The Rosso could be similarly described. It may have less concentration, complexity, and weight than the Brunello, but it is also less demanding. This is a wine that can happily be drunk from its second year but has the bones to last a good 5–10 years.

Poderuccio [V]

By contrast, the remaining two Camigliano reds are both more obviously international in style. Poderuccio, a sort of mini Super-Tuscan, consisting of 60% Sangiovese, 20% Cabernet Sauvignon, and 20% Merlot, is aged for a few months in second-passage barriques. Like the Rosso, it is designed to be drunk relatively young, and is particularly interesting for its modest price.

Sant'Antimo DOC [V]

Camigliano was one of the first Montalcino estates to plant Cabernet Sauvignon. This 100% Cabernet, aged in new barriques, is one of the best of its type—and certainly the best value—in Tuscany.

Camigliano was one of the first Montalcino estates to plant Cabernet Sauvignon. This 100% Cabernet is one of the best of its type—and certainly the best value—in Tuscany

Left: The view out from Camigliano, a watchtower in the Middle Ages and now one of the largest estates in Montalcino

Camigliano
Total area: 530ha (1,310 acres)
Area under vine: 90ha (222 acres)
Average production: 350,000 bottles
Via d'Ingresso 2,
Località Camigliano, Montalcino, Siena
Tel: +39 05 77 84 40 68
www.camigliano.it

Il Poggione

Il Poggione is your archetypal Brunello. When others all around seem to be overoaking or underachieving, overpricing or underproducing, illicitly irrigating here and spraying too much there, artificially concentrating here or adding Merlot there, you can buy a bottle of Il Poggione Brunello safe in the knowledge that you are getting the real thing at a reasonable price from genuine, modest people who know their business. To call it archetypal, mind you, is not to suggest it is middle-of-the-road. Rather, it is the sort of wine you put in a blind tasting when you really want your audience to recognize what it is. It is the benchmark: You may be able to find better, but you will not find anything more authentic.

One of the five largest estates in this boomtown wine zone, which has grown from a handful of producers to several hundred in less than a handful of decades, Il Poggione is one of the few that can claim a history. The property has been in the ownership of the Franceschi family for five generations—it used to be much larger but was split between two Franceschi brothers in 1958, the other part now called Col d'Orcia. But 1958 was crucial for Il Poggione for another reason, it being the year when they were joined by the late great Pierluigi Talenti, who set the high standards for which they are renowned and ruled supreme until his death in 1999. Seamlessly, his place was taken by his assistant Fabrizio Bindocci, who had been responsible since 1976, under Talenti, for the estate's extensive vineyards and who now took over as enologist as well, secure in his master's teaching that the way to make great wine was to minimize intervention in the cellar.

Obviously, therefore, fruit quality is paramount, and to that end Il Poggione adopted certain measures that others might not agree with but that work for them. One was to adopt the traditional

Right: Winemaker Fabrizio Bindocci and his son Alessandro, who craft archetypal Brunello from one of its largest estates

*You can buy a bottle of Il Poggione Brunello safe in the knowledge
that you are getting the real thing at a reasonable price from
genuine, modest people who know their business*

double-arc method of training, which they claim gives the grape greater exposure to the sun for an enhanced maturation. And while others may push their vine density per hectare upward toward the 10,000 mark, Il Poggione keeps its down to 5,000—the most, they say, one can get away with in a drought-prone zone like southern Montalcino, where not even emergency irrigation is allowed.

As for clones, while in the past they practiced massal selection, since 1990 they have been planting the best clones to emerge from the various experiments on Montalcino. Two of these—R5 and R6—are of in-house origin, being clones developed by Talenti and Bindocci from their own material and currently offered without exclusivity by the Rauscedo (R = Rauscedo) nursery in northern Italy.

Back in the cellar, there have been a few changes since Talenti's day, but nothing dramatic. The Brunello is still aged for three years in large *botti*, and the Brunello Riserva for four years, but the oak today is of French origin rather than Slavonian. And from 1997 they have adopted a method for dealing with the wine's solids in fermentation that seems more retro than avant-garde: submerged cap. Indeed, they may be alone in Montalcino in still using this traditional system.

FINEST WINES

Brunello di Montalcino

This is the mainstay of production (an average of 200,000 bottles each year). The 2004 has the intensity, balance, and grace one has come to expect from this producer. I also tasted a remarkable range of older vintages.

1997 Good color and upfront tertiary aromas of leather and sandalwood, with plenty of sweet, evolving fruit on the palate. Abundant but smooth, showing ripe tannins and good acidity. Probably at its peak now, but it may hold another ten years.

1991 Slight reduction on the nose blows off after a few minutes to reveal a nose similar to that of the 1997, but of less intensity. A bit weaker, too, in the mouth, but it retains its characteristic elegance.

1988★ Perhaps the most youthful wine of the tasting in terms of color and development. Still chunky, with cherry/liqueur fruit and some coffee notes on the nose. Fresh and dried fruit on the palate, which is ripe and sweet, but still with firm tannins and sufficient acidity to carry it through another 20 years.

1980 Displays leather, tobacco, and juicy, sweet, raisiny fruit. On the downward slope, at almost 30 years of age, but into a noble decline.

1970 A wine of fading charm, with tertiary aromas of leather and sandalwood. Still lively on the palate, so it can go on for several more years, but it will not now improve.

1966 Light color, oranging at the heart. Toffee, dried fruit (fig/prune) on the nose, then a sweet and savory palate, with enough structure to carry it further still.

Brunello di Montalcino Riserva

This selection is from a single vineyard called I Paganelli, which was planted in 1964, and the wine is produced in top years only.

2001★ This is poised and subtle but vital, and should reward some serious time in the cellar.

1999 Deep color. Tobacco and chocolate on the nose: very forthcoming. Concentrated fruit and a creamy texture on the palate, which has nerve and length. This also needs time, but should drink well from around 2012 to 2030.

Rosso di Montalcino [V]

Although lower down in the hierarchy, this is, in its serious but drinkable way, as archetypal as the Brunello (also 200,000 bottles per annum).

San Leopoldo IGT Toscana

A Super-Tuscan-style, barrique-aged blend of Sangiovese plus the two Cabernets.

Left: Drawing a cask sample from one of the traditional large wooden casks that contribute to the wine's classic style

Il Poggione
Total area: 588ha (1,453 acres)
Area under vine: 116ha (287 acres)
Average production: 550,000 bottles
Località Sant'Angelo in Colle,
53024 Montalcino, Siena
Tel: +39 05 77 84 40 29
www.tenutailpoggione.it

Sesti (Castello di Argiano)

Giuseppe Maria Sesti is no ordinary winegrower. A Venetian, his background is astronomy and music, not wine, but this has not prevented him from eschewing the usual enological consultant and taking on the role of winemaker-in-chief at the 13th-century castle that he acquired in the mid-1970s—not to be confused with the more famous Argiano of Noemi Cinzano. It was not until 1991 that he got serious about planting vines, using material selected from a research program undertaken during the 1980s in the commune of Sant'Angelo in Colle, on the southern slopes of the Montalcino zone, where the Argiano subzone is located.

Given the astronomical leanings of the proprietor, the approach to viticulture takes account of heavenly movements, though not, they emphasize, in a biodynamic manner, Steiner's astrology being founded (according to Sesti in his books on the subject) on erroneous data. Nor are they officially organic, though every bottle of Sesti wine carries the mention "eco-friendly," indicating their "maximum respect for the environment."

For the rest, production (of the Sangiovese wines, at least) is strictly traditional, with long maceration and lengthy aging in 30hl *botti*: up to 60 months for the Brunello Riserva, around 40 months for the Brunello, and 18 for the Rosso, followed in all instances by up to 12 months in bottle.

I have been to this property a couple of times, in the late 1990s and the late 2000s. The first time I was not overly impressed with the wines, which I found a little too artisanal, shall we say? Recent tastings have been much more positive. The style (of the Sangioveses) is definitely leaning toward a Burgundian rather than a Bordelais interpretation, with evolved, sweet fruit of an almost decadent character, nicely controlled with velvety and seductive tannins.

Right: Giuseppe Maria Sesti, who brings his knowledge of astronomy to bear on winemaking but is not biodynamic

Giuseppe Maria Sesti is no ordinary winegrower. A Venetian, his background is astronomy and music, and his wines lean toward a Burgundian rather than a Bordelais interpretation

FINEST WINES

Brunello Riserva Phenomena

Top of the range here is the Brunello Riserva Phenomena, based on astronomical happenings during the year of production. The label of the 2001 vintage, for example, depicts the meteor shower of the Leonids that took place in November 2001. The style is highly individual, with a brooding cherry liqueur nose and a way of seizing hold of the palate with the intensity of its fruity acidity. Plenty of grip, but all elements come together harmoniously, and the finish is long. It could be drunk happily now, or could equally well be kept until its 20th birthday and beyond. One can taste that it is made by one who does not follow a well-trodden path.

Brunello

The mainstay is the Brunello *annata*, a wine that looks and tastes mature even from the moment of release—which is not to say that it will not develop well, displaying, as it does, a considerable, if well-managed, tannic backbone. The 2003 was round and mature, almost jammy (a feature of the vintage) but saved by fresh acidity and a firm tannic base. There is an earthy quality about it, which adds to the impression of terroir.

Rosso di Montalcino

The Rosso di Montalcino is in the same vein as the Brunello—less concentrated, naturally, but soft and highly drinkable.

Terra di Siena Sant'Antimo

This Bordeaux-style red is made from Merlot and Cabernet and aged in barrique. Although it is well made, my vote goes unhesitatingly to the Sangioveses.

Left: A view of Castello di Argiano, its vineyards tended with "maximum respect for the environment"

Sesti (Castello di Argiano)

Total area: 102ha (252 acres)
Area under vine: 9ha (22 acres)
Average production: 60,000 bottles
Località Castello di Argiano
53024 Montalcino, Siena
Tel: +39 05 77 84 39 21
elisa@sesti.net

Soldera (Case Basse)

Small as his vineyard is, and tiny his production, Gianfranco Soldera is one of the big guns of Montalcino. Not a Tuscan in origin, nor a farmer, nor a wine man except in respect of drinking it (though he is hugely critical of other people's efforts at making wine), Soldera came to Montalcino in 1972 from Milan (where he worked as an insurance broker until 2003) in search of a few hectares where he and his horticulture-loving wife Graziella could "produce one of the best wines in the world." After a long search, they found their present little paradise, on the southern side of Montalcino, facing southwest, at an altitude of 1,050ft (320m). The fact that it was uncultivated and that there were no vines there at the time did not deter him at all. Trusting nobody's work but his own, he wanted to be in charge of the entire operation from A to Z.

The essence of making "great wine" is that every grape is healthy and fully ripe. A central aspect of fruit health and ripeness is the ecosystem in which the fruit is produced

The essence of making "great wine," as Soldera modestly describes his and that of practically no other grower in the world, is to ensure that every grape that goes into it is healthy and fully ripe. This means not only looking after every vine throughout the season, but also ensuring a rigorous selection process at the harvest and in the winery. A central aspect of fruit health and ripeness is the ecosystem in which the fruit is produced, and Soldera does everything possible to encourage a living soil and an insect- and bird-rich environment. In this, Graziella, with her amazing 2ha (5-acre) garden, which features a pond teeming with animal and vegetable life, is his great ally. She even discovered a new type of rose.

On the winemaking side, Soldera, despite his distrust of others, did find an ally, if not a kindred soul, in the person of Giulio Gambelli, the master taster from Poggibonsi. This was in 1976, shortly after he brought in his first crop (1975). Gambelli's techniques, with which Soldera found himself in more or less complete accord, involve minimum interference in the natural processes, even to the extent of not controlling fermentation temperature, lengthy maceration on the skins, and long—sometimes five years or more—aging in large, neutral *botti* of Slavonian oak. In other words, a case of the famous but all-too-often-fallacious notion of "letting the wine make itself."

Accordingly, when Soldera is describing his technique, the word that crops up most frequently is "no." "No operation of concentration of the must. No addition of clarifying agents or filtration. No barriques. No grapes besides Sangiovese. No grapes from anyone else's vineyards." And when you are tasting his wines, in the winery, there is strictly no spitting. "The rule in Case Basse [I quote from my own earlier volume, *Brunello to Zibibbo*] is that one spits only bad wine. Therefore, no one spits at Case Basse."

I said above that Soldera is one of the big guns of Montalcino, and it is true that others quake at his name—either from fear or from anger. In the great debate over the 100 percent Sangiovese purity of Brunello, Soldera is an implacable and wily enemy of those who would compromise it, even by a tiny percentage. Some of the largest producers suspect him of calling in the authorities at the time of Brunellogate, the blending scandal that broke over the zone in 2008, though he denies responsibility and lays it elsewhere. He was, however, proud of his ability to help maneuver the *consorzio* into a vote endorsing the 100 percent rule—which effectively ruled out change for the foreseeable future.

Left: Gianfranco Soldera, who created a paradise from scratch in Montalcino and, with it, unsurpassed Brunellos

FINEST WINES

Case Basse and Intistieti

Soldera concentrates almost all of his efforts on producing Brunello Riserva, which may come from the Intistieti vineyard (usually) or from the Case Basse vineyard. Occasionally he also makes an IGT Toscana called Pegasos, which spends much less time in wood (a mere 33 months for the 2005). His wines, as should be the case with pure Sangiovese, are light in color and, after a few years in *botti*, display complex aromatics in the form of leather, spice, fresh and dried fruit, mushrooms, and tea leaf. The structure on the palate is always very firm but integral, but the wines are more or less concentrated and intense according to the vintage. Even lesser vintages can work in the hands of one who will allow no poor-quality fruit through the system, and he takes delight in demonstrating that even off-years like 2002 and 1987 are delicious.

In top years such as 1999★, 2001, 2004, 2006, and 2008 (the last three, with the difficult 2005 and 2007, all tasted from barrel for this book) the perfumes can be quite heady and the complexity of sensations in the mouth almost awe-inspiring. Soldera would no doubt claim that if you have not tasted his Brunello, you have not tasted Brunello. It will cost you, but he is right.

Above and far left: The exquisitely crafted Case Basse gardens
Above right: Giulio Gambelli, the estate's long-time consultant

Case Basse
Total area: 23ha (57 acres)
Area under vine: 10+ha (25+ acres)
Average production: 15,000 bottles
Località Case Basse,
53024 Montalcino, Siena
Tel: +39 05 77 84 85 67
www.soldera.it

Villa Argiano

Villa Argiano claims that it may be the oldest wine estate in Montalcino. The imposing villa itself is situated below Sant'Angelo in Colle, some 5 miles (8km) southwest of Montalcino, on a high plateau supposedly known to the Romans as *Ara Jani*, the altar of Janus. (An alternative explanation of the name is that it once belonged to a Roman family called Argia.) Visible for miles around, it was built in 1581 and passed from owner to owner, finally ending up in the hands of Noemi Marone Cinzano in 1992. A London resident, Countess Noemi has conferred the responsibility of wine production on various experts: Sebastiano Rosa (now back with his stepfather Nicolò Incisa della Rocchetta at Tenuta San Guido) until 2002, and Giacomo Tachis (about as expert as they come) until 2003, at which time the Bordeaux-trained Hans Vinding-Diers took over.

One of the most radical innovations in recent years, not just at Argiano but in the whole of Montalcino, is Suolo, meaning "soil," the definitive expression of Argiano's terroir

With Tachis around, it was inevitable that Argiano would take a livelier-than-most interest in Bordeaux varieties and styles of vinification, and this may or may not have led to the trouble they experienced in 2008 when, among others, their 2003 Brunello was blocked from sale by the authorities. In any case, Argiano claims its Brunello has always been 100 percent Sangiovese (certainly the sample I tasted for this book was unimpeachable), so let us give them the benefit of the doubt and move on.

Their French leanings are evident in the fact that 30 percent of their vineyard area is planted to Cabernet Sauvignon, Merlot, and Syrah, and that two of their wines, Solengo and Non Confunditur, are completely or principally made from these grapes. They have for several years been leading proponents of the use of top-quality French barriques for aging and, in the case of Solengo and Suolo, for the malolactic fermentation as well. They do, however, continue with the larger *botti* for a part of the Brunello aging period.

Solengo and Suolo, indeed, are probably Argiano's most interesting wines, both of them idiosyncratic in totally different ways. Solengo, which means "lone wild boar," was, when the 1995 vintage first appeared in 1998, a revolutionary blend of Sangiovese, Cabernet, Merlot, and Syrah. The Sangiovese has since been dropped, and the wine has become thoroughly international, but it is none the less excellent for that. In order to create a Bordeaux-style first- and second-wine situation, and so as to reserve only the finest fruit and best parcels for the first wine, Non Confunditur was created from the 2002 vintage. Non Confunditur means "not to be confused"—presumably with Solengo. Certainly no one could confuse it with Sangiovese, though the grape is supposedly still there at 20 percent.

But the most radical innovation in recent years, not just at Argiano but in the whole of Montalcino, is Suolo (meaning "soil" in Italian, because it is presented as the definitive expression of Argiano's terroir). This is Hans Vinding-Diers's baby, a pure Sangiovese (but IGT, and neither Brunello nor Rosso di Montalcino) from some of the estate's oldest vines, vinified in such a way as to give it a smooth creaminess of texture highly unusual for a Sangiovese and yet not necessarily out of keeping. I may get into trouble with my purist friends over this, but in my view Suolo is a perfectly valid and indeed adventurous expression of Sangiovese—at least in respect of its texture, though the flavor is still slightly compromised by the new-oak aromas that, at least for me, somewhat spoiled the earlier vintages.

Right: Villa Argiano winemaker Hans Vinding-Diers, who has created Montalcino's most innovative wine of recent years

FINEST WINES

Suolo

Whether you like it or not, approve or not, Suolo is a must-taste for anyone who wants to understand Sangiovese—in particular, for anyone who wants to make connoisseur-pleasing wine with the recalcitrant Tuscan grape. I did not like it in its earliest manifestations, but I am beginning to wrap my palate round the most recent ones and believe it will be seen as a milestone in the development of Montalcino wines. It should not be criticized for lacking Brunello typicity, because it does not present itself as Brunello. [2005★]

Brunello di Montalcino

The contrast between this, which strikes me as being of very good and correct character (even in 2003, which I tasted), and Suolo, could not be greater. These should be tasted side by side to understand the range of which Sangiovese is capable.

I can see the point of **Solengo**, but it is not what I look for in Montalcino. **Non Confunditur** still less so.

Above: Argiano's crest proudly proclaims its antiquity
Left: The 16th-century villa dominates the local landscape

Villa Argiano
Total area: 134ha (331 acres)
Area under vine: 51ha (126 acres)
Average production: 300,000 bottles
Sant'Angelo in Colle, 53024 Montalcino, Siena
Tel: +39 05 77 84 40 37
www.argiano.net

Castello Banfi

The giant of Montalcino is something of a love/hate figure among producers, press, and public alike. American-owned, by the Lambrusco-rich Mariani family (brothers John and Harry Mariani, with their offspring Cristina and James), it is indeed a massive presence in what was, before it came, a relative backwater of the Tuscan viticultural scene. Alas, it is all too human for the small to dislike the big, especially when the latter behave with ostentatious largesse. Banfi has created a tourist complex—restaurant, tavern, museum, *agriturismo*—at the ancient but somehow Disneyfied castle whose name it has changed from Poggio alle Mura to Castello Banfi, where it has many times hosted the gala dinner offered by the *consorzio* to visiting journalists and others during the four-day Benvenuto Brunello tasting held every February.

Castello Banfi, the giant of Montalcino,
is a massive presence in what was,
before it came, a relative backwater
of the Tuscan viticultural scene

There are those who blame them for bringing too international a culture to Sangiovese specialist Montalcino, principally in the form of those grape varieties that they (with others) have been accused, and cleared, in the course of the so-called Brunellogate scandal, of sneakily blending into Brunello. Indeed, with around 500ha (1,235 acres) planted to Cabernet, Merlot, Syrah, Chardonnay, Pinot Grigio, and Sauvignon (to say nothing of the 95ha [235 acres] dedicated to Montepulciano, the black, full-colored grape of Abruzzo, making Banfi the biggest producer of that variety west of the Apennines), you might consider there is substance to the argument. Banfi answers, predictably, that it does no such illicit blending; that the internationals are strictly for use in their Super-Tuscans and consumer-oriented wines; and that, anyway, there is documentation to show that the Bordeaux grapes were present in Montalcino as far back as the 19th century.

The other aspect of the "internationalization" that they are accused of importing into Montalcino is their introduction of French oak barriques (they have around 7,000 of their specially-designed 350-liter type). Banfi argues, again predictably, that the enhanced gentle oxygenation of the wine afforded by this notable increase in the ratio of wine to wood surface helps soften and give roundness to the potentially fierce tannins of Sangiovese, as well as aiding in the retention of color; and that, furthermore, far from abandoning the traditional *botte*, it retains some 14,000hl capacity in large Slavonian oak.

There are those, too, who say Banfi was seriously mistaken in the late 1970s and '80s, when, during the setting up of its viticultural empire, bulldozers were used to rearrange hills and redesign the contours of the land, thus changing the natural soil characteristics as given by nature in the wine zone of Montalcino. Unpredictably, but very courageously, Banfi has admitted, in private if not in public, that this was indeed perhaps a mistake.

Clonal and zonal research

This, however, is not what I want to home in on. Banfi's contribution to viticultural research in Tuscany generally, and Montalcino particularly, is something for which even its critics should be grateful. It was in 1982, years before the Chianti Classico 2000 project got under way, that Banfi got together with the University of Milan (Professor Scienza et al) to research Sangiovese clones—work that was then practically untouched. More than 600 "presumed clones" were discovered among

Right: Castello Banfi, formerly known as Poggio alle Mura, with its extensive vineyards and impressive tree-lined drive

the vineyards of their own estate, purchased from previous owners Poggio alle Mura. Of these, 180 were selected and subjected to analysis and microvinification, which boiled the group down to 15. Simultaneously, they undertook a *zonazione*, or soil analysis, program, in which 29 different soil types were distinguished in their vineyards—from solid clay, to stone and sand. From 1992, they began a replanting program for some of the older fields, in which three or four massal-selection types per vineyard were selected according to the prevailing soil types. Carrying the process one step further, they developed three clones—Janus 50, Janus 10, and BF 30, each with very distinctive characteristics—that have since been propagated and made generally available through Rauscedo and other nurseries. These three go to make up their most recently introduced cru Brunello, appropriately named Poggio alle Mura. Other studies—on density (they reckon 4,500 vines per hectare is about right for Sangiovese; this is less, in some cases much less, than others recommend, but Banfi is more mechanized than most), training, rootstocks, canopy management, and irrigation—have also been undertaken in conjunction with the universities, with published results.

FINEST WINES

Banfi makes three types of Brunello di Montalcino and three Super-Tuscan blends (Sant'Antimo Rosso), as well as an IGT Toscana introduced in 2009 called Belnero, a blend of 90% Sangiovese and 10% "other grapes". From my tasting, it emerges that the latter have the beating of the former (and interestingly, they precede the Brunellos on Banfi's website). One possible reason for this is that the mesoclimate at this relatively low altitude of southernmost Montalcino—around 800ft (250m), in a zone where the most elegant and subtle wines come from 1,150–1,600ft (350–500m)—is, as in the Maremma, more suitable for Bordeaux and Rhône varieties than for Sangiovese. Banfi, then, has chosen wisely in planting so many vineyards to Cabernet, Merlot,

etc. Indeed, perhaps their most successful French variety is Syrah, as shown by the gutsy, almost Rhône-like 100% Syrah called Colvecchio.

Summus
Best of the blends, as it should be according to its superlative name, Summus is a blend of Sangiovese, Cabernet, and Syrah. Both the 2005 and 2001★ showed opulence and sumptuousness of fruit—red berry, cherry, and plum—combined with firm structure and very good length.

Excelsus
A 60/40 Cabernet Sauvignon/Merlot blend, Excelsus is almost as fine as Summus, the 2001 displaying ripe but balanced blackcurrant fruit against a structure of fine but dense tannins, with hints of woodsmoke on the medium-long finish.

Cum Laude
A blend of Cabernet Sauvignon, Merlot, Sangiovese, and Syrah, this was less impressive in the two vintages that I tasted (2002 and 2005), but one would not expect great things from either (especially 2002).

Brunello di Montalcino Poggio alle Mura
In 2000 and 2003, this wine suffered from the excessive heat of those vintages, there being good underlying fruit but a lack of real finesse. The 2001, from a classic year, was much better.

Poggio all'Oro
From a single vineyard called La Pieve, this was the finest of the Brunellos, being structured and elegant, with plenty of cherry and plum fruit and subtle power.

Brunello di Montalcino
The basic Brunello is made in astonishing numbers (700,000+ bottles) and, in my view, shows it. If you're going to pay a Brunello price, you'd be better off with one of the crus.

Castello Banfi
Total area: 2,830ha (6,993 acres)
Area under vine: 945+ha (2,335+ acres)
Average production: 10 million+ bottles
53024 Montalcino, Siena
Tel: +39 05 77 84 01 11
www.castellobanfi.com

Col d'Orcia

As the figures suggest, Col d'Orcia is one of the largest estates in Montalcino—third, actually, in terms of vineyard, after Banfi and Castelgiocondo. Count Alberto Marone Cinzano bought the property in 1973 from a member of the Franceschi family. Its vineyards, at an altitude of 1,050–1,150ft (320–350m), lie on the southern, south-facing slopes of Montalcino and have been producing Brunello grapes, and wine, since the early 20th century. In 1933, then called Fattoria di Sant'Angelo in Colle, it presented as many as three vintages of "Brunello" at the first Italian wine show in Siena.

Col d'Orcia is one of the largest estates in Montalcino, and has been producing Brunello grapes, and wine, since the early 20th century

Even more important than its history and position, however, is the spirit of Col d'Orcia—and the people who collaborate to maintain that spirit. With an operation as large as this, it is inevitable, indeed desirable, that there should be a measure of industrialization. But Count Alberto's son, Count Francesco, now runs the property, and he and his team—which includes consultant enologist Maurizio Castelli; resident winemaker Pablo Harri, who cut his enological teeth at nearby Banfi; and managing director Edoardo Virano, who has been with the firm over 30 years—know where to draw the line, mixing the advanced with the traditional in just proportion.

In the field, they have done a lot of work on plant selection, in collaboration with the University of Florence, and recently planted vineyards include specially selected clonal material, as well

Right: Col d'Orcia's Banditella vineyard, planted with carefully selected clones, is the source of its superior Rosso

as Sangiovese and Moscadello vines developed from their own genetic stock. Experiments in density have run as high as 7,000 plants per hectare (compared with densities as low as 2,500 per hectare), and they are currently running tests, supervised by Professor Attilio Scienza of the University of Milan, on the suitability of particular rootstocks for particular soils. Inter-row grassing and mulching, bunch-thinning, and bunch and grape selection, both in the field and on arrival at the winery, are routine.

In the cantina they use specially designed, temperature-controlled, stainless-steel fermenters of such a wide and short shape "that the surface of contact between juice and skins ensures optimal extraction of polyphenols and coloring matters." But maceration is quite extended—up to 25 days on the skins—and aging takes place, for Brunello, in *botti* of mainly Slavonian oak, plus 10 percent in French barrique, and for a period that, in the case of top cru Poggio al Vento, can last up to four years—twice the legal minimum.

Even more important than its history and position is the spirit of Col d'Orcia— and the people who collaborate to maintain that spirit

FINEST WINES

Brunello di Montalcino Riserva Poggio al Vento
The pride and joy of Col d'Orcia's production is Brunello di Montalcino Riserva Poggio al Vento, from a single vineyard planted at an altitude of 1,150ft (350m) in 1974. Made only in the best vintages, this is a wine that needs to reach a certain age—say ten years—before revealing its full splendor. This should certainly be the case with the excellent 2001★ version, which I rated highly for its complexity, perfume, structure, and youthfulness on my most recent tasting. In other

good vintages, the nose can mingle wild cherry fruit with mushroom, as well as a certain (agreeable) medicinal note. It is tannic, with firm acidity, but fruit is there in abundance, without ever being easy or obvious.

Brunello di Montalcino
Far more important in terms of numbers and regularity is the non-riserva Brunello di Montalcino, of which some 230,000 bottles may be produced annually. A bit more approachable in its youth than the Riserva, even this from a good year needs six years before the fruit begins to dominate the structure. A bottle of the 1999 that I tasted at nine years of age was just beginning to flower: "very Sangiovese, very elegant," I noted. The 2004, at less than half that age, was classic but still a bit closed and clearly needing more time.

Rosso di Montalcino Banditella and Rosso
Another wine to look out for from Col d'Orcia is Rosso di Montalcino Banditella, of which some 25,000 bottles are produced yearly (as compared with the 120,000 bottles of the simpler, more immediately enjoyable **Rosso**). This is made from grapes of an otherwise designated Brunello vineyard planted with carefully selected, high-quality clonal material. The wine is aged in French tonneaux and barriques and nicely combines the international and Montalcino styles. The 2006 [**V**] is a good example of this successful marriage.

St Antimo Cabernet Sauvignon Olmaia
Col d'Orcia is also very proud of its St Antimo Cabernet Sauvignon Olmaia, from a vineyard planted in 1984. Rich and powerful, with the characteristic dark-chocolate and coffee finish that rounds off Cabernet Sauvignon aged in barriques (for up to 18 months in this case), it is no doubt one of the best wines of its type from central Italy. The 2005 seems to be particularly successful.

Right: Count Francesco Marone Cinzano leads the talented team responsible for this large and historic Montalcino estate

Col d'Orcia
Total area: 540ha (1,334 acres)
Area under vine: 142ha (351 acres)
Average production: 750,000 bottles
53020 Sant'Angelo in Colle, Montalcino, Siena
Tel: +39 05 77 80 891
www.coldorcia.it

Salvioni (La Cerbaiola)

Salvioni wines more than compensate in quality for what they lack in quantity, just as their maker, Giulio, makes up in verbiage and showmanship what he lacks in grand cellars and luxurious premises. Turn Giulio Salvioni on at a dinner or gathering of any sort, and he will keep his audience enthralled with witticisms and penetrating, sometimes painful, or at least overly honest observations, until he is forcibly quieted.

This is a seriously small operation with a reputation of global proportions, constructed from regular offerings of wines of the highest quality and purest typicity of which Montalcino is capable— genuinely hand-crafted and strictly according to traditional precepts.

Salvioni's vineyards find themselves a few miles south and east of the town at an average altitude of over 1,300ft (400m), and they are planted exclusively to Sangiovese. In good years, only Brunello is produced. In lesser years, a bit of Rosso is made, with the express aim of saving the best material for the top wine. In poor years, only Rosso is made.

La Cerbaiola has been in the Salvioni family for generations, if not centuries—Giulio's grandfather was another Giulio. It was in the early 1980s that he began to train his attention exclusively on wine (and olives—they have 3ha [7.5 acres] of olive grove), taking on Attilio Pagli as consultant enologist. The first vintage was the mythic 1985, released in 1990, the year of the death of his father, who had always wanted to see his wine in bottle. Today Giulio's son David, a trained agronomist, is taking over in the vineyards. Every few years, a small part of the vineyard is replanted, using the latest and best of the available clones. At 5,300 plants per hectare, the most recently replanted vineyards have virtually double the density of the original ones.

Right: Salvioni's small cellar, where large Slavonian oak *botti* with a capacity of around 20hl contribute to the wines' purity

This is a seriously small operation with a reputation of global proportions, constructed from regular offerings of wines of the highest quality and purest typicity

As for Giulio, he can generally be found in the family house-cum-aging cellar in Piazza Cavour in Montalcino town.

Try a bottle of Salvioni. It will cost you—but try it once. If you like it, keep looking for other producers of this style. If you do not like it, you do not like Brunello

FINEST WINES

Brunello di Montalcino

What can I add to the assessment made above of Salvioni's Brunello di Montalcino—even in the hot 2003★ vintage? That it gets 20–30 days' maceration with submerged cap in stainless-steel fermenters? That it is aged about three and a half years in Slavonian oak *botti* (two years is the legal minimum, but Giulio says, "If you have wines of structure, a longer stay in wood does them no harm")? That these barrels have a capacity of around 20 hectoliters ("which gives you about the right amount of interchange between wood and wine")? That he "absolutely!" has no barriques, does not use cultured yeasts, does not have any cooling system other than pouring water over the fermenters when threatened with rapidly rising fermentation temperatures, does not filter...?

It all adds up to this: Try a bottle of Salvioni. It will cost you—but try it once. If you like it, keep looking for other producers of this style, who might not be so expensive. If you do not like it, you do not like Brunello.

Left: Giulio Salvioni at his family house-cum-aging cellar in Montalcino, from where he has forged a global reputation

Salvioni (La Cerbaiola)
Total area: 20ha (49 acres)
Area under vine: 4ha (10 acres)
Average production: 15,000–20,000 bottles
Piazza Cavour 19,
53024 Montalcino, Siena
Tel: +39 05 77 84 84 99
aziendasalvioni@libero.it

Brunelli (Le Chiuse di Sotto)

Gianni Brunelli passed away prematurely, at the age of 61, toward the end of my writing of this book. It is customary to heap praise on the dead, and much has been heaped on Gianni, but in his case it was all very merited and sincere. A man of *montalcinese* origin (with a name like Brunelli, how could it be otherwise?), whose father had planted a vineyard at Le Chiuse di Sotto during the difficult postwar times, Gianni worked hard to build a beautiful business at his Siena restaurant Le Logge, just off the Piazza del Campo, where customers were treated like friends, and friends like gods—and still are, by the faithful Mirko. His ultimate ambition, however, was to return to Montalcino to work with grapes, olives, and the wonderful vegetables with which he knew his native country was capable of regaling man—"without additives, without anti-parasite sprays, having the courage to trust in what nature offers us. I want to bring the land of Montalcino to the table." The same rule prevailed in his approach to wine, which was to be brought forth gently from the earth, with no forcing, with respect for Sangiovese, and devotion to the principles of elegance and restraint, aging in medium-sized *botti* of Slavonian oak. Gianni sought the taste of fruit and the complexity brought by the soil's minerals and other components. To help him, he enlisted the consultancy of Laura Bernini on the viticultural side, and on the enological side that of Paolo Vagaggini, whose advice is sought by many in Montalcino precisely because he does not impose his style on the wine but leaves it to the grower.

Gianni began his return to Montalcino when, in 1987, he repurchased the family's old 2ha (5-acre) vineyard at Le Chiuse di Sotto, on gentle slopes above which loom the ramparts of the medieval town. It was small even for Montalcino, but in 1996 he acquired a magnificent 4.5ha (11 acres) of vines at Podernovone, on slopes adjacent to Barbi Colombini, facing south with, in the distance, a magnificent view of Monte Amiata. It was and is a paradise, and Gianni dreamed of finishing his days there with his beloved wife Laura. He used to say, "I want my heart to be buried at Montalcino, like the Indians of Wounded Knee."

And so it has come to pass. As Laura said of him, he may have been taken before his time, as we survivors see it, but he fulfilled his destiny. And as the song goes, he did it (writes Laura) "his way—not in the silly sense of not needing others, but in the true and beautiful way of knowing how to win the hearts and minds of others in a common enterprise."

FINEST WINES

Brunello di Montalcino
This is the Gianni Brunelli calling card. There is something unique about the Brunelli style that reflects its author's mix of pride and humility, the wine combining elegance with unique personality, brilliance of flavor with seamless velvetiness of texture. A real connoisseur's Brunello, of which the 2004, from a great vintage, is a splendid example.

Brunello di Montalcino Riserva
In exceptional years there is also a Riserva; 2001★ is the most recent (no 2002 or 2003). For elegance and intensity, one would have to rank this as Gianni's *chef d'oeuvre*. What can one say? A great Brunello!

Rosso di Montalcino [V]
Another triumph of its type: light and fruity, yet structured so as to age well for a dozen years.

Amor Costante
The name of this IGT appropriately links Gianni and Laura. Even this Sangiovese/Merlot blend is stamped by the subtlety and the joie de vivre that Gianni carried with him throughout his life.

Gianni Brunelli (Le Chiuse di Sotto)
Total area: 15ha (37 acres)
Area under vine: 6.5ha (16 acres)
Average production: 25,000 bottles
Azienda Agricola Le Chiuse di Sotto
Località Podernovone, 53024 Montalcino
Tel: +39 05 77 84 93 42
www.giannibrunelli.it

Cerbaiona

Diego Molinari, originally from the province of Pavia in Lombardy, was working as an airline pilot for Alitalia when he was bitten by the wine bug in 1960. He did a month's wine course and became an *appassionato* of Burgundy. By the mid-1970s, he had had enough of the city (Rome), the jet lag, and the hassle. The call of wine became ever more insistent, and in 1977 he bought his modest property in Montalcino and became a wine grower full time. It was not complicated, because in those days there were relatively few producers and he was not interested in technology —only in growing grapes and turning them, or rather letting them turn themselves, into wine.

The fact that Molinari is one of the few in Montalcino to boast no e-mail address says something about his attitude toward the 20th, never mind the 21st, century

The fact that Molinari is one of the few in Montalcino to boast no e-mail address says something about his attitude toward the 20th, never mind the 21st, century. He does things like forgetting to sign official documents, resulting in the downgrading of his wine to IGT Toscana. He refuses to attend promotional tastings such as the annual Benvenuto Brunello. And he fails to provide a spittoon for visiting journalists, thus joining an elite group that includes, as far as I am aware, Gianfranco Soldera (*qv*), Giuseppe Quintarelli, and no one else in Italy.

He does not appear to be in the best of health, so I ask, "Who looks after the vineyards?" "I do," he says, "with a couple of Romanians. I made myself a peasant. I also look after the wine—no barriques, no chemicals, very little control—just grow the grapes, ferment them, and age the wine in Slavonian *botti*. There's nothing else to it."

All fair enough, and indeed at the top of their form his wines can be phenomenal, capable of great complexity, and, of course, very "terroir." But there does seem to be a question mark over their consistency, as indeed there is over the consistency of some of his beloved Burgundies. Caveat emptor would therefore seem a prudent motto to bear in mind in relation to Molinari's vinous wares, which are certainly not modest in price—but bear in mind also that, if you hit it right, you can find yourself in wine-magic land. At least in this important respect, Diego Molinari reminds me of no one so much as the late great Bartolo Mascarello of Barolo.

FINEST WINES

Molinari produces **Brunello di Montalcino**, **Rosso di Montalcino**, and a bit of **Cerbaiona Sant'Antimo Rosso**, which adds small portions of Cabernet, Merlot, and Syrah to Sangiovese.

The Brunello is clearly the big one in this range. The 1998★ vintage he cracked open for my elucidation proved superb, with fresh and dried fruits on the palate and a roundness, ripeness, and sensuousness that had nothing forced about it and that could, one felt, go on improving over another decade at least. Indeed, Molinari reckons his wines are best at 20 years of age. So the 2004 we tasted together was a mere babe (it had not even been released), and while the palate was marvelous, the nose needed time to come round. The 2003 had the sweet, almost jammy character of the vintage, lower acidity, and less freshness, but was distinctly nearer to drinkability than the 2004 on the day.

Cerbaiona
Total area: 14.5ha (36 acres)
Area under vine: 3ha (7.5 acres)
Average production: 16,000 bottles
Località Cerbaiona,
53024 Montalcino, Siena
Tel: +39 05 77 84 86 60

Ciacci Piccolomini

I confess that until I actually visited, by way of preparation for this book, I naively assumed that the ownership of this large, illustrious, and historic estate belonged to the aristocratic family that displays its name proudly on every label. My surprise on learning the truth would have been minuscule compared with that of Giuseppe Bianchini, general manager, who in 1985 was informed that Contessa Elda Ciacci Piccolomini d'Aragona, who died in that year without direct heirs, had bequeathed it all to him.

Giuseppe was probably prepared for the windfall, since he wasted no time in moving his family into the 17th-century episcopal palace and rationalizing the estate's properties, selling the lands removed from the center and concentrating his viticultural efforts on those fields in the immediate vicinity of the palazzo's cellars. There followed

Today, Ciacci Piccolomini are seen as placed somewhere between the modernists and the traditionalists. They emphasize Sangiovese while experimenting with French grapes

years of consolidation and experimentation as the estate's reputation grew, thanks in part to consultant enologist Roberto Cipresso, then to his successor Paolo Vagaggini.

In 2004, Giuseppe passed away and his shoes were filled by those of his progeny, Paolo and Lucia Bianchini, who continue to run the estate according to their father's lights.

Today, Ciacci Piccolomini is seen as placed somewhere between the modernists and the traditionalists. On the latter side, they continue to emphasize Sangiovese, both on their Montalcino lands and on those, purchased in 2001, in the nearby zone of Montecucco. When planting new fields, they retain a modest density of 4,500 to 5,000 vines per hectare, following up with viticultural methods that they describe as being of the "traditional system," including longish maceration (up to three weeks) and no filtration for Brunello. Aging of Brunello (up to three years) and Rosso (one year) takes place in the old cellars of the palazzo in *botti* with a capacity of up to 85hl.

They have, on the other hand, been at the forefront of those *montalcinesi* experimenting with French grapes, and their now iconic alternative wine Ateo ("Atheist," because it breaks the tradional rules, blending as it does Cabernet and Merlot with Sangiovese) dates all the way back to 1989. A more recent contribution in the international mode is Fabius, a 100 percent Syrah. Both are aged in barrique, French and American, in the new cantina below Castelnuovo, where all enological operations other than *botte* aging are now carried out.

FINEST WINES

Ciacci produces a straight **Brunello di Montalcino**; a **Brunello Pianrosso [2001★]**, with selected grapes from the nearly 12ha (30-acre) vineyard of that name; and a **Brunello Riserva Vigna di Pianrosso** from the same vineyard in exceptional years. All are capable of power-cum-elegance, the Pianrosso having an extra dimension in terms of concentration and, probably, longevity (especially the Riserva, obviously).

I have never been a great fan of the once-revolutionary **Ateo**, nor am I of the newly revolutionary **Fabius**, both of which strike me as overextracted. The **Rosso di Montalcino**, however, is a model of its type—lively cherry fruit and highly drinkable. But beware the alcohol, which can be as high as 14.5% (+).

Ciacci Piccolomini
Total area: 200ha (494 acres)
Area under vine: 40ha (99 acres)
Average production: 200,000 bottles
Località Molinello, 53024 Montalcino, Siena
Tel: +39 05 77 83 56 16
www.ciaccipiccolomini.com

Il Colle

This small property stands tall among the purist producers of Montalcino. Purchased by Sienese notary Alberto Carli in 1972, Il Colle's original vineyards were (and are) just below the town to the south. The first plantings followed in short order, and the first Brunello was released in 1982. In 1985 came the massive winter frost that killed so many olive trees throughout Tuscany; thereafter, grapes, rather than a mix of olives and grapes, became the azienda's principal crop.

In that year, too, Carli engaged the master taster Giulio Gambelli to look after his wine quality, thus nailing his colors firmly to the traditionalist mast. Perhaps during the 20th century they were a touch too traditionalist, their vineyard at Il Colle being at some 1,475ft (450m) altitude, facing north, and their wines sometimes displaying a rasping acidity and leathery thinness. So in 1998 they bought another small property—lower down, at 720ft (220m), and farther south, near Castelnuovo dell'Abate. The grapes from this vineyard, which ripen up to ten days earlier, provide a firm and rich body to balance against the perfumes and elegance of their more northern counterparts.

Alberto Carli died in 2001, and his daughter Caterina took over the running of the estate. She did not hanker after modernization, as many a rebellious son, eager to establish his own credentials against those of his father, might have done. Rather, she determinedly followed in her father's footsteps, proud of the fact that they still macerate for more than three weeks, use only natural yeasts, age Brunello in large Slavonian (and French) *botti* (15–50hl in size) for four years, sometimes have the malolactic carrying over into a second year, and never filter any wine, including the Rosso di Montalcino.

FINEST WINES

Brunello di Montalcino is far and away the most important wine here, **Rosso di Montalcino** being considered a mere outlet for wines that Gambelli does not rate at Brunello level. Only in outstanding years do they make **Brunello di Montalcino Riserva**. There is, to come, a **Sant'Antimo Rosso**, which will blend Sangiovese with a drop of Merlot, but Caterina says none of the blends she has tried so far has convinced her.

I tasted a range of young Brunellos from barrel and bottle. There is a great purity to the house style, and an elegance that it is not easy to find in these days of power worship. Unusually, the oldest vintage I tasted (and the only one from glass) was 2004★, a wine of correct Sangiovese color (not deep, but bright), with a nose of wild cherry and tea leaf, plenty of ripe fruit on the palate, but also firm acidity and some assertive tannins. This is a wine one could drink young, but that would obviously reward a wait of at least 10–12 years.

Il Colle
Total area: 20ha (49 acres)
Area under vine: 7.5ha (19 acres)
Average production: 40,000 bottles
Località Il Colle 102B, 53024 Montalcino, Siena
Tel: +39 05 77 84 82 95
ilcolledicarli@katamail.com

Fuligni

The Fulignis of Montalcino derive from a family of Venetian viscounts who have held land, and made wine, in Tuscany since the 18th century, transferring from the Maremma to Montalcino in the early 20th century. They are proud of the fact that their vineyards are in the "classic" zone of Montalcino, having been purchased in 1923 by the father of current proprietress Maria Flora Fuligni from a certain Gontrano Biondi Santi. *Il Brunello è nato qua* ("Brunello was born here"), Maria Flora is fond of proclaiming. These are fine, east- and southeast-facing lands, not far from the town at elevations of 1,250–1,475ft (380–450m). The aging takes place in two locations: at Cottimelli, a former convent that also serves for tasting and reception, where the 5hl tonneaux and smaller *botti* are deployed for the early part of the oak aging; and, most impressively, in the depths of the family's

The Fuligni range of wines has attracted considerable praise from guides. Deservedly so, if somewhat surprisingly, since the style is on the traditional side

discreetly palatial 18th-century ex-Medici palazzo in the center of Montalcino, where the wine completes its refinement in bulk in larger Slavonian oak *botti*.

In recent years, the Fuligni range of wines has attracted considerable praise from guides and pundits, mainly American and Italian. *The Wine Advocate*, *Wine Spectator*, and *Wine Enthusiast*, as well as *Gambero Rosso*, *L'Espresso*, and *Veronelli* have fairly lined up to heap the honors. Deservedly so, if somewhat surprisingly, since the style, overseen by ubiquitous Montalcino consultant enologist Paolo Vagaggini, is if anything on the traditional side—something that these influential publications do not normally go for, tending as they have (until recently, admittedly) to reward

impenetrability of color, concentration of flavor, oakiness of aroma, and massiveness of structure, over the orange-rimmed, sour-cherry, subtle, slightly decadent, almost Burgundian style of classic Sangiovese. A fair measure of the credit for this success on the PR side probably goes to Roberto Guerrini, the friendly, ever-welcoming nephew of Maria Flora, who combines his real-life function as a professor of jurisprudence at Siena University with that of putting forward at every opportunity the very genuine virtues of his family estate to the world of wine.

FINEST WINES

Brunello di Montalcino Riserva
Pride and joy of production, from the oldest vines of the estate, is the Riserva, of which I tasted a pair straddling the Millennium. Both were excellent, the 1999★ in particular showing a structured durability and noble decadence, with an aromatic scale that included fresh and dried fruit, herb and spice, hints of leather, and, happily, very little oak. These are wines for drinking at around the ten-year mark but will easily last twice that long.

Brunello di Montalcino
Aged two and a half years in oak compared with the Riserva's three, this is from younger vines. It has a fresher, more immediate appeal, echoing the class of the Riserva but less insistently, as in the 2004 vintage.

Rosso di Montalcino
The Rosso is nicknamed Ginestreto after the vineyard of that name, which used to be full of *ginestra* (broom). It receives less extended aging, in French tonneaux for around six months and is more for early drinking. There is also a highly drinkable Sangiovese/Merlot IGT called **San Jacopo**.

Fuligni
Total area: 100ha (247 acres)
Area under vine: 11ha (27 acres)
Average production: 40,000 bottles
Via S Saloni 32, 53024 Montalcino, Siena
Tel: +39 05 77 84 80 39
www.fuligni.it

Lisini

Property of the Lisini-Clementi family, whose archives date them back to the 16th century, Lisini is one of the historic producers of Montalcino. It is also one of the most devoted to tradition, growing only Sangiovese and the bit of Malvasia Bianca and Trebbiano (which they call Procanico) needed for making Vin Santo.

The grandfather of nonagenarian current owner Elina Lisini came to Montalcino from Chianti in the final third of the 19th century. Elina, one of the original founders and a former president of the Brunello *consorzio*, has kept faith with her grandfather's precepts, which included the use of Sangiovese *in purezza* for their red wines.

Elina's nephews and niece, Lorenzo, Carlo, and Ludovica Lisini Baldi, going completely against the tide of the times, have proved even more traditionalist than their forebears—to the extent that, a couple of years ago, they decided to part company with their consultant Franco Bernabei, feeling that even he, one of the least modernist enologists of Tuscany, was too modernist for them. They asked their longtime agronomist Filippo Paoletti to take over, and he in turn requested that they enlist the services of the greatest traditionalist winemaker of them all: Giulio Gambelli. Paoletti takes all the Lisini wines to Poggibonsi twice a year for approval by Gambelli, who asks no questions as to how they are made but only tastes them and judges them with a "yes" or a "no"—and if "no," insists that "you must precisely follow my instructions."

The Lisini estate is between Sant'Angelo in Colle and Castelnuovo dell'Abate, at an altitude of 1,000–1,150ft (300–350m). All vineyards are planted with massal-selected material from older fields, with the exception of a trial that Filippo is carrying out with a clone of Biondi-Santi. The mature vineyards, where planting density is about 3,300 plants per hectare, are up to 75 years old, 60 percent of them having an average age of more than 30 years. This, too, is against current accepted wisdom.

Vinification takes place in glass-lined concrete tanks. Maceration time is between 18 and 26 days, depending on the wine being made, and aging time—in large, Slavonian-oak *botti* of between 11 and 40hl—is up to 36 months for the Brunello.

FINEST WINES

Brunello di Montalcino Ugolaia
Made only in the best years, this is now Lisini's proudest product. They used to make a Brunello di Montalcino Riserva from the best grapes of the estate, but finding that these were almost invariably from the Ugolaia plot, they switched to this single-vineyard wine, the first vintage being 1990. Ugolaia can age for up to 42 months in oak plus six months in chestnut (a wood that was previously employed quite widely, but that can add too much bitterness if not sensitively used), followed by an extended period in bottle. It can have quite a deep color, turning a characteristic brick, and in youth it shows cherry and plum fruit of great concentration on a hefty tannin-acid base. Thanks to its heroic structure, this is definitely a wine built to last. I described a bottle of the 1995★, broached in early 2009, as "one of the best Sangioveses I've tasted: notes of leather and mushroom, almost truffle, with ripe, evolved fruit and smooth tannins, but also that firm Sangiovese acidity running right through it and keeping it very much alive."

Brunello di Montalcino
The straight Brunello is more approachable than Ugolaia, the 2004 displaying an elegance and definition that belie its considerable alcohol, acidity, and tannin. Very Sangiovese, very sour cherry.

Rosso di Montalcino
Although friendlier than the Brunello and Ugolaia, this is nevertheless a serious wine and more substantial than the **San Biagio**, a Toscano IGT made with abbreviated maceration and no wood.

Lisini
Total area: 200ha (494 acres)
Area under vine: 18ha (44 acres)
Average production: 100,000 bottles
Sant'Angelo in Colle, 53020 Montalcino, Siena
Tel: +39 05 77 84 40 40
www.lisini.com

Mastrojanni

This estate changed ownership while I was writing this book. It was in 1975 that the Mastrojanni family initiated operations here in the extreme southeast corner of the Montalcino zone, near the village of Castelnuovo dell'Abate, above the valley where the Asso stream meets the Orcia River, while looming over the area to the south is Monte Amiata. It is a dramatic situation for a dramatic wine, the Mastrojanni having agreed from the start that top quality was what they were aiming for. Unfortunately, in recent years, there was not much else that they managed to agree upon, so the property was sold to Gruppo Illy, whose fame is based not on wine but on coffee, but whose member Francesco Illy, the new president of Mastrojanni, has a small wine-holding nearby called Le Ripi.

It is a dramatic situation for a dramatic wine, the Mastrojanni having agreed from the start that top quality was what they were aiming for

Francesco also has much respect for Andrea Machetti, the man who has been making things work at Mastrojanni since 1992; he has been appointed managing director, with responsibility for all decisions relating to administration and production. He is helped, as before, by consultant enologist Maurizio Castelli, one of the longest-serving and most dedicated to terroir of his ilk. In other words, apart from ownership, not much has changed at all: The name remains the same; the production criteria remain the same; they will continue to source their clones from those selected by the University of Florence plus those sourced by Castelli from Col d'Orcia. They will, as ever, age their Brunellos for about three years in Allier oak *botti* of 16–54hl capacity and their Rosso in Styrian oak casks for around eight months. They will make the same wines plus one new one: a single-vineyard Brunello cru called Vigna Loreto, the 2007 vintage to be released in 2012—but even that is not new, since it was planned before the sale of the azienda.

FINEST WINES

Brunello di Montalcino
This is the lead wine in terms of volume, as well as of regularity of production. It is not an easy wine to come to terms with—partly because of the complexity of the aromas, and partly thanks to a tight structure in which acidity and tannins are never in short supply. But it certainly rewards keeping, as an 11-year-old 1997 vintage demonstrated, the aromas moving more toward the tertiary (so leather, Mediterranean herbs, mushrooms, and dried fruit).

Brunello di Montalcino Schiena d'Asino
Still more complex, but retaining great elegance, is this cru, made every year but only released (that is, not blended with the Brunello *base*) in the best vintages. This is a single-vineyard wine, not a Riserva, whose wood aging is similar to that of the basic Brunello, but it gets more time in glass before release. This is a connoisseur's Brunello of such complexity yet harmony that I described the 1990★, in my book *Brunello to Zibibbo*, as "one of the finest Brunellos I have ever tasted"—an opinion that I have not had occasion to alter.

Rosso di Montalcino
This has the house finesse but is much more approachable in youth.

IGT Toscana San Pio
Although this is 80% Cabernet Sauvignon and 20% Sangiovese, and it is for aged 18 months in Allier oak *botti*, it is still more Tuscan, and less international, than one would expect from such a blend.

Mastrojanni
Total area: 90ha (222 acres)
Area under vine: 24ha (59 acres)
Average production: 90,000 bottles
Poderi Loreto e San Pio
Castelnuovo dell'Abate, 53020 Montalcino, Siena
Tel: +39 05 77 83 56 81
www.mastrojanni.com

Pian dell'Orino

This, since 1997, is the property of Caroline Pobitzer from Alto Adige, aided as both agronomist and enologist by her German husband Jan Erbach, who arrived in 2000 having studied at Geisenheim and worked for several years in France. They would appear to have links with both of the biggest names in Montalcino—Biondi-Santi and Soldera—the first for the simple reason that the main part of their estate (which is divided between four different vineyards) is adjacent to the famous Greppo vineyard of Biondi-Santi, at about 1,500ft (450m) altitude; the second because their approach to viticulture in particular smacks of the intensity, not to say fanaticism, of the great if difficult Gianfranco Soldera.

To say that they were organic would be putting it mildly. Let's say they have an individual if strongly committed approach to biodynamics, seeking, in Caroline's own words, "the maximum harmony between vineyard, climate, soil, and mankind." In organizing their daily work, they follow the phases of the moon, and eschewing all such industrial poisons as herbicides, pesticides, and so on, they protect and bolster their vines' immune systems with preparations of nettles, horsetail, and yarrow, to say nothing of propolis, which they use against fungi and bacteria.

As at Case Basse, flowers are planted and encouraged all around in order to attract bees, butterflies, and other insects. Pruning is severe, with only four bunches left on the plant, and their average yield is around 750ml per plant (at 5,000 plants per hectare, equivalent to 37.5hl/ha). At harvest time every bunch is inspected and moldy grapes are removed. In the cellar (a new one, round in shape, was completed in time for the 2007 vintage), they use only natural yeasts, and all wines are either vinified or at least subjected to the malolactic in oak. The Brunello, following the Gambelli formula, does not even receive temperature control during the fermentation, and maceration is long (up to eight weeks for the Brunello), as is aging (as much as 40 months in large Slavonian oak barrels). Not surprisingly, there is no filtration for the Brunello. Both it and the Rosso have a striking purity about them.

FINEST WINES

Rosso di Montalcino

This has an alluring and penetrating aroma of pure berry-cherry fruit, with not a whiff of wood, despite being aged 14 months in French tonneaux. Although uppish in alcohol (at around 14%), it is almost dangerously drinkable. [2005 V]

Brunello di Montalcino

The top wine is of the same ilk but more sturdy and structured, requiring more time. The 2003★ showed no signs of being from an overheated vintage. Again, almost irresistible.

Pian dell'Orino

Total area: 11ha (27 acres)
Area under vine: 6ha (15 acres)
Average production: 25,000 bottles
Località Piandellorino 189,
53024 Montalcino, Siena
Tel: +39 05 77 84 93 01
www.piandellorino.it

Agostina Pieri

Agostina Pieri is one of three sisters whose father Alessandro bequeathed them each valuable vineyard land in the Piancornello section of the Montalcino zone. The azienda began life in 1991 as a producer of grapes to sell to other winemakers. Not long thereafter, Agostina's elder son Francesco Monaci got involved in production and, a rudimentary cantina having been established, started vinifying and bottling the estate's own wine.

At first, production pretty well followed traditionalist lines. The first wine to emerge was the Rosso di Montalcino, which stimulated immediate interest at a time when fruit-driven, lightly oaky Montalcino reds were entering into vogue. It was not until 1999 that the first Brunello, of the 1994 vintage, came on the market—aged, as today, partly in barrique/tonneau, partly in larger *botte*.

Meanwhile, Francesco had been bitten by the technology bug, a direction in which he was

Francesco Monaci is a fruit-quality perfectionist, and it shows in the wines, which have a very individual character—smooth, with velvety tannins

encouraged from 2001 by his adviser in matters viticultural, Fernando Sovali, and from 2002 by his new enological consultant, Fabrizio Moltard. There followed what he describes as a "restructuring of the production mechanisms, with a view to adapting them to better winemaking techniques, including equipment to enable berry selection of the harvest, ability to adjust temperature up or down during the fermentation, and constant renewal of aging wood."

So far, nothing particularly unusual, but Francesco's passion for bringing technology into the production process does not end there. He introduced what he describes as an "automatic winemaker"—an electronic system that, once set

takes care quite independently of such functions as *délestage*, pumping over, and breaking the cap. "He [as Francesco calls the machine] makes his own decisions as to what to do. The machine makes the wine himself!"—apparently with the aid of various computers, which also, among other things, decide how long the picked grapes should be kept in cool conditions before crushing. All Francesco has to do is enter the information about rainfall and humidity relative to the vintage-time weather.

Of course, all this presupposes great attention to quality in the vineyard during the growing season, but this is something that Francesco—and his younger brother Jacopo—takes for granted. Francesco is a fruit-quality perfectionist, and it shows in the wines, which have a very individual character—smooth, with velvety tannins, and the spicy-herby aromas typical of this relatively southerly, low-altitude terroir.

FINEST WINES

Rosso di Montalcino
This displays an intensity and sheer fruitiness, yet with very rounded edges unusual for the genre. The 2007★ follows a line of successful vintages, including tricky ones like 2003 and 2002.

Brunello di Montalcino
More robust, deeper, and richer than the Rosso, but still with the hallmark elegance-cum-fruitiness. Francesco managed an impeccable if lightweight 2002, a vintage that many declassified for Brunello.

Sant'Antimo J&F
A recent addition to the range is this Cabernet/Merlot blend: juicy, round, and for mid-term drinking.

Agostina Pieri
Total area: 18ha (44 acres)
Area under vine: 10.5ha (26 acres)
Average production: 70,000 bottles
Via Fabbri 2, Località Piancornello,
53020 Castelnuovo Abate, Siena
Tel: +39 05 77 84 39 42
www.pieriagostina.it

Poggio Antico

What a lot can change in a quarter of a century! It was in 1984 that Milanese investment banker Giancarlo Gloder bought this estate, 7 miles (4.5km) south of Montalcino, transferring from a smaller one he had purchased for holiday purposes in 1970. It had belonged to a friend who had to introduce electricity and running water, so primitive were things then. The friend had also introduced vines but sold his wines through a distributor, GIV. Gloder wanted to make his own wine, but 1984 was one of the bad years; and to make matters worse, the winemaker died. Undaunted, in 1985, Gloder broke with GIV.

But Gloder was—is—not a wine man, and in 1987 he was able to persuade his youngest daughter Paola to take over. This 20-year-old, straight from school in Milan, did not know a tannin from an anthocyanin but was willing to learn. For a year, Paola

Poggio Antico is one of the highest vineyards in Montalcino. You know the proximity of the Tyrrhenian Sea is a factor, because it is visible in the far distance on a clear day

worked her socks off in the vineyard, staggering into the office at the end of the day to handle the admin. She was helped by Claudio Ferretti, son of the manager, who had been born at Poggio Antico, and after a decade further help came in the shape of her new husband Alberto Montefiori, who took over production, though he had no experience of enology either. Fortunately, there were Ferretti and the consultant Paolo Vagaggini to oversee things.

Paola likes to make a point of the fact that Poggio Antico is, at an average altitude of 1,475ft (450m), one of the highest vineyards in Montalcino. You know the proximity of the Tyrrhenian Sea is a factor, because it is visible in the far distance on a clear day. The constant breezes keep the vineyards free from humidity and insects, and this, combined with a south-southwest exposure plus classic soil structure of limestone and *galestro*, increases the chances of ripe, healthy grapes, despite the relative lateness of the harvest. Another particularity is that the estate is open to the public 365 days a year and boasts one of the finest restaurants in the area.

FINEST WINES

Brunello di Montalcino Riserva
The top wine is from selected grapes of a 30-year-old vineyard. The wine is made semi-traditionally, with one year's aging in French tonneaux and two and a half years in large Slavonian oak *botti*. The 2001★ was still youthful at seven years of age, with plenty of fresh fruit on the palate, ripe tannins, and good acidity. An elegant wine, needing time.

Altero
The most modern of their Brunellos, this is aged two years in tonneaux and two in bottle. Altero has been their "alternative" Brunello for years, and it was only after the minimum aging time for Brunello was reduced from four years to two that this came into the DOCG from the cold of IGT.

Brunello di Montalcino
Non-cru Brunello constitutes the bulk of the production here (they also make limited amounts of **Rosso**, which Paola dismisses as "declassified Brunello"). Aged three years in Slavonian oak *botti* and a year in bottle, it is a classic of its type, with good fruit definition and structure, though able to be drunk relatively young. The 2004 is very good.

Madre
"Mother" is not a Vin Santo but an IGT Rosso combining Cabernet Sauvignon and Sangiovese in a thoroughly convincing "Tuscanized American" style, as Paola poetically puts it.

Poggio Antico
Total area: 200ha (494 acres)
Area under vine: 32ha (79 acres)
Average production: 120,000 bottles
53024 Montalcino, Siena
Tel: +39 05 77 84 80 44
www.poggioantico.com

Poggio di Sotto

Piero Palmucci is certainly one of the few uncompromising traditionalists of Montalcino. He is a perfectionist who is in wine not primarily for business reasons but in order to create a thing of beauty in vinous form, and this has been his driving motivation ever since he arrived on the Montalcino scene in 1989.

He came, as he puts it, from "another world," that of container shipping, and settled on his beloved Poggio di Sotto site, near the village of Castelnuovo dell'Abate, only after a comprehensive search for the perfect place. Today, he revels in the superb views that his property affords him (of Monte Amiata, of the Orcia Valley) and in the exquisite fruit his vines and olive trees—organically tended at an altitude of 650–1,300ft (200–400m)—deliver to him.

The idea of mixing any grape variety other than Sangiovese into his wine appalls him. "I take that as an insult," he replied when I asked him whether he grew other varieties. Some years ago he gave up attending the annual press and trade tasting Benvenuto Brunello because he felt the *consorzio* was not capable of organizing the tasting in an "adequate ambience," the event being held in a huge tent in the month of February, when the wines were either freezing or soupy. (Actually, the authorities seem to have rectified this problem, but Palmucci is happy with the world coming to him and does not intend to return.)

When Palmucci first came to Poggio di Sotto, there were about 3.5ha (9 acres) of vineyard. Acknowledging his amateur status, he researched the market for the best consultants he could find and came up with the University of Milan, in the persons of Dr Brancadoro and the now-famous Professor Attilio Scienza. It was they who analyzed the various parcels of his soil, to a depth of at least 7ft (2.2m), and recommended the right clones (between six and ten) and rootstocks to complement them, the latest additions being 3ha (7 acres) in 1997, with the same area again in 1999.

On the enological front, Palmucci has placed his wines in the care of Giulio Gambelli, the octogenarian master taster who believes in minimal intervention, extended maceration (up to four weeks) with no temperature control, and aging in large *botti* of traditional Slavonian oak. Palmucci, who abhors barriques, having experimented with various sizes between 20 and 45hl, has settled on 30hl barrels of oval shape. Like another client of Gambelli—Gianfranco Soldera of Case Basse—Palmucci ages his Brunellos in wood for a good four years, and longer for Riserva, which he makes only in exceptional years (2004, 1999, and 1995). Even the Rosso gets two years in oak. There is no filtration.

FINEST WINES

Brunello di Montalcino
Palmucci made no 2002, very little 2003, and the 2001★ had still to be followed by the 2004 in 2008. It is a wine of balance and elegance rather than power, holding its 14 degrees lightly, medium-light of hue, almost floral and Pinot Noiresque on the nose, together with notes of Mediterranean *macchia*. Still tight and taut, with firm acidity and plenteous but ripe tannins, one feels it could age in bottle much longer. The 1999 Riserva, tasted at a dinner a couple of years ago, was subtle but complex, ethereal yet sure of itself. Five of the six journalists at my table thought it magnificent; the sixth (who was working for a very famous American wine critic at the time) thought there was "nothing there." That's wine.

Rosso di Montalcino
It is tempting to describe this as a "mini Brunello," since it is made in a similar fashion to many of that ilk. Complex and very individual, it is a fine bottle that, thanks to its price as well as its lighter style, can be drunk more readily than its senior partner.

Poggio di Sotto
Total area: 33ha (82 acres)
Area under vine: 21ha (52 acres)
Average production: 40,000 bottles
Castelnuovo dell'Abate, 53024 Montalcino, Siena
Tel: +39 05 77 83 55 02
www.poggiodisotto.com

Le Potazzine

There is nothing outwardly extraordinary about this youthful husband-and-wife team—except, perhaps, the fact that, as well as their little gem of an estate 2.5 miles (4km) south and west of Montalcino town, in the *contrada* called Le Prata, they also run a *vineria* (a sort of wine bar) right in the middle of town, where it is possible to taste various Rosso and Brunello wines (not just theirs) together with simple local dishes.

In fact, this is a kind of happy-ever-after story that the reader—or better still, the taster—picks up after all the adventures are over and the rest of the heroes' lives has already begun.

Giuseppe Gorelli, with a diploma in agriculture and enology plus 15 years' work experience at the Brunello *consorzio* behind him, acquired the property at Le Prata with his wife Gigliola in the

Somehow, one can taste in Le Potazzine wines the contentment and harmony that prevail at this estate. These are wines you just want to drink, sold at reasonable prices

early 1990s, planting some 3ha (7.5 acres) to Sangiovese here in 1993 and another 2ha (5 acres) at a site that they subsequently purchased near Sant'Angelo in Colle in 1996—a site, he maintains, that adds "structure" to the "elegance and perfume" of the fruit from Le Prata. These two dates happened to coincide with the birth years of their two daughters—the estate was originally called Viola after the elder, then Le Potazzine when the second, Sofia, came along (the name alludes to the little birds—tits—depicted on the labels).

Vineyards are planted to a cordon system at around 5,000 plants per hectare—nothing unusual there. The recently constructed cellar is functional, while being in character with the countryside—

nothing unusual there, either. Production is sufficient to fill around 50,000 bottles between Rosso and Brunello—par for the small-producer course. If there is an unusual aspect to their production, it is that Giuseppe uses barriques for the Rosso only, preferring to age the Brunello in medium-large *botti*.

FINEST WINES

Brunello di Montalcino and **Rosso di Montalcino**
Somehow, one can taste in Le Potazzine wines the contentment and harmony that prevail at this estate. I tasted a range of Brunellos from 1997 to 2001, and all save the relatively lean 1998 had a sweetness, ripeness, and intensity that made them delicious to drink early, which is not to say that they won't age well. These are wines without great pretensions, of sappy fruit together with excellent varietal typicity, sold at reasonable prices. The Rosso is even more forward, ideal for wine-bars such as their own. We can only hope, for everyone's sake, that the happiness does indeed continue into the ever-after.

Tenuta Le Potazzine
Area under vine: 7ha (17 acres),
including 3ha (7.5 acres) rented
Average production: 40,000 bottles
Tenuta Le Potazzine, 53024 Montalcino, Siena
Tel: +39 05 77 84 61 68
www.lepotazzine.it

Salicutti

Francesco Leanza knew nothing about winemaking when he decided to take the reins at this small but stunning estate. There was a bit of agriculture in his background, in that his family had grown citrus fruits in Sicily. And as a chemist in Rome for most of his working life, he had analyzed wine but never made it. All he knew about Montalcino, from his occasional visits prior to 1990, was that it exercised a strange attraction for him, and in 1990, yielding to the pull, he purchased this powerfully suggestive site on a fairly steep slope, facing south toward mysterious Monte Amiata, at an average altitude of 1,475ft (450m).

By 1994, he had planted a couple of hectares, using a clone developed by the late, great Pierluigi Talenti; by 1996, he had moved permanently from Rome; by 1999, he had built the cantina, and from then on, it was all systems go. Not that it had not

Francesco Leanza comes across, in his quiet, studious way, as a fanatic for quality. But the quality he seeks, he insists, can never be contrived

been all go up to that point, as he studied the principles of viticulture and winemaking from books, as well as under the guidance of teachers such as Jan Erbach (*see Pian dell'Orino*) and his current enological consultant Paolo Vagaggini. He had also supervised the building site of his cellar while getting the property recognized as organic—the first in Montalcino—from 1996.

This latter move, Leanza insists, was "more for reasons of quality than ideology," and indeed he does come across, in his quiet, studious way, as a fanatic for quality. But the quality he seeks, he insists, can never be contrived. "Wine can only be great if it comes from land of great vocation," he likes to say. "You need passion and feeling. You can't make wine

by reason alone. For it to be unique, it must reflect its unique terroir."

He does not sound much like a scientist, does he? Indeed, one senses in Leanza a fiery, emotional intensity—one of his pet hates, apparently, being journalists who come and poke their noses around his farm and issue pontifications on the fruits of the unremitting labors of artists like him, thus creating false expectations in the market. Journalists have misunderstood the soul of Montalcino, which is elegance, perfume, lightness of touch à la Bourgogne, not power and depth. And you know what? He is absolutely right.

FINEST WINES

Leanza is essentially a non-interventionist, using (from 2003, at least) wild yeasts and no additive other than SO_2, and that at a very low level. There is no fining, no filtration, and no cold stabilization. The only technology he admits is temperature control in his stainless-steel fermenters. Wood aging for **Brunello di Montalcino Piaggione** (named for a nearby stream) is in *botti* of between 10 and 40hl capacity, and for **Rosso di Montalcino**, which he makes in roughly equivalent amounts, it is tonneaux, one quarter of which are renewed annually. Brunello gets more than a year in bottle before release, and this will increase for the **Brunello Riserva** that he will be bringing out shortly.

Far be it from me to judge these works of vinous art. I am sure, however, that Leanza will not object to my affirming that his creations, which are indeed of a Burgundian delicacy and lightness of touch, particularly the 2004 Brunello Riserva★, are among those from Montalcino most to my taste. Except, perhaps, for the mainly **Cabernet Sant'Antimo Rosso Dopoteatro**, which does not seem to fit.

Podere Salicutti
Total area: 11ha (27 acres)
Area under vine: 4ha (10 acres)
Average production: 17,000 bottles
Località Podere Salicutti 174,
53024 Montalcino, Siena
Tel: +39 05 77 84 70 03
www.poderesalicutti.it

Siro Pacenti

Giancarlo Pacenti is the scion of two *montalcinese* families. In 1971, his father, Siro Pacenti, founded the currently 7ha (17-acre) vineyard at Pelagrilli, northeast of the medieval hilltop town of Montalcino, which looms above it. He was also one of the founding members of the Brunello *consorzio* in 1967. His mother, Graziella, is a Pieri, from the southern section of Piancornello, near Sant'Angelo Scalo. One of three sisters, she inherited 13ha (32 acres) from her father Alessandro, the other two thirds of his property going to Agostina Pieri of the estate of that name (*see p.243*), and Silvana Pieri, proprietress of the estate called Piancornello.

Giancarlo, who first got involved at Pelagrilli in 1988 (though he does not look older than mid-30s), is often cited as an example of the arch-modernist in the Montalcino context, but this image ignores

Giancarlo is often cited as an example of the arch-modernist in Montalcino. But those who reject Siro Pacenti on the basis of oak aging are missing out on a good thing

certain realities of his production. True, he is deeply influenced by classic French methods, being a regular visitor to Bordeaux and an appreciator of Burgundy. But classic France is far from the New World. His enological mentor is Yves Glories, ex-teacher to Giancarlo Pacenti during the latter's time at the University of Bordeaux. Professor Glories is a committed partisan of barrique aging (as he would be), but let's face it, the French are much more expert than the relative newcomers of Italy in the art of using the small barrel as an instrument to manage polyphenols rather than as a flavoring device. Indeed, one of Giancarlo's proudest boasts—backed up triumphantly by the wines—is the knowledge he has gained in

balancing the wine with the *cessioni* (aromas and tannins drawn from the barrel).

So Giancarlo is a modernist if barrique aging is all you go by. But he claims his aim has always been to "bring out to the maximum the characteristics of our land as expressed by Sangiovese." He does not practice abbreviated maceration (average is 15–20 days) and is a strong believer in the extra complexity, if lesser power, derived from old vines, having a vineyard more than 40 years old in Sant'Angelo Scalo and another over 30 years at Pelagrilli.

One aspect of Giancarlo's pursuit of excellence is his involvement with a research program run by Roberto Bandinelli of the University of Florence, aimed at identifying different biotypes of Sangiovese. There could, according to Bandinelli, be up to 70 different types in the vineyard planted by Giancarlo's maternal grandfather in the 1960s. Giancarlo has planted an experimental vineyard with 50 of these biotypes, and the experiment will be followed up with microvinifications.

FINEST WINES

Giancarlo is proud of his attention to the quality of his raw material, with three stages of fruit selection: one in the vineyard, where only the best fruit is picked, and two in the winery, where first imperfect bunches and then poor berries are discarded on the selection belt. As a result, his **Brunello di Montalcino** is a model of impeccability as far as purity of fruit is concerned, with bright, well-defined flavors, crisp, clean, fruit-acid balance, and wild-cherry and herb prevailing quite definitely over oak. Those who reject Siro Pacenti on the basis of oak aging are missing out on a good thing. [2004 ★]

Siro Pacenti
Total area: 60ha (148 acres)
Area under vine: 20ha (49 acres)
Average production: 60,000 bottles
Località Pelagrilli,
53024 Montalcino, Siena
Tel: +39 05 77 84 69 35
pacentisiro@libero.it

Valdicava

Vincenzo Abbruzzesi recalls his grandfather, Bramante Martini, in order to illustrate how poor people were in early 20th-century Montalcino. As a boy, he used to get up at 5am to walk several miles to fetch milk, returning in time to escort his younger siblings to school. Later, he got into meat, specifically the trading of that prized Tuscan bovine breed called Chianina.

He bought what is today Valdicava in 1953, and while his principal revenue came from beef, he also planted a vineyard. He was sufficiently taken with viticulture that he helped form the Montalcino *consorzio* in 1967, being acquainted with the leading lights of what was then the embryonic wine scene of Montalcino: Tancredi and Franco Biondi Santi and Dr Colombini of Fattoria Barbi. Vincenzo remembers his grandfather's 1967, as well as those of Il Poggione and Barbi, as being good Brunello. Before 1964, he further recalls, there was no good Brunello apart from that of Biondi-Santi.

Vincenzo started helping in his grandfather's cantina in 1975, at 14 years of age. By 1980, he was working in the cantina and loving every minute—so much so that he managed, in 1987, to scrape together the money to pay the comparatively modest asking price for the property. He persuaded consultant enologist Attilio Pagli to come on board, and by the time the fabulous 1990 vintage rolled around, Vincenzo Abbruzzesi was off and running.

Vincenzo was among the first to realize that the way to great wine was through great grapes, so he planted an experimental vineyard to four types of rootstock and four different biotypes—16 combinations in all. All subsequent plantings have been informed by this material. Later on, to help him use and extend this knowledge, he hired agronomist Andrea Paoletti of what is today called the Aminea group. The daily work in the vineyards, however, is overseen by Vincenzo with 16 field-workers, Vincenzo describing himself as "one of the few hands-on *viticoltori*" in Montalcino.

Today, the most recently planted vineyards on the Valdicava estate contain 5,500 plants per hectare, and Vincenzo is getting significantly less than one kilo of grapes per vine, ending up, after *triage*, with an average of 30hl/ha—a small amount even by the best French standards. But he is getting ever greater concentration and complexity, as well as deeper color—sometimes remarkably deep for a genuine Sangiovese, as we shall see.

FINEST WINES

Vincenzo likes to say he produces five Brunellos and four Rossos, since he divides his various plots for purposes of vinification and aging, but the commercial reality, after blending, is two and one.

Brunello di Montalcino
Made in all but the worst years, this is a forceful, full-fruited style of Brunello, with plenty of backbone, yet by no means lacking elegance. The 1999 is classic, the 2000 good for a forward vintage.

Brunello Riserva Madonna del Piano
Made in the better years, this is richer still and can be so deep of color as (in Vincenzo's own words) to be "embarrassing for a Sangiovese." So much so that many journalists at the Benvenuto Brunello annual press tasting thought the 2001 was not bona fide. Vincenzo swore up and down that it was not blended, and he strikes me as an honest man. His explanation for the color is simply all the hard work they are doing in the vineyard, plus the excellent vintage. The 1999★ is a model of power-cum-restraint.

The wines have good staying power. I tasted the 1990 vintage of both Brunellos, and wrote of the *normale*: "Mushroom and leather, dried fruits, herbs, firm tannins well disguised by richness of fruit. Still quite youthful, time to go." Of the Riserva I noted: "Firm, almost pointed acidity, very fresh. Classic, traditional Sangiovese, made well. Excellent."

Valdicava
Total area: 43ha (106 acres)
Area under vine: 20ha (49 acres)
Average production: 50,000 bottles
Località Val di Cava, 53024 Montalcino, Siena
Tel: +39 05 77 84 82 61
www.valdicava.it

Montepulciano

If any wine zone of Tuscany deserves the description "historic," Montepulciano is it. Livy mentioned it in his *History of Rome*, some 2,000 years ago. There exists a document relating to the transfer of vineyard rights going back to the end of the 9th century AD. Another, from 1350, establishes trade and export conditions for Montepulciano wine. In the 16th century, Sante Lancerio, a much-cited wine steward of Pope Paul III, recorded His Holiness's partiality for it. Then there is the famous description of Montepulciano by Francesco Redi, in his book *Bacchus in Tuscany*, as "the king of all wines." No one is quite sure when it started to be known as "noble," but that epithet was well established by the early 19th century. Voltaire mentions Montepulciano wine in *Candide*; Thomas Jefferson drank it with pleasure. All these, admittedly, are snippets you will find in any promotional blurb on Montepulciano, and I claim no credit for original research. Indeed, it could all have been invented by some clever spin doctor of yore for the rest of us to trot out obediently every time an introduction to the wines of Montepulciano is called for, following that noble discipline that a friend of mine once described as *l'arte del copiare* ("the art of copying"). But it does sound good, doesn't it?

Anyway, how then, with all that history, did the late 20th and early 21st centuries see the image of Montepulciano wine fall so far behind that of the other major wine commune of the province of Siena, Montalcino? Could it be simply that the wine-bibbing public, encouraged by American wine publications, the myth-makers of our vinous times, bought the line of the wine supposedly (with almost no evidence) capable of aging 100 years, in preference to the history-packed but somewhat hackneyed blurb? Or could it have something to do with wine styles?

Certainly, Montalcino wine, apart from being about twice as expensive (and therefore twice as good?), is in general a more polished product, its tannins being rounded and softened by the extra wood aging (minimum two years out of four, as compared with Montepulciano's minimum one year out of two), while the acidity of Vino Nobile tends to be more aggressive and less integrated than that of Brunello. Indeed, the acid/tannin structure of Vino Nobile is such that one might be forgiven for thinking that this—not Brunello—is the one that might, in exceptional circumstances, be able to last a century. It is, as I have said elsewhere, the taming of these structural obstacles that has constituted the drama of Vino Nobile in our time.

What might account for this hardness? Could it be that Montepulciano is that much farther inland than Montalcino, less in line to benefit from those mitigating sea breezes (though they have the large Lake Trasimeno nearby)? Altitude and soil types are similarly mixed, though some of the vineyards around the town of Montepulciano itself, as distinct from the farther-east-lying and sandier Valiano section, are a bit heavy on the clay, which can make for hardness. It does rain more in Montepulciano— or perhaps one should say it rains less in famously dry Montalcino—and the average temperature is slightly lower (we look forward to the effects of climate change, quipped one grower).

The major difference lies in grapes employed. While Brunello is (or is supposed to be) 100 percent Sangiovese, Vino Nobile can be anything from 70 to 100 percent Sangiovese, the balance being made up of Canaiolo and Mammolo, on the indigenous side, or (more frequently) Merlot or Cabernet among the internationals. The law even permits up to 10 percent Trebbiano or Malvasia, but almost no one avails themselves of this allowance.

More to the point, Montepulciano boasts a different version of Sangiovese called Prugnolo Gentile ("gentle wild plum")—a curious name in view of its tendency to austerity. But even this

Right: Montepulciano's cooler climate is among the reasons why its wines tend to be firmer than those of Montalcino

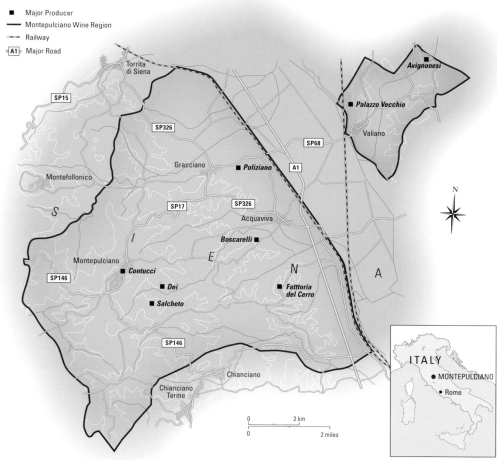

Torrita
di Siena

SP15

SP326

SP68

SP326

A1

Gracciano ■ *Poliziano*

Montefollonico

■ *Avignonesi*

■ *Palazzo Vecchio*

Valiano

SP17

SP326

Acquaviva

■ *Boscarelli* ■

Montepulciano

SP146

■ *Contucci*

■ *Dei*

■ *Fatttoria del Cerro*

■ *Salcheto*

SP146

Chianciano

Chianciano
Terme

0   2 km
0   2 miles

N

S   I   E   N   A

ITALY
● MONTEPULCIANO
● Rome

does not quite explain the difference between Montalcino and Montepulciano, because most *poliziani* in the replanting period—which, as elsewhere in Tuscany, has been taking place over the past 10–15 years—have used clones developed by the universities and nurseries, or research groups such as Chianti Classico 2000, rather than clones specifically designated as Prugnolo Gentile.

Nevertheless, the Montepulciano *consorzio*, which consists of 40-odd producers (many fewer than Chianti Classico or Montalcino), has carried out research on specifically Montepulciano clones of Sangiovese, and these have recently reached the stage of being planted out. It is much too early in the vine/wine cycle to say what kind of product can be expected from them.

Before concluding, it is necessary to mention the second wine of Montepulciano, called Rosso di Montepulciano. Like Rosso di Montalcino, it is intended to give growers a product they can sell younger, but since Vino Nobile's aging requirement is only half that of Brunello, it has about half the significance as a wine. Whereas almost everyone in Montalcino makes Rosso di Montalcino, many here do not bother with Rosso, perhaps also because it gets confused in the public mind with Montepulciano d'Abruzzo, with which it has no connection, being of a different grape variety. As in Montalcino, the best alternative wines from Montepulciano will likely come under the IGT Toscano.

Right: Historic Montepulciano has some of its most traditional producers, including Cantine Contucci, whose door this is

Poderi Boscarelli

The Marchesi de Ferrari are Genovese in origin and maintain their roots in that Tyrrhenian city. They were among many northerners who took advantage of low Tuscan land prices in the decade following the ending of *mezzadria* (sharecropping), acquiring this Montepulciano property in 1962. In fact, it was Paola de Ferrari's father who made the purchase, but it was she and her husband who, following her father's early death in 1967, carried on looking after the estate. For 16 years the couple worked at tending and improving the property, doing what they could while commuting from Genoa at weekends and during holidays, starting with vineyards of mixed cultivation and working up to 9ha (22 acres) of specialized vineyard by the early 1980s. Tragically, the arrangement was brought to a sudden end by the premature death of Ippolito de Ferrari. Paola was at that point left alone to deal with the farm, on top of raising two teenage boys.

In 1984, she recruited one of Tuscany's top consultant enologists in Maurizio Castelli, former adviser to the Chianti Classico *consorzio*, and one of the first freelancers in what is now a thriving and generally most lucrative business. It was from this point that Boscarelli began to attract attention as being among the most serious Vino Nobile producers. By 1988, Paola's son Luca was old enough and interested enough to take over the reins, tending mainly to the enological side of things (with Castelli's counsel). Luca's younger brother Nicolò, a qualified agronomist, later came on board, settling on the estate, while Paola and Luca continue to commute from Genoa.

Boscarelli is essentially a smallholding, a fact that Castelli considers a boon. "Their fortune was that they never expanded. It is not difficult to make very good wine on a large property, because you have more choice. But to make wine of real individual character, it is best to have a small estate."

They sorted out the cantina in the 1970s, and it has remained essentially the same ever since, the major exception being the introduction of stainless steel. As elsewhere in Tuscany, however, the main focus since the early 1990s has been on fruit quality. In 1991, they began a program of slowly replanting all the vineyards, the best zones being reserved for Sangiovese derived partly from massal selection. The oldest vineyard still standing today is from 1975—a mix of Sangiovese (principally), Canaiolo, Colorino, Malvasia Nera, Mammolo, and Ciliegiolo. Today, of course, they no longer do *uvaggi di vigneto* but tend to keep all varieties separate, though there is also an "experimental" vineyard with various French and Italian grapes. Density has moved upward from the original 2,000–3,000 plants per hectare to the present level of 6,000–7,000.

These days they try to keep production per plant down to 1.5–1.7lb (700–800g). They are switching from cordon training to Guyot simple or double, following Castelli's dictum that "no great wine has ever been grown on cordon."

FINEST WINES

Vino Nobile di Montepulciano Nocio dei Boscarelli
There has been some chopping and changing in respect of Boscarelli wines' grape make-up. This one, since 2001, has been 100% Sangiovese. It is a wine of lengthy maceration (more than 40 days) and aging (18 months in tonneaux and barriques), and is probably their finest product, released only in good vintages. I tasted a range from the 2004 vintage back.
2004 Very fine, elegant, fruit and herb aroma. Plenty of depth and structure promising much, and plenty of flavor, too, but needs laying down and forgetting till 2012.
2001 An earthy, spicy, plummy character on the nose and plenty of class on the palate—quality fruit with that stony, earthy character that distinguishes

Right: Paola de Ferrari and her sons Luca (left) and Nicolò, who together have taken their estate to the top

the rather austere style of Montepulciano. Big but "very elegant," I remark. Castelli responds: "Sangiovese, if it isn't elegant ..." He wags his finger negatively.

1999 There is around 7% Merlot in this, and the color is correspondingly deeper and more purply. Seems younger than the 2001. Plenty of sweet fruit, but plenty, too, of that Montepulciano austerity. Compared with 2001 it is slightly less characteristic of the zone, perhaps because of the Merlot. Only just becoming ready to drink at ten years of age.

1997 Merlot and Mammolo in this one. It has the ripeness, almost mellowness, of the vintage, and an opulent palate in which oak (25% of which was new) plays perhaps slightly too prominent a part. As Luca admits, "with Sangiovese you have to be more attentive concerning the wood."

1991 Vino Nobile Riserva Vigna del Nocio From Sangiovese and Mammolo, this was a bit dilute (due to the vintage), but had a sweet, somewhat decadent palate, comparable with a good Pinot Noir, demonstrating Castelli's point that Sangiovese is comparable in character not so much with the Bordeaux grapes but rather with Pinot Noir and Nebbiolo.

1983 Riserva This boasted a complex and inviting nose—vegetal, leathery, and lively—showing, if proof were needed, that Sangiovese & Co., properly stored, can deliver exciting old bottles.

Vino Nobile Riserva

The Vino Nobile Riserva of today is 90% Sangiovese and 10% Merlot. The latter, in the case of the 2004, does not, in my view, detract from its intensely Tuscan character, merely adding sweetness and concentration. The wine is excellent and very typical, if more concentratedly fruity than Nocio—but is it (the law aside) a true child of Montepulciano? I rated it highly, though it needs a few more years in bottle.

Boscarelli

The grape mix of this IGT Toscana is subject to change, and may consist of varying proportions of Sangiovese, Merlot, or Carmenère. The 2005 successfully combines the characteristics of its home soil (some pretty firm tannins) with those of its French components (oaky and berry sweet). A worthy Super-Tuscan. Boscarelli, indeed, was the name of the finest wine I tasted from this estate, a 1985 vintage (great year), which in those days was 100% Sangiovese. An outstanding example of the

grape's ability to age nobly in the right conditions; great charm and drinkability. Herby, spicy, fruity, almost Christmasy. One to remember.

Vino Nobile di Montepulciano

The straight Vino Nobile is a traditional blend of 90% Sangiovese plus Malvasia Nera, Colorino, Mammolo, and Canaiolo. The 2005 displays the typical wild-cherry aroma on the nose, followed by layered, complex, and concentrated fruit of considerable interest. The tannins are typically firm in the Montepulciano style, and there are herbal notes and something savory on the finish. In short, a well-made and interesting bottle.

Above and left: Attention at Poderi Boscarelli has been focused on ensuring the highest possible fruit quality

Poderi Boscarelli
Total area: 18ha (44 acres)
Area under vine: 13ha (32 acres)
Average production: 70,000 bottles
Via di Montenero 28,
53040 Cervognano di Montepulciano, Siena
Tel: +39 05 78 76 72 77
www.poderiboscarelli.it

Fattoria del Cerro

Saiagricola is the agricultural arm of the insurance firm SAI, and Fattoria del Cerro, purchased in 1978, is the most important of its several farms, currently including four in the viticultural mode, all in central Italy—one in Umbria and three in Tuscany. As befits a successful business, the estate at Acquaviva near Montepulciano—the largest private producer of the Montepulciano zone, with vineyards at altitudes of 1,148–1,476ft (350–450m)—is a model of efficiency, with a good dollop of quality consciousness thrown in. Lorenzo Landi, the long-serving consultant enologist for all Saiagricola's wine estates, a colleague and disciple of French enologists Denis Dubourdieu and Christophe Olivier, proved elusive (as is often the case, I have found) on my most recent visit. I was shown around by youthful resident enologist Roberto da Frassini, who seemed enthusiastic about the work of the group.

Da Frassini explained that what they are aiming at is an individual yet typical style of Vino Nobile —one that reflects the character of the terroir yet can be drunk with pleasure and also speaks a unique language recognizable as theirs alone. In pursuit of this, they had been involved over a period of many years with the universities of Florence and Pisa, in the development not just of massal-selected Sangiovese culled from their oldest vineyards (examples of which had been used to further research into Montepulciano's supposedly unique Prugnolo Gentile), but also of such alternative indigenous varieties as Colorino, Abrostino, and Pugnitello. In respect of the first of these—a grape much favored by Landi for blending purposes—they are among the largest producers in central Italy. Since the 1990s, da Frassini averred, some 85 percent of Fattoria del Cerro's vineyards had been replanted, at an average density of 5,000 plants per hectare.

Vinification takes place in purpose-built, fully equipped cellars, as you would expect, but the wines are a judicious compromise between the modern and the traditional. No French grapes are used in any of the three Vino Nobiles, the *normale* and the Riserva adding Mammolo to the blend of Colorino and Sangiovese. Aging takes place in a mix of barrique and Slavonian oak *botte* for these two, while the cru Antica Chiusina gets 15 months in barrique, followed by a year in bottle.

FINEST WINES

Vino Nobile di Montepulciano
There is no doubt that del Cerro produces one of the best Vino Nobiles in terms of seriousness-cum-drinkability, having a gamut of aromas including tea leaf, cherry, and something floral, with ripe, reasonably smooth tannins—though being third in line for fruit selection, its intensity on the palate can be a little attenuated.

Vino Nobile di Montepulciano Riserva
This has a similar aromatic character to the *normale* above but delivers much more in terms of fruit succulence. [2006 V]

Vino Nobile Vigneto Antica Chiusina
As one would always expect, the top selection (no longer single-vineyard) has easily the most to it, with velvety tannins and a concentration that more than compensates for the oak flavors mingling with those of berry fruit, plum, and balsam. [2004★]

Among the numerous other wines of this estate are a varietal **Sangiovese IGT Manero** and a varietal **Merlot IGT Poggio Golo**, neither of which has ever convinced me as being top level.

CÒLPETRONE
Saiagricola's second most important estate is Còlpetrone, at Gualdo Cattaneo in the Montefalco zone of Umbria, where 63 of the 140ha (156 of 346 acres) are planted to Sagrantino, Sangiovese, and Merlot, the latter being blended at 15% with Sagrantino (15%) and Sangiovese (70%) in the **Montefalco Rosso DOC**. The two major wines, **Montefalco Sagrantino** and **Montefalco Sagrantino**

Right: Saiagricola's managing director Guido Sodano (*left*), and long-serving consultant enologist Lorenzo Landi

Passito, both DOCG, are 100% varietal. These are wines of heroic structure with, in the case of the first, a Porty finish overlaying an impressive but ripe tannic base, great length, and penetration. A recent innovation is **Montefalco Sagrantino Gold**, a selection of the best fruit of two separate vineyards in top years only. The one I tasted was very backward, but everything was there for a great bottle of the future. As for the Passito, from grapes given two months drying in the manner of Recioto, I found it less impressive than the dry version, having an unsubtly high level of residual sugar.

LA PODERINA
The group's third estate is in the Montalcino zone near the village of Castelnuovo dell'Abate. Here, of the 49ha (121 acres), half are planted to vines, with almost half of these being registered for Brunello. The main wine is the **Brunello di Montalcino**, aged in oak for two years, mostly in *botte*—a wine of good concentration and elegance, a model of the type if not especially inspired. The **Brunello di Montalcino Poggio Banale** is in a modern, barriqued style, having greater concentration plus the dark-chocolate/roasted-coffee aromas of the genre.

MONTERUFOLI
This 1,000ha (2,471-acre) estate, of which 16ha (40 acres) are planted to the vine, finds itself at Monteverdi Marittima, in the province of Pisa. Curently, there are two wines—a dry white Vermentino IGT called **Redenzione [2008★]**, unoaked, that I found fresh and clean with plenty of saline/mineral flavor ("One of the better Tuscan whites I've tasted," I noted), and a Sangiovese/Cabernet/Merlot called **Malentrata**, which lacked ripe fruit and about which I noted: "Back to the drawing board."

Left: The simple structure of Fattoria del Cerro belies its status as the largest private producer of Montepulciano

Fattoria del Cerro / Saiagricola
Total area (Montepulciano): 600ha (1,483 acres)
Area under vine: 170ha (420 acres)
Total production: 800,000 bottles
Via Grazianella 5,
53040 Acquaviva di Montepulciano, Siena
Tel: +39 05 78 76 77 22
www.saiagricola.it

Avignonesi

The name Avignonesi is a historic one in Montepulciano wine circles. In the old days, several Vino Nobile producers, including Avignonesi, kept cellars inside the town walls—a tradition that continues with Contucci. By the early 1970s, however, Avignonesi's reputation had fallen quite far in the wine world's esteem, as, indeed, had that of Montepulciano generally.

It was then that, through marriage, the Falvo brothers of nearby Chianciano Terme entered the fray. And it was they—mainly Ettore and Alberto Falvo, with the help, from 1992, of resident winemaker Paolo Trappolini—who over the ensuing years raised the company's profile, both viticulturally and enologically, to the point where it is arguably the most prestigious presence in this ancient wine zone. In 2008, the Falvo brothers sold 90 percent of their shares to Virginie Saverys.

The world-famous Vin Santo and Occhio di Pernice are in the Venice league of things one must experience before the kicking of the bucket

Today, Avignonesi embraces four separate estates, growing grapes of both indigenous and international types. I Poggetti is their main source of Sangiovese (Prugnolo Gentile), as well as of Mammolo and Canaiolo, for Vino Nobile. La Selva (in the wine zone of Cortona) and La Lombarda are dedicated to international varieties, of which Merlot is the most significant, but they also include Cabernet Sauvignon, Pinot Nero, Chardonnay, and Sauvignon. It is perhaps Le Capezzine, however (the smallest in vineyard terms), that is the most interesting, for several reasons.

Apart from housing the impressive cantina, Le Capezzine offers tourist attractions in the form of a very fine restaurant linked with cookery classes and winery tours. More importantly from a wine point of view, it is the site of a 7ha (17-acre) vineyard planted to the ancient *settonce* system, whereby every vine is the center of a hexagon of vines planted at an equal distance in all directions (7,158 plants per hectare) and trained according to the *alberello* method. This equidistance between vines, and the absence of wires, allows tractors to travel in several directions from any given point. Another notable viticultural feature at Le Capezzine is the *vigna tonda*, or round vineyard, an experiment in vine density and rootstock suitability that would take longer to explain than we have space for here (further details are on their website). There is also a vineyard "dedicated to growing ancient varieties indigenous to Montepulciano and the surrounding area."

The most amazing feature of Le Capezzine, however, is the *vinsantaia*, where the world-famous Vin Santo and Occhio di Pernice wines are aged in 50-liter *caratelli* for ten years before being blended and bottled. On a winery tour, if you are very lucky, you might get a tiny taste of these nectars. Certainly they are in the Venice league of things one must experience before the kicking of the bucket— though fewer than 1,000 half-bottles per type are produced in a given year, so they are extremely hard to find, even if money is no object.

FINEST WINES

Vino Nobile Riserva Grandi Annate
This ought to be the top wine, and as the title indicates, it is produced only in great years such as 2004, 2001, 1997, and 1990 (the first vintage). Made from 85% Sangiovese and 15% Cabernet Sauvignon, the 2004 was aged 30 months in new barriques, which seems on paper excessive for any Sangiovese, as indeed it proved in practice. Oak dominates the nose and palate, covering some very fine plum and cherry fruit, with hidden herbal depths. Probably needs to be left till at least 2012.

Right: Paolo Trappolini, the winemaker at Avignonesi, which is among Montepulciano's most prestigious producers

Vino Nobile (*normale*)

On the day I tasted it, the Riserva was trumped by the 2005 Vino Nobile *normale*, from a lesser vintage but aged 50% in *botti* and 50% in used barriques. Again, 85% Sangiovese, but the remaining 15% is made up of Canaiolo and Mammolo. A bright, expressive wine; fresh fruit and garden herb; tannins reasonably harnessed, no rough edges; well typed, clean, and long. An archetypal Vino Nobile.

Desiderio

The 2005 vintage of this 100% Merlot was not my cup of tea at all—plenty of fruit but rather monolinear and no great length. There are several better Merlots from Tuscany.

Occhio di Pernice ★

What can one say about 1992 Occhio di Pernice Vin Santo di Montepulciano, made entirely from Sangiovese grapes (as distinct from the other Vin Santo, made from Grechetto, Malvasia, and Trebbiano)? Superlatives are not adequate. Deep brownish hue. Intense, ethereal nose, whose uppish volatility only adds to the magic—toffee, crème caramel, dried apples. It is more a food than a beverage. One can but give it maximum points.

Above: A barrel of Avignonesi's precious Vin Santo, which like Occhio di Pernice remains sealed with wax for ten years

Avignonesi

Total area: 225ha (556 acres)
Area under vine: 109ha (269 acres)
Total production: 700,000 bottles
53040 Valiano di Montepulciano, Siena
Tel: +39 05 78 72 43 04
www.avignonesi.it

Contucci

The name Contucci embodies the best of tradition in Tuscan wine. "The second-longest-serving wine producer of Montepulciano, Fanetti, established 1925, has been going 900 years less than we," quips present paterfamilias Alamanno Contucci, with a jolly chuckle. "I suppose we have been both *bravi* and *fortunati*. *Fortunati* [lucky] because there was always someone to whom we could pass the baton and someone willing to receive it. *Bravi* [clever] because those who took on the business were always good enough to keep it going for the following generation."

Their occupation of their present headquarters —a handsome early 16th-century palazzo designed by Antonio da Sangallo the Elder—has been relatively brief, too: a mere 360 odd years. It is an

"When the zone has seemed to be going too fast for its own good, our role has been to apply the brakes"
Alamanno Contucci

impressive place, being positioned in the old town wall on the edge of the main cathedral square of this famous medieval town. The interior, a veritable warren of nooks and crannies, with barrels here and fermenters there, is the sort of cantina you would dream up for a film set. It perhaps accounts for the fact that a staggering 60 percent of their sales are now to private individuals who have been touring the cellars.

"Our philosophy," Alamanno continues, "has always been to act as *precursori* [movers and shakers], almost revolutionaries, when the zone seemed in danger of dying. When, on the other hand, it has seemed to be going too fast for its own good, our role has been to apply the brakes. The thrust of the past 25 years has seemed to be to

want to throw all tradition into the nettles. Fair enough when tradition is *sbagliato* [wrong], but surely not everything in the past was done badly.

"There are times, admittedly, when we are made to pay for our stance, and in the past 20 years or so we have taken some hard knocks from critics in the trade and press. But somehow, thanks to our history, to our perceived seriousness, to the fidelity of our clients, we have survived, and we've even done rather well. It's not the only way, no doubt, but it's our way."

Alamanno explains, matter-of-factly, not proudly, that Contucci is a traditional Tuscan azienda "in the strictest sense," buying neither grapes nor wine and producing, as well as wine, oil and seed crops, mainly wheat. Until the 1950s, wheat was their principal crop, and it remains important.

In the wine department they have stuck to the traditional grapes—Prugnolo (he does not use the word Sangiovese), Canaiolo, and Mammolo, and they are also bringing Colorino into the equation increasingly. Nothing French.

For a quarter-century, Alamanno was president of the Consorzio del Vino Nobile di Montepulciano. He was instrumental in launching the study of clones of Prugnolo Gentile that has already seen three clones officially authorized from 140 originally taken from vineyards in various sectors of the Montepulciano macrozone. He is convinced that these studies, and in particular these clones when they have grown to maturity in the vineyards and are making wine, will help lift Montepulciano wine back to the preeminence that it enjoyed in centuries past. He is equally convinced that Prugnolo Gentile is a distinct biotype of Sangiovese and not just a marketing gimmick. "You can see [the difference] in the bunch, in the leaf. I can't describe the differences to you, but I can take you into a vineyard and show you. When the new clones come into production, the differences will be evident."

Alamanno Contucci delivers these next words with his characteristic, self-deprecating laugh: "The family is continuing the work. My son is employed in the vineyards, and my daughter looks after the administration. My nephew helps me on the commercial side. Our thousandth anniversary is coming soon, but we don't see any reason why we should not last another thousand years."

FINEST WINES

Vino Nobile di Montepulciano

The main production, obviously, is of Vino Nobile, a blend of 80% Prugnolo Gentile and 20% Canaiolo, Colorino, and Mammolo. I tasted a selection of Vino Nobiles going back to a 1967 Vino Nobile Riserva Speciale, a designation that no longer exists and a wine still containing a significant proportion of white grapes. Contucci's style, it has to be said, is uncompromisingly traditional, with some fairly chewy, sometimes drying tannins and some pretty firm acid levels, plus the odd bitter kick on the back palate coming probably from the chestnut. But the wines have great purity of fruit—sour cherry, fresh-picked blackberry, blueberry—and

certainly no lack of personality or ageability, and definitely no excess of oak. "We maintain our Vino Nobile at a certain level," he says, "and keep a thick skin against the insults. We have our market, our production is limited, and we can continue to make wine as we see fit, even against the tide." The tasting did not offer conclusive evidence that old wines from Contucci can be excellent, but there was enough to suggest that there are probably some exceptional bottles lying in those old cellars.

Vino Nobile Pietra Rossa, from the same grape mix, is a selection of the best in good years, and there is also a single-vineyard **Mulinvecchio [2004★]**. The more approachable **Rosso di Montepulciano** is 80% Prugnolo, 20% Canaiolo and Colorino.

Above: The cellar of Cantucci's 16th-century palazzo
Left: Alamanno Contucci, revolutionary and traditionalist

Contucci

Total area: 172ha (425 acres)
Area under vine: 21ha (52 acres)
Average production: 100,000 bottles
Via del Teatro 1, 53045 Montepulciano, Siena
Tel: +39 05 78 75 70 06
www.contucci.it

Poliziano

This large estate may attract negative noises from some traditionalists because of its owner's unrelentingly rationalist approach to viti-viniculture, but Federico Carletti, Liberace-like, is crying all the way to the bank.

Who would have predicted such enormous success at the beginning of the story, in 1961, when Federico's father Dino acquired his first 22ha (54 acres) of land in this home commune of Montepulciano? For fine wine in Tuscany, those were dark days, even though with hindsight we can see that it was the dark before the dawn. Undaunted, Dino planted "the first specialized vineyards in the area," according to Federico, though I dare say Contucci might have something to say about that.

Carletti is happy to take advantage of technological advances but maintains passionately that everything he does is to exalt the character of the land he farms

Federico took his degree in agrarian studies at Florence University in 1978 but did not join the family firm immediately. That came in 1980, when "despite the economic crisis, [he] decided to accept the challenge" and to impose his clear vision of how "a vineyard, a variety, and a wine" should be handled in order to realize their potential. He has been planting and replanting vineyards ever since, sometimes with massal-selection material from his oldest vineyards, sometimes with the latest clones to be approved. Densities vary from 3,300 plants per hectare in the oldest vineyards to 6,000 in those more recent.

A key component in the success equation has been the help he has received from his old classmate Carlo Ferrini—today one of Tuscany's most successful consultant enologists, advising Federico to this day—and from Maurizio Castelli, another of that ilk.

Carletti, like Ferrini, has always been a believer in the measured use of the "improving" varieties of Bordeaux, though he is not rigid on the subject. For example, his top Vino Nobile, Asinone, is made entirely from Prugnolo Gentile in the best years, while he reserves the right to call in the aid of Merlot or Cabernet when quality demands—that is, when pure Sangiovese lets him down, as it will. He feels sorry for the *montalcinesi*, who do not enjoy this resort, at least not legally.

Also like Ferrini, Carletti is a great believer in the fixing of color and smoothing of tannins achieved by the refinement of Montepulciano's notoriously tough wines in small French (and American) oak. Again, however, he is not rigid, and still ages around a third of his Vino Nobile in what he describes as "traditional *botti*."

Carletti is happy to take advantage of whatever technological advances are made in the field of enology, such as the precisely shaped conical fermenters with automatic punching down and pumping over, lined up in his spotless, ordered winery, completed in the late 1990s. But he maintains passionately that everything he does is in order to exalt the character of the land he farms. "We are not industrial," he insists, "just very efficient." Something wrong with efficiency?

FINEST WINES

Vino Nobile di Montepulciano

The Vino Nobile (200,000 bottles a year) is the lead wine. Subtly referring to the notorious acidic and tannic astringency of the genre, Carletti comments: "We make it structured and long-lasting, but not a caricature of itself, with intense perfumes that faithfully express its Tuscan origins and the link between earth, man, and culture." Which translates as: It tastes like Vino Nobile, but you can drink it.

Right: Federico Carletti at his state-of-the-art winery in Montepulciano, where he harnesses the latest technology

Vino Nobile Asinone
Selected from a large single vineyard, this is a limited-production wine (maximum 45,000 bottles) made only in the best years. First produced from the 1983 vintage as a riserva, it represents "the most complete synthesis between tradition, territory, and enological innovation." Which translates as: You can drink it with even greater satisfaction but need to pay more and to wait longer. [2004★]

Other wines of the original estate include the very quaffable **Rosso di Montepulciano [2007 V]** and the deep but elegant if chewy-tobaccoey Cabernet Sauvignon **Le Stanze IGT Toscana**. Nor should we forget the wines of Carletti's estate in the Maremma,

Lohsa, where he produces one of the best wines of Morellino di Scansano.

Above: Carletti relies on barriques to soften Montepulciano's tannins, though one third of his Vino Nobile is still aged in *botti*

Poliziano
Total area: 240ha (593 acres)
Area under vine: 140ha (346 acres)
Total production: 600,000 bottles
Via Fontago 1,
53040 Montepulciano Stazione, Siena
Tel: +39 05 78 73 81 71
www.carlettipoliziano.com

Dei

As tourists travel from all over the world to escape their humdrum lives in the marvels of medieval Siena, so the Sienese flee their overcrowded city in the summer in search of the peace and cool of the Tuscan countryside. Such was the motive for the acquisition by the Dei family of this splendid estate, in a circular park within sight of, but well detached from, the almost equally touristy medieval jewel-town of Montepulciano.

It was in 1964 that Alibrando Dei made his purchase. His vinous ambitions—at a time, it must be said, when the market for historic Vino Nobile was at its nadir—went no further than to make a decent brew for consumption by family and friends. He planted a vineyard, Bossona, but it was to the prevailing mix of red and white, at low density, and what fruit he did not need for his wine he sold as grapes. It was his son, Glauco, with no experience

Dei is making refined, elegant wines from four vineyards: Bossona, Martiena, La Ciarlina, and La Piaggia, a mix of soils that enables considerable differentiation in style

and no consultant but an inkling of what might one day be, who first bottled the family product, by good fortune from the outstanding 1985 vintage, renting a cantina in town. In the late 1980s he built a winery of his own (a new one is currently being constructed to take its place) and, acquiring new vineyards just as Tuscan wine began reacquiring a positive image in the world of wine, set the wheels in motion for the reality of today.

Said reality consists of a sizable estate making refined, elegant wines from four vineyards: Bossona, Martiena, La Ciarlina, and La Piaggia, at an average altitude of 1,000ft (300m), and with a mix of soils that enables considerable differentiation in style. In charge of the estate since 1991 is Glauco's daughter,

Maria Caterina, while responsibility for the wine has fallen, since 1992, to the noted Tuscan consultant enologist Nicolò d'Afflitto. New plantings (most of the vineyards have been renewed in the past 15 years) have been to a mix of massal-selected Sangiovese and the latest clones. French grapes like Merlot and Syrah now seem to be getting preference over the likes of Canaiolo and Mammolo—which is fine so long as these grapes are for IGT, not Vino Nobile.

FINEST WINES

Vino Nobile di Montepulciano
Commercially, this is the important wine: Sangiovese, with some 20% of Canaiolo and Mammolo, aged 24 months in traditional Slavonian oak *botti* of 33hl. The style goes more toward elegance of perfume than opulence of fruit, as is typical for Vino Nobile. From a good year it will have the fruit to age well; the structure is almost guaranteed to be there.

Riserva Bossona
The highest expression of Vino Nobile, this Riserva is Sangiovese *in purezza* from the oldest vineyard. Aging time in wood is similar, though there is an element of tonneau (7.5hl Allier) refinement. Limited production ensures a wine that, if not generous in youth, can gain great complexity over time. [2004★]

Sancta Catharina
Caterina is particularly proud of her namesake wine, named for Catharine of Siena. This is a Super-Tuscan blend of Sangiovese, Cabernet Sauvignon, Syrah, and Petit Verdot, aged one year in French barrique. I asked Caterina what the role of Sangiovese would be in such a blend, given that perfume-wise it tends to get lost against such strong bedfellows. She said it was in part to hold the others in check, so that no single variety dominated. Somewhat to my surprise, I thought that this, though lacking typicity, was their best wine.

Dei
Total area: 100ha (247 acres)
Area under vine: 40ha (99 acres)
Total production: 200,000 bottles
Villa Martiena, 53045 Montepulciano, Siena
Tel: +39 05 78 71 68 78
www.cantinedei.com

Palazzo Vecchio

We find ourselves in Valiano, the smaller, eastern section of the Vino Nobile di Montepulciano DOCG zone. Palazzo Vecchio means "old palace," and a 15th-century palace is indeed what we find when entering the courtyard of this impressive building. We are on top of a round hill offering a 360-degree view that includes Montepulciano to the west, Cortona to the east, and the Apennines to the northeast.

Marco Sbernadori is a large, hearty, good-natured man who comes across as quite passionate about his work in wine. Originally he came from the Oltrepò Pavese part of Lombardy, where as a child he enjoyed the time of the grape harvest, though he was not himself of a wine family. His chance came when he married Maria Alessandra Zorzi, whose father had acquired this estate in 1952. They moved here full time in 1982, at a low point in the history

At Palazzo Vecchio, they are firm believers in staying out of the wine's way and letting the fruit quality, on which they place their major emphasis, express itself

of Montepulciano. In 1987, they adopted the name Fattoria di Palazzo Vecchio. Restructuring of the house and cantina was complete by 1988 (the cellar was modernized again in 2007), and their first Vino Nobile was the mythic 1990 vintage.

Since then, they have grown from the original 5ha (12 acres) of vineyard, at a density of around 3,000 plants per hectare, to their present size of 28ha (69 acres), the latest vineyards, planted mainly with the most recently approved clones of Sangiovese (they prefer small berries and small, loose bunches, whereas Prugnolo Gentile is a larger-berried version), having a density of around 5,000.

Since 2003 the consultant enologist has been Andrea Mazzoni, one of the more traditionalist

and non-interventionist of that fraternity. Most important, according to him, is a relatively brief maceration—maximum two weeks for the normal Vino Nobile—long maceration being a major culprit behind Montepulciano's notoriously tough tannins (others being a high proportion of clay and high yields). Aging takes place for up to two years in French oak *botti* of 27–31hl, followed by an extensive bottle refinement (barriques being used only for the Merlot in the IGT Rosso dell'Abate Chiarini). Otherwise, they are firm believers in staying out of the wine's way and letting the fruit express itself.

FINEST WINES

Vino Nobile di Montepulciano
(Sangiovese 85% plus Canaiolo and Mammolo) This is of course the most important wine here. It is plummy/pruney, with a rich, ripe aroma and surprisingly soft tannins for the genre. Good acidity, a whiff of balsamic and of tar; quite complex and, compared with Brunello, very good value. [2005 **V**]

Vino Nobile di Montepulciano Riserva
Made only in better years, from selected fruit, and given an extra 12 months in *botte*, this has more structure but also more concentration of fruit and is made for medium-long aging. [2000★]

Vino Nobile di Montepulciano Terrarossa
This cru wine, from the old vines of the iron-rich, red-earthed (hence the name) Vigna del Bosco vineyard planted in 1951, is made in top years only and gets 18 months bottle aging before release.

Rosso dell'Abate Chiarini IGT
This is a Sangiovese (70%) and Merlot (30%) blend of considerable distinction.

Palazzo Vecchio
Total area: 85ha (210 acres)
Area under vine: 28ha (69 acres)
Total production: 50,000–60,000 bottles
Via Terrarossa 5,
53040 Valiano di Montepulciano, Siena
Tel: +39 05 78 72 41 70
www.vinonobile.it

Salcheto

Salcheto is not your typical wine estate. Purchased in 1984 by Cecilia and Fabrizio Piccin, it began life as a general farm, with the accent on goats and their cheese. The fact that it was within the boundaries of one of Tuscany's iconic wine-production zones, however, could hardly escape notice, and even though Montepulciano at the time was going through a sticky patch, by 1987 the Piccins had realized that their best chance of viability was through the fermented juice of the grape.

They engaged one of southern Tuscany's most influential and ubiquitous consultants, Paolo Vagaggini, and in the early 1990s they launched their first Vino Nobile. But times were still tough and they needed support, so in 1997 they decided to team up with a certain Michele Manelli, whom they had met in 1994. He set to, renovating the goat barn for use as a cantina, and they worked together for a few years.

The Vino Nobile Salco Evolution is a
rich, tannic wine with lots of sweet fruit—
a wine that achieves that elusive ideal:
the blending of power and grace

In 2003, for reasons that are still unclear (at least to me, and I think I am not alone), the Piccins decided to split to Basilicata, and Manelli took over. He in his turn, having no wine background and little money, needed support and has brought in investors, retaining a one-third share. He says that he will one day—in the not-too-distant future, one gets the impression—trade it in for pastures new, perhaps in South Africa.

Michele Manelli is not your typical wine man, though he seems quite passionate about raising wine to the level of art. His principal avenue in this respect has been the establishment not only of a wine but of a whole project, called Salco Evolution. "'Evolution,'" says the blurb, "because that is the concept that inspired and inspires our work: the evolution of the balance of our vineyard [part 30 years old, now replanted, part planted in the early 1990s with grapes of massal selection], the evolution of the concept of bottle refining [now three years in glass, used to be four], and the professional and cultural evolution we who chart this path of growth undergo." Hmm... In any case, what it boils down to is the creation of original labels of an artistic nature, the latest being a mini series of three photos from art photographer Paolo Pellegrin, depicting various political and social horrors of our time. The proceeds of the sale of the program for this exhibition were all donated to Médecins Sans Frontières.

FINEST WINES

Vino Nobile di Montepulciano Salco Evolution
This is obviously the prized creation of the estate— a riserva in spirit, though not so called, 100% Sangiovese aged two years in large *botti* and French barrique. This is a rich, tannic wine with lots of sweet fruit—a wine that achieves that elusive ideal: the blending of power and grace.

Vino Nobile di Montepulciano
Also 100% Sangiovese and aged two years in a mix of oaks, this is a brighter, brisker, but also more classic Vino Nobile than the Salco Evolution, its tannins a little tough in youth but boasting good purity of fruit. [2003★]

Rosso di Montepulciano
A blend of Sangiovese with a bit of Canaiolo and Merlot, this wine is aged entirely in stainless steel. As such, it is clean, fresh, and eminently drinkable.

Salcheto
Area under vine: 15ha (37 acres) in
Montepulciano, 10ha (25 acres) in Colli Senesi
Total production: 130,000 bottles
Via di Villa Bianca 15,
53045 Montepulciano, Siena
Tel: +39 05 78 79 90 31
www.salcheto.it

San Gimignano

As you motor along the *autostrada* from Florence to Siena, you can't help but spot on your right, about halfway along, the amazing (or ridiculous, depending on your point of view) towers of San Gimignano, looking like a poor man's Lower Manhattan. Silly they may seem, but people travel from all over the globe to see them, stand under them, climb them, photograph them. Apparently, there was a time when there were a great many more—in the late Middle Ages, there seem to have been 70-something—each newly arrived ego needing to build that bit higher in order to lord it over the previous biggest ego. And we, the public, are always suckers for the display of strutting peacocks. You'd almost expect Donald Trump to make a bid for the one that rises into the clouds. *Plus ça change…*

Chameleon-like Vernaccia

All this might well color one's attitude toward the wines of this town, though it shouldn't. The foundation of their vinous image is Vernaccia, which, it should be remembered, is not akin to any other grape of that name, such as the one in Sardinia, for example, that makes Sherry-like, *flor*-affected wine, or the one in Le Marche, which is red and aromatic. The Tuscan Vernaccia makes a dry white wine of chameleon-like character. I say that because there seems to be no clearly identifiable overall style, with one producer achieving a crisp, minerally wine, and another something broad and fat, or oaky, or even slightly oxidized. One could make a positive argument along the lines that such variation proves Vernaccia's versatility, similar to that of Le Marche's Verdicchio. But somehow Verdicchio is always essentially Verdicchio, whatever the differences in yield or winemaking technique. Vernaccia seems to morph into different things altogether. That may have something to do with the fact that Vernaccia producers take greater advantage than Verdicchio makers do of the allowance within their respective *disciplinari* to add a small proportion of other grapes (mainly Chardonnay, but also Sauvignon, Vermentino, and who knows what else?).

Raising the red

Perhaps because of their inability to persuade the world that Vernaccia was a great wine, around 20 years ago the producers started cultivating quality red wines—something they had not previously done (red, yes; quality, no). Perhaps they felt aggrieved by the fact that prices for top red wines were shooting up all around them, while white-wine prices remained relatively and stubbornly stable. Lacking a tradition in fine red-wine production, they took advantage of the prevailing lax attitude to the blending of indigenous grapes with internationals, or the making of pure internationals, and as a result some quite innovative and interesting wines have emerged.

In 1996, a new DOC was created: San Gimignano (as distinct from Vernaccia di San Gimignano), for red wines, with all kinds of grapes invited along, including Sangiovese, Cabernet Sauvignon, Merlot, Syrah, Pinot Nero, Uncle Tom Cobley, and all. But try as they might, they could not, nor probably did they wish to, overturn the association with white wine that the name San Gimignano implies. In the final analysis, these are proud people: proud of the fact that theirs was the first wine, red or white, to gain the DOC, in March 1966; proud that Vernaccia is still one of the few white DOCGs of Italy; proud of the phenomenal success of their venerable town as a universal tourist attraction; proud, indeed, of their amazing towers.

Right and over: San Gimignano's architectural fame may have led its wines to be by turns overestimated and undervalued

Falchini (Casale)

The house of Falchini represents history in two guises. As an old Florentine family, they can cite documents of the 17th century referring to their service to the commune—and specifically to its leaders, the Medici. In 1720, one of their ancestors, Domenico, brought out a treatise on agriculture that spoke of methods of vine-pruning in the context of producing "noble white and red wines."

But perhaps the most interesting story behind this estate is more recent. It was in 1964—two years before Vernaccia di San Gimignano became the first Italian DOC—that Riccardo Falchini, still the active head of the azienda, bought the Casale property on the outskirts of the famous town of towers. In 1976 he had a fateful meeting with one of the doyens of modern Tuscan viniculture, Giacomo Tachis, who advised him, among other things, to remove the white grapes from his red wines, get rid of his old chestnut barrels, and introduce temperature-controllable stainless-steel fermenters. A builder by trade, Falchini, who professed no expertise in winemaking, obeyed every one of the master's instructions (he was eight years ahead of the San Gimignano competition in respect of temperature control), and a lifelong friendship was established. (Tachis is no longer the hands-on consultant—his protégée Elisabetta Barbieri has taken over—but the friendship continues.)

Another piece of advice the Piedmontese guru gave to Falchini was to plant small parcels of international varieties—Cabernet Sauvignon, Chardonnay, Merlot—for purposes of "improving" his blends. To this day, Riccardo Falchini, backed by his American-Italian sons Michael and Christopher, speaks up for the Tuscan/international blend, saying by way of musical analogy that a single variety makes for a "monotone," while two or three other notes give you a melody. He does admit, however, that the new, improved clones of today can obviate the necessity for the kind of blending that Tuscany, led by Tachis, rightly deemed essential in the 1970s and '80s.

FINEST WINES

From its three vineyards—Casale, Colombaia, and Savomaia—Falchini offers a broad range of wines: various versions of the famous dry white named after their home town; a traditional-method sparkler called Falchini Brut (not at all bad considering this style has been abandoned by virtually everyone else in Tuscany); an outstanding Vin Santo; and a selection of successful reds.

I am on record (and I am not alone) as being unconvinced that Vernaccia di San Gimignano merits its lofty status among Italy's top wines, but I was impressed by the dry whites of Falchini. The unoaked **Vernaccia di San Gimignano Vigna a Solatio**, from the original Casale vineyard—first released in 1965 and a 100% varietal despite Falchini's views on blends—is a wine of freshness (only 12%) and flavor, with a mineral-savory style, good for early drinking. The richer, more complex **Vernaccia di San Gimignano Ab Vinea Doni**, with 5% Chardonnay (or Muschio, as they call it), is intensely savory and salty-mineral, with a creamy texture and no obtrusive oak aromas—more the effect of wood aging than the perfumes. [2006★]

On the red side, **Paretaio IGT** (the name of a vineyard at Casale), with 95% Sangiovese and 5% Merlot, does have a slightly sweet-berry nose from its French component, but the Sangiovese comes through loud and clear on the palate, with a firm acid/tannin structure overlaid by expressive sour cherry fruit. As for **Campora IGT** (95% Cabernet Sauvignon/5% Merlot): one would expect the Tachis influence to bring forth something special in this category, and at least from the better years, one would not be disappointed. A vertical tasting back to 1999 showed the wine's elegance and poise, as well as its ability to gain complexity and improve over time. The hand of a master was upon it.

Finishing with something sweet, you really shouldn't forget that "outstanding" **Vin Santo Podere Casale I**. Once you taste it, you won't. [2002★]

Falchini (Azienda Agricola Casale)
Total area: 60ha (148 acres)
Area under vine: 35ha (86 acres)
Total production: 280,000 bottles
Via di Casale 40, Località Casale,
53037 San Gimignano, Siena
Tel: +39 05 77 94 13 05
www.falchini.com

Montenidoli

Elisabetta Fagiuoli was a young lady when, in the pre-DOC era, she came from her native Veneto to Siena to study art and somehow found herself in possession of a vineyard on the slopes above San Gimignano. There were no amenities—no electricity, no water, no phone—just a house and a small, abandoned, "promiscuous" vineyard. She had nine children in tow, some hers, some not, and little experience of farming or viticulture beyond what she had observed on her father's vineyard in Valpolicella. But she had grit and determination and a quasi-mystical sense of mission. It was not for her to beat the land into submission; instead, she wanted to work with it, to serve the earth and its creatures (in her case, vines and olive trees and a few animals). She was biodynamic "from the beginning"—something she defines, in comparison with mere organic agriculture, as "what you *do* do as distinct from what you *don't* do." She was her own agronomist, or rather that role was filled by "the earth from 250 million years past." She was also her own enologist, or rather it was "the earth—from the time of the Etruscans." Expanding on the history of her vineyard, she wrote:

"The mollusks and crustaceans were the first inhabitants of this land, when it was covered by the Ligurian Sea, in the Quaternary Period. They left their precious sediments. The Etruscans came with the vine. The Romans followed with their coins, found beneath an olive plant. The Templars refined the art of vinification. Generation followed generation in the peasant tradition. This land was abandoned due to the wars and industry of the past century. We arrived in 1965. We knelt down upon this earth. The old vines and the olive trees were covered by thorns. We loosened the chain that time had cast upon this enchanted land. Many great ones have climbed upon the hill of Montenidoli and have left their message. Many volunteers have given their work. Every day, every season brings its contribution to Montenidoli, the hill of little nests" (*nido* = nest).

You get the picture. It is a one-off. And the work goes on "slowly, for lack of money." I saw a recently cleared field, saw the massive blocks and masses of lesser rock that had been removed in preparation for planting, and understood that Montenidoli, after more than 40 years, is still a work in progress. The children are long gone now, but "the vines are my children, and I am their servant. You have to talk to them, as you talk with children. The new-age winemakers think they have all the answers, but the moment you think you're right, you're wrong."

FINEST WINES

The essential ingredient of Elisabetta Fagiuoli's wines is soul, and you can't describe soul. You have to sense it, taste it, relate to it. So I won't attempt to describe her wines, except to say they're different. I will merely give you their names and a little information, urging you to track them down.

Whites: **Vernaccia di San Gimignano Tradizionale**, 100% Vernaccia, maceration on the skins, no oak; **Vernaccia di San Gimignano Fiore**, 100% Vernaccia, free-run juice, stainless steel only; **Vernaccia di San Gimignano Carato**, 100% Vernaccia, free-run must, 12 months on fine lees in barrique; **Il Templare Toscana IGT**, 70% Vernaccia, 20% Trebbiano, 10% Malvasia Bianca, barrique-fermented, 12 months on the lees.

Reds: **Chianti Colli Senesi Il Garrulo**, 75% Sangiovese, 20% Canaiolo, 5% whites grapes—the classic Ricasoli Chianti blend; **Chianti Colli Senesi Montenidoli**, 70% Sangiovese, 30% Canaiolo, 12 months in barrique; **Sono Montenidoli Toscana IGT**, 100% Sangiovese, 18 months in barrique. [1999★]

Rosé: **Canaiuolo Toscana IGT**, 100% Canaiolo, no oak.

Montenidoli
Total area: 200ha (494 acres)
Area under vine: 22ha (54 acres)
Total production: 100,000 bottles
Località Montenidoli 28,
53037 San Gimignano, Siena
Tel: +39 05 77 94 15 65
www.montenidoli.com

Panizzi

Giovanni Panizzi is a Lombard by origin but a Tuscan, it seems, at heart. In the late 1970s he bought a small property at Santa Margherita near San Gimignano and, for the next decade and a half, divided himself between business activities in the environs of Milan and his Tuscan second home. Having taught himself about vine growing and winemaking, and having excavated a working cantina out of the clay soil (a more modern cellar has recently been constructed alongside), helped by Professor Salvatore Maule of San Michele all'Adige, in 1989 he made his first wine: 10,000 bottles of Vernaccia di San Gimignano. His single hectare of vineyard became 4ha (9 acres), expanded to 30ha (74 acres), and finally—with the establishment in 2008 of a new company called Società Agricola Panizzi, in which Giovanni is a shareholder, and the acquisition of Fattoria di Larniano with 18ha (44 acres) in the San Gimignano area—grew to 48ha (119 acres). There are also 7ha (17 acres) at Montalcino and 8ha (20 acres) at Seggiano in the Montecucco zone.

I consider these wines unusually interesting of concept, even if not necessarily typical— which, in the context of San Gimignano, is not necessarily a bad thing

Currently the president of the San Gimignano *consorzio*, Giovanni Panizzi seems, like his wines, to be something of a like/dislike figure among his fellow producers. What he does not do is evoke feelings of neutrality. I will not say to which side I inclined during our single, somewhat brief meeting, but I can say that not only did I like his wines, which I have known for a considerably longer period than I have known him, but I consider them unusually interesting of concept, even if not necessarily typical—which, in the context of San Gimignano, is not necessarily a bad thing.

Before broaching the wines, it is worth noting that Panizzi, in the course of its long collaboration with the Istituto Agrario di San Michele all'Adige, has, as far as Vernaccia is concerned, followed the unusual course of planting/replanting with material obtained by massal selection. In particular, it has come up with a clone that has been multiplied by the French nursery Guillaume and made available to other growers. Panizzi does not make a charge for this, but Giovanni admits he would be gratified if it were known as the Panizzi clone. It is not.

FINEST WINES

The basic **Vernaccia di San Gimignano** is surprisingly fresh and lively: pale, pineappley/appley, with good persistence and penetration. Two steps up is the single-vineyard **Vernaccia di San Gimignano Vigna Santa Margherita** from a 35-year-old vineyard. Like the *base*, this is a pure Vernaccia, but with greater intensity and complexity. [2007★]

Of the other two DOCG whites, easily the more interesting is the Gravner-like, oak-fermented, three-months-macerated-on-skins, ten-months-on-lees, unfiltered **Evoè** (the cry of the Bacchantes). This wine is made as much in the spirit of a red as of a white—"like they used to make whites in the past," says Giovanni. "It was a gamble, the sort of wine you love or you hate, but it paid off and has sold out." I found it fascinating: oxidized, yes; oaky, yes; fat and tannic, yes; but with a good line of acidity, ripe fruit, complexity, and bags of personality. Definitely an experiment worth doing and worth continuing.

On the red side, the most arresting wine is the **Chianti Colli Senesi Riserva Vertunno**, 100% Sangiovese, very bright and clean, with just enough acid and tannin for the sweet, almost jammy fruit not to be cloying on the finish.

Azienda Agricola Panizzi Giovanni
Total area: 67ha (166 acres)
Area under vine: 48ha (119 acres)
Total production: 300,000 bottles
Località Santa Margherita 34,
53037 San Gimignano, Siena
Tel: +39 05 77 94 15 76
www.panizzi.it

Umbria

Umbria is the only Italian region south of the River Po that has no outlet to the sea. It is bordered to the north and west by Tuscany, to the south and west by Lazio, and to the west, across the mountains, by Le Marche. It is Lazio, Latium, or more precisely Rome that has largely determined Umbria's political and economic history over the years. But culturally, the main influence has come from Tuscany. And that includes grapes and wines.

Perhaps that is a little unfair. Umbria has plenty going for it in its own right. Was the most influential Christian of the second millennium, St Francis of Assisi, not an Umbrian? Is the region not full to bursting with such delicious art-and-culture-filled towns as Orvieto, Todi, and Spoleto, to say nothing of the capital Perugia? And wine-wise, are Sagrantino on the red side and Grechetto on the white not two of Italy's most interesting grapes?

Orvieto: neutral to wonderful

Once again we are looking at three separate production zones—or rather, two limited ones and one general. The limited are Orvieto, named after the superb, high-perched town overlooking the main Florence–Rome *autostrada*, and Montefalco, home of Sagrantino. Orvieto is a blended wine based on Grechetto and Procanico (Umbria's euphemism for Trebbiano) but including others like Drupeggio (Canaiolo Bianco), Verdello, and Malvasia Bianca. You might also sometimes find Chardonnay and Riesling getting in on the act. The soil conditions here, mainly tufaceous, as in the Loire Valley's Vouvray, seem to be ideal for white-wine production, ensuring firm acidity and a variety of floral, fruit, and mineral flavors. Alas, Orvieto's image has been dragged down somewhat by versions cheap and, if not exactly nasty, at least very neutral (all that Procanico). The same law applies here as it does everywhere else: If you

want a complex and balanced wine, you have to restrict yields and spend time in the vineyard, all of which costs money. Encouragingly, more and more producers today are pushing quality in an upward direction, whether for the dry versions or for those semi-sweet (*amabile* or *abboccato*) or fully sweet, indeed botrytis-affected, wines, which can be wonderful.

Montefalco and Torgiano

More specialized still is Montefalco, which rejoices in a variety grown in its very small, limited area and nowhere else. Sagrantino, which DNA tests indicate has no close relation in the pantheon of grapes, is the variety with the highest tannin content in the world. You might think that this dubious distinction would make it undrinkable—and in not a few cases you would be quite right. But the growers of Montefalco are getting the hang of it, with improved clones and viti-vinicultural methods. Bit by bit the wines are shedding that *noli me tangere* ("don't touch me") style that they had when they first began, only about 30 years ago, to be made as dry table wines as distinct from the traditional, sweet, *recioto*-like *passitos*.

Sagrantino can have a powerful effect, too, in a blend, and indeed Montefalco's most produced wine is her Rosso, which is mainly Sangiovese with a bit of Sagrantino, and sometimes a bit of Merlot, mixed in. Which brings us to our general zone, or rather wine style—Sangiovese—the most famous example of which, from a recent historical perspective, is Torgiano Riserva. Along with Montefalco Sagrantino, this is one of the two DOCGs that Umbria has to offer. But Sangiovese in Umbria is as ubiquitous as it is in Tuscany, even though it goes under a variety of names. The famous local enologist Riccardo Cotarella has done well in bringing Umbrian Sangiovese-based wines out of the Middle Ages and into the modern world.

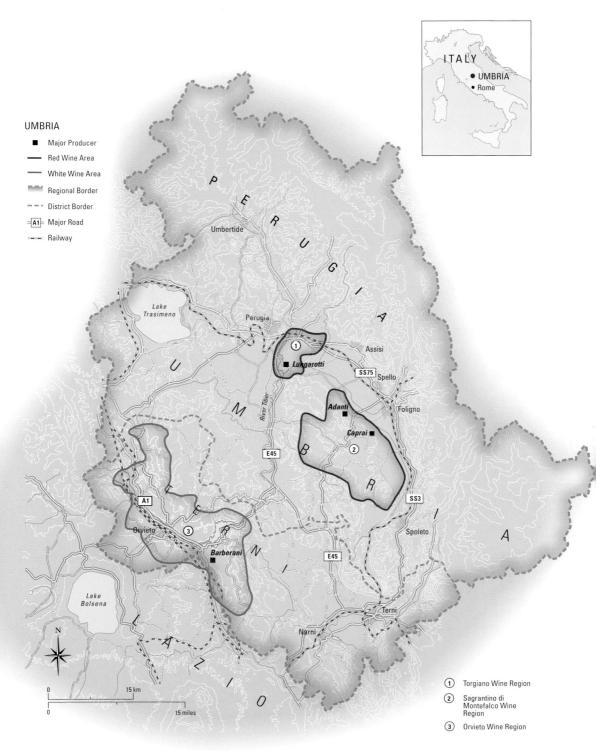

UMBRIA

■   Major Producer

──   Red Wine Area

──   White Wine Area

▨   Regional Border

┈   District Border

⟦A1⟧   Major Road

┈   Railway

ITALY

● UMBRIA

● Rome

P E R U G I A

Umbertide

Lake
Trasimeno

Perugia

Assisi

① Lungarotti

SS75 Spello

U

Adanti ■

Caprai ■ Foligno

M

River Tiber

②

E45

B

R

SS3

A1

E45

Orvieto

③

Spoleto

Barberani ■

N

I

A

Lake
Bolsena

N

L

Terni

A

Narni

Z

I

O

0   15 km

0   15 miles

①   Torgiano Wine Region

②   Sagrantino di
   Montefalco Wine
   Region

③   Orvieto Wine Region

Arnaldo Caprai

Although named for his father, a textile manufacturer who bought it in 1971 and maintained it through the 1970s and 1980s as a kind of hobby, this property as it stands today —the "azienda leader of Sagrantino di Montefalco production," according to its own propaganda, which in this case is accurate—is really the baby of Marco Caprai, one of vinous Italy's most dynamic entrepreneurs. Marco arrived on the scene in 1988 and immediately increased vineyard area from 3ha to 15ha (from 7 to 37 acres). In 1989, he enlisted the research facilities of the University of Milan, in the person of Professor Leonardo Valenti, a relationship that thrives to this day and has given rise to some extraordinary experiments and results. In 1990, Marco recruited the services of one of Tuscany's most respected

The "azienda leader of Sagrantino di Montefalco production" is really the baby of Marco Caprai, one of vinous Italy's most dynamic entrepreneurs

consultant enologists, Attilio Pagli, and since that time he has invested considerable time and expense in equipping his winery with all the most modern techniques and technology while, he maintains, giving full and due respect to tradition.

But it is in the field that the efforts of Caprai— together with the University of Milan—have been most notable, particularly in the area of research into the nature of Sagrantino, a remarkable and unique grape variety that, as we have seen, is world champion in respect of tannicity.

Today, Caprai, with 30 of a total 130ha (74 of 321 acres) devoted to research, has no fewer than 20ha (49 acres) set aside for clonal study, where almost 300 different clones of Sagrantino are grown and multiplied. Three of these clones

have already been approved for general use by the National Registry of Varieties. Since 1998, they have been carrying out parallel work on Sagrantino biotypes grown from seed, while at the same time, since 1997, they have been researching into Sagrantino's polyphenolic content in particular. Similar if less intensive work has been taking place in respect of Grechetto and Trebbiano Spoletino, while elsewhere on the estate, research continues into the suitability of numerous other grape varieties of Italy and farther afield (such as Negroamaro, Pinot Noir, and Tempranillo). Nor has research into various viticultural practices been neglected, with studies continuing into subjects such as planting density, rootstock compatability and suitability, training, and inter-row seeding.

FINEST WINES

Sagrantino di Montefalco 25 Anni
A selection of the best grapes and wines of the estate, effectively a riserva, Sagrantino di Montefalco 25 Anni was first released in 1996 (the 1993 vintage), 25 years after the establishment of the winery in 1971. Aged two years plus in barrique, the 2005★ is a huge wine, with massive but ripe tannins, brambly, spicy, almost Christmassy or fruit-punch notes riding on a faintly sweet, Porty fruit base, but with a dry, dark-chocolate and coffee-grounds finish. Big, but not without elegance, it is certainly one of modern Italy's most remarkable vinous creations.

Collepiano
This is the name of the azienda's other Sagrantino di Montefalco, made similarly to 25 Anni and at almost as elevated a quality level, receiving slightly less time in barriques. Fewer of the barriques are new, and as a consequence, Collepiano is somewhat more forward in terms of drinkability, even though it (the 2005) has its massive aspect, too, with an almost explosive palate and a long coffee-and-spice finish.

Right: Marco Caprai, son of the eponymous founder, who has raised the profile of his winery and that of the wider region

Montefalco Rosso Riserva

With this, we enter a land of less impenetrability and easier drinkability, even though the 70% Sangiovese, 15% Sagrantino, and 15% Merlot blend, aged 20 months in barrique, is no pushover on the palate. Aromas (of the 2006) are fruity and spicy, with morello-cherry, mocha, and licorice notes coming through, riding on a wave of firm but ripe tannins. It has the power of Montefalco plus the nervosity of Sangiovese.

Sagrantino di Montefalco Passito

This has predictably huge concentration and monstrous tannins, but the sweetness of the raisined grapes trumps the structure, and the finish is almost dry and very long. Not an easy wine to pair with food, a mature pecorino cheese probably being the most suitable partner.

Above: The Arnaldo Caprai winery, where almost one quarter of the vineyard is devoted to pioneering viticultural research

Arnaldo Caprai

Total area: 150ha (371 acres)
Area under vine: 130ha (321 acres)
Total production: 700,000 bottles
Località Torre di Montefalco,
06036 Montefalco, Perugia
Tel: +39 07 42 37 88 02
www.arnaldocaprai.it

Lungarotti

Giorgio Lungarotti was thinking quality above quantity before almost any other winemaker in Italy. Already in 1962 he was transforming his large family farm in the hills of Perugia province into a modern wine- and oil-producing estate. In the same year, for the first time, he made his soon-to-be-famous Rubesco Torgiano (from the Latin *rubescere*, to redden), a Sangiovese/Canaiolo blend (no doubt, in that era, also containing some white grapes), which came on the market in 1964, before the DOC system had really got going. Then from the outstanding 1964 vintage he created his *chef d'oeuvre*, Rubesco Torgiano Riserva, from the prime site Vigna Monticchio, a wine to be produced only in top years and designed to stand at the top of the Italian quality-wine tree.

The classics remain, updated and improved, and there are some additions as well. Lungarotti are bidding to re-take first place in the Umbrian wine hierarchy

It stood there for many years, together, some time later, with one of the first of central Italy's "super-wines," the Cabernet/Sangiovese/Canaiolo blend San Giorgio, the first vintage of which was 1977. Then, sometime around the mid-1980s, either they began to slow down or others sped up and began to pass them, and the luster on the reputation of the name of Lungarotti began to fade somewhat.

Giorgio Lungarotti died in 1999, and for whatever reason it was from that point on that the house of Lungarotti began making its comeback. From being very much a patriarchal operation—Giorgio was an Italian male of the old school—the Lungarotti organization found itself in the role of one of the most female-dominated wine businesses in the land, with Giorgio's widow Maria Grazia at the head of the Lungarotti Foundation (which also looks after the famous wine museum, founded in 1978; the olive-oil museum, founded in 2000; and the five-star hotel Le Tre Vaselle, also founded in 1978). Giorgio's daughter Chiara, a qualified viticulturist, was chief administrator, and his stepdaughter Teresa Severini, a qualified enologist, became head of marketing and communications. Not all operations, however, were run by women. Attilio Pagli was taken on as vineyard manager in 2000, the same year that Vincenzo Pepe became resident winemaker and, highly significant, that Denis Dubourdieu of Bordeaux, Chiara's ex-teacher, took over as visiting consultant in both departments.

Today, Lungarotti wines are reclaiming lost territory. The winery has been modernized, and a large majority of the vineyards have been replanted. The classics remain, updated and improved, and there are some additions as well, notably the wines of Chiara Lungarotti's 20ha (49-acre) estate, purchased in 1999, in Turrita, in the Umbrian wine zone of Montefalco. Lungarotti is bidding to retake first place in the Umbrian wine hierarchy.

FINEST WINES

Rubesco Torgiano Riserva DOCG Vigna Monticchio
This is still the Lungarotti wine that best expresses their love and and respect for the territory in which they work. A blend of 70% Sangiovese and 30% Canaiolo grapes, selected for their perfection from a large single-vineyard site at an altitude of around 1,000ft (300m), it is a wine of relatively brief (one year) barrique maturation and long bottle aging (previously ten years, now more like four) prior to release. It is not a wine that tries to impress through strength (though 13.5% alcohol is normal) but rather through subtlety and grace. Its junior version, **Rubesco Torgiano DOC** [V], is a wine remarkable for its freshness, vigor, and—best of all—sheer drinkability, as evidenced by the 2005. The Rubesco Torgiano Riserva and Rubesco Torgiano are made from the same grape mix, the difference being that for the latter the grapes may be sourced anywhere in the Lungarotti estates and not just the Monticchio hill; and of course the process is considerably less extended for what

they call their Classico (in order to avoid the word *normale*); also, aging takes place in large *botti* (55hl barrels, all today in French oak, the Slavonian ones having by now all been phased out). Our tasting, however, centered on the Riserva, brought up from the reserve cellar wherein are stored old bottles of Riserva going back to 1969 (as well as of Classico back to 1968, and Teresa has a couple of bottles of 1962 Classico in her private cellar).

We tasted old to young, starting with:

1970 From a good vintage, this wine of 12% alcohol had a mid-depth if aging color, and a still lively nose of dried fruits (prunes, figs), as well as something minty or eucalyptus. Lively acidity, smooth tannins, sweet figgy fruit, decadent but still very valid.

1977 A great vintage, as reflected by the wine. Somewhat deeper in color, with a lively, almost fresh, minty/eucalyptus nose. Firm acidity but smooth tannins, figgy/plummy, balanced, and with great length. Still in excellent condition.

1978 Tobacco and menthol on the nose. Firm acid, and the tannins a bit more present, too, the fruit less sweet than in the '77, with pipe tobacco again on the aftertaste. Teresa says this is the first year they would have used a few barriques.

1982 First released in 1992. Medicinal, herby, leathery notes, with hints of menthol and tobacco on the nose. Very ripe fruit on the palate, with good balancing acidity and firm tannins. Medium concentration, and still the fruit and structure to go on for a few more years.

1985 Relatively closed at first, later opening thrillingly to reveal mushroom and truffle, onion and garlic, and flowers as well as sour cherry; sweet, figgy fruit on the palate, and the firm, ripe tannins capable of carrying it on.

1988 Deeper color than previously, with some fresh fruit on both nose and palate, yet also something slightly old-style about it, the acid pointy and the tannins not quite polymerized.

1990 First released in 2000, as indicated on the label. A significantly deeper color than the previous wines. Menthol and tobacco on the nose, with something meaty, herby. A firm tannin/acid backbone, but sweet fruit dominates, concentrated and elegant. Among the best.

1992 Not a great year, as the wine demonstrates. Good color, but an artificial nose; lacks elegance.

1997 ★ Released in 2003. Deep, still youthful color, little evolution. Nose restrained. After a while it opens out nicely but remains backward. This was Giorgio's last Riserva, since the wine was not made in 1998 or 1999.

2000 Deep, youthful, virtually impenetrable color, and quite a break with the past; the first Dubourdieu/ Landi wine. Fresh nose, with notes of tobacco, which presumably come not from wood but from terroir. This has modern, post-Parker concentration, but also Sangiovese austerity and firmness. Some elegance lost to power. This needs another five years, perhaps justifying the earlier policy of holding it for up to ten years before release.

2001 Similar depth of color. Closed at first, hints of dark berry fruits. Sweeter, less austere fruit than in the 2000, tobacco and spice coming through on the palate. Needs several years to achieve drinkability. This is an example of a top Sangiovese that will only come into its own after several years—rather like a Bordeaux Cru Classe of a good year.

San Giorgio Umbria Rosso

This is today a blend of 50% Cabernet Sauvignon, 40% Sangiovese (sourced from the Monticchio vineyard), and 10% Canaiolo. A wine of fairly intense cassis, coffee, and mint-chocolate aromas, with the sour cherry of Sangiovese cutting right through. Like the Riserva, it is made to last, though I suspect the Riserva will outlive it.

Montefalco Rosso

A blend of Sangiovese, Sagrantino, and Merlot, this Montefalco displays licorice and meat-extract flavors, with well-managed tannins, a certain grip on the finish, and good length. Sangiovese has some difficulty in dealing with two quite such forceful partners, but it helps keep the wine in balance, and the ripeness of the fruit shines all the way through it.

Sagrantino di Montefalco

This is predictably a strapping, muscular wine with characteristically tough tannins and a very dry finish. Apparently a wine needing plenty of time.

Lungarotti
Total area: 400ha (988 acres)
Area under vine: 290ha (717 acres)
Total production: 2.7 million bottles
Via Mario Angeloni 16, 06089 Torgiano, Perugia
Tel: +39 07 59 88 661
www.lungarotti.it

Left: Teresa Severini and half-sister Chiara Lungarotti have helped restore the family winery's proud reputation

Adanti

"I did not have a scientific knowledge of what I should do. I did it because I felt it. I sensed that such and such needed to be done. A question of instinct, of love for the vineyard. Today people are more scientific, precise, but without emotion. The search for balance is fundamental. It is not enough to say, 'I have low production in the vineyard.' That way, you end up with an imbalance equal to that that comes from overproduction."

These are the words of Alvaro Palini, ex-cellar master of the house of Adanti, an estate in Arquata Bevagna near Montefalco purchased in 1970 by Domenico Adanti, father of the current owners, just as Alvaro was father of the current winemaker, Daniele Palini. Alvaro, a tailor, who lived for many years in Paris before returning to his native Umbria, was a man without any training in winemaking but

The wines of Adanti are very like those that Alvaro succeeded in creating 30 years ago. That means picking only the best bunches and extended aging in Slavonian oak botti

with sufficient palate to understand when a wine is good and when it is not—like the one his old friend Adanti offered him in the early 1980s. "Do you really think it's no good?" asked Domenico, querulously. "No, it's rubbish," said the straight-talking Alvaro. "Then make it yourself," replied Domenico irritably. And so Alvaro, ex-tailor, did precisely that (according to Roberto Spera's *Il Sagrantino di Montefalco*).

Today, the wines of Adanti are very like those that Alvaro succeeded in creating nearly 30 years ago, his son and Domenico's progeny all agreeing to continue the house tradition. That means picking only the best bunches and extended aging in Slavonian oak *botti*; for the rest, mainly tasting until the decision is made to bottle. They did update a bit in 2007, with a new barrel-storage area, and in

2008 they brought in help on the technical side with the appointment of consultant enologist Maurizio Castelli. But these steps are aimed at improving the existing wines rather than doing anything radically new. Alvaro himself was not beyond a bit of modernization. One example of this is his planting in the 1980s, among the first in Montefalco, of Merlot and Cabernet, which he used to bolster the Montefalco Rosso, as well as to make the idiosyncratic Rosso Arquata.

FINEST WINES

Montefalco Rosso DOC [V]
A blend of 70% Sangiovese with 15% Sagrantino, 5% Barbera, 5% Merlot, and 5% Cabernet. First produced in 1979, this intense, juicy wine, with a hint of licorice and cumin, has the structure to carry it forward several years and a long, sweet finish, its almost jammy fruit cut by firm but ripe tannins.

Sagrantino di Montefalco DOCG
A deep-hued brew made from the world's most tannic grape variety, aged two years in *botte* and a further two in bottle, this has the concentration and grip you would expect but enough ripe fruit to stand against these. Rich but dry, the 2004 is a wine of contrast, personality, power, and yet finesse.

Sagrantino di Montefalco Passito DOCG
The grapes for this wine, first produced in 1975, are dried for two months before being pressed. The result is thick and sweet but cut dry on the finish by a mass of tannin. There is a medicinal character, and you cannot help feeling that it is doing you good. Powerful, long, balanced. [2003★]

Rosso dell'Umbria Arquata IGT
A blend of Cabernet Sauvignon (50%), Merlot (40%), and Barbera—yet far more "Italian" than "French."

Adanti
Total area: 40ha (99 acres)
Area under vine: 30ha (74 acres)
Total production: 160,000 bottles
06031 Arquata di Bevagna, Perugia
Tel: +39 07 42 36 02 95
www.cantineadanti.com

Barberani

This is a family operation involving father Luigi (managing director), mother Maria (in charge of the Barberani shop, opposite Orvieto's superb duomo, and of their *agriturismo*, near the vineyards above Lago di Corbara), and sons Bernardo (sales, from 2000) and Niccolò (production, from 2005). A fifth and essential "human resource" is consultant enologist Maurizio Castelli—one of the first and still one of the best of his breed in central Italy.

The azienda's origin goes back to 1961, when Luigi's father Vittorio began commercializing his wines in Italy and abroad. Luigi entered the business in 1971. A large, good-humored man, as he walks through the streets of Orvieto the locals all greet him, and he has a smile and a wave for everyone.

All their grapes come from their own vineyards, which are tended, to all intents and purposes, organically (though it does not say so on the label). They have quite a host of varieties, in keeping with the *disciplinare* for Orvieto, which calls for a blend of two or more varieties. Barberani's *normale* contains five, while the cru Castagnolo contains no fewer than six: Grechetto at 50 percent; Procanico (which is Trebbiano); Chardonnay; Vermentino; Verdello; and Riesling.

FINEST WINES

Orvieto Classico Secco [V]
The extensive range begins with this basic Orvieto, which is fresh, fruity, and a lot more interesting than much of the drab brew that emanates from under the Orvieto label.

Orvieto Amabile
This is an admirably flavorsome (medium-sweet) version, for which style Orvieto has long been renowned.

Orvieto Classico Superiore Castagnolo
On the next level up, still mercifully unoaked, is this wine– a more complex offering than the previous two, full-bodied yet racy. [2008★]

Some may prefer the pure varietal **Grechetto dell'Umbria** to the more sophisticated **VIlla Monticelli Bianco**, which from the 2005 vintage contains 60% Grechetto with 40% Trebbiano and, although vinification no longer takes place in barriques but in 20hl *botti*, may still come across as a bit too oak-influenced.

Also under the Villa Monticelli label is a red wine called **Polvento**—50% Sangiovese, 25% each Cabernet Sauvignon and Merlot—which can achieve considerable heights of complexity and nuance. It justified Barberani's desire to be taken seriously as a red-wine producer when it was awarded the coveted *tre bicchieri* in the 2009 *Gambero Rosso* wine guide.

Despite that welcome recognition, however, the *chef d'oeuvre* remains **Calcaia ★**, a botrytis-affected Orvieto Classico Superiore of luscious noble-rot (*muffa nobile*) character that is fully deserving of a place in the pantheon of the great sweet wines of the world.

Barberani
Total area: 110ha (272 acres)
Area under vine: 55ha (136 acres)
Total production: 350,000 bottles
Località Cerreto,
05023 Baschi, Terni
Tel: +39 07 63 34 18 20
www.barberani.it

Romagna

Romagna is the eastern half of the region of Emilia Romagna. Administratively it may be linked with Emilia, but ampelographically and enologically, the two are not related. Emilia, the part to the west of Bologna, is mainly about wines with gas, be it in the form of Lambrusco, Barbera, Bonarda, Pinot Nero, Chardonnay, or whatever. Romagna is much more eco-friendly, with very little CO_2 rising to heat the atmosphere, and lots of what you will find in the rest of vinous central Italy—Sangiovese and Trebbiano.

Allowing the cream to rise

Romagna, however, has in the postwar period suffered in wine terms from adverse publicity—partly because some of Italy's largest producers of cheap, industrial plonk are located here, and partly because the quality producers have not found a way to separate their product, image-

Left: Recognition of the quality of Zerbina's wines came early on, as shown by this commemorative plaque

wise, from that of the giants. The big boys are generally to be found in the flatlands to the north of the Via Emilia, in zones where grapes may be grown in the hundreds of quintals per hectare, if they use grapes at all, while the quality producers are all located in the foothills of the Apennine ridge, south of the motorway. True, the epithet *Superiore* may be added to the name of the wine only if it comes from south of the road. But the killer blow has already been delivered in the name "Sangiovese di Romagna," which they still share with the industrialists. In the circumstances, it is not surprising that some top producers, such as Castelluccio, avoid the DOC for their best wines and use the name "Sangiovese di Romagna" only for their cheapest.

In the past few years, an attempt has been made to deal with this situation via the formation of a group of quality producers called the Convito di Romagna. Apart from two of our featured producers—San Patrignano and Zerbina—members include Tre Monti, Ferrucci, Calonga, Drei Donà, and San Valentino. The aim of the consortium is to bring the wine world's attention to the quality aspects of Romagnan production, including particular expensive viticultural methods such as Zerbina's *alberello* or the nurturing of obscure or endangered vine varieties like La Balsamina (Calonga), Bianchino Faentino (Ferrucci), Uva Longanesi (Drei Donà), Terrano (Tre Monti), and Ancellotta (Zerbina). But as long as they are stuck with the same basic DOC name as the industrialists, they are, frankly, fighting an uphill battle.

Distinguished raw materials

As for Sangiovese itself, the grape behind most of the best Romagnan wines (and virtually all of her top reds) boasts an illustrious history. The

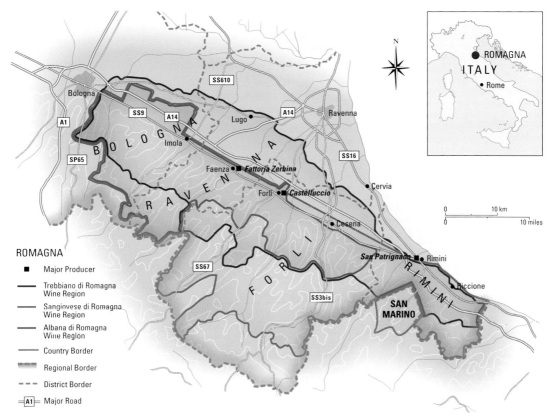

ROMAGNA

- ■ Major Producer
- ▬▬ Trebbiano di Romagna Wine Region
- ▬▬ Sangiovese di Romagna Wine Region
- ▬▬ Albana di Romagna Wine Region
- ▬▬ Country Border
- ▬▬ Regional Border
- --- District Border
- =A1= Major Road

Convito di Romagna's notes say that it has been "grown" here since 1700, though it might be truer to say it has been "known" here since 1700. It might actually go back a lot further than that and may even—at least the small-berried variety—have originated here.

The University of Bologna began actively researching Sangiovese clones in the early 1960s—the first such study in Italy—and after 20 years they came up with two low-yielding, loose-clustered, small-bunched, virus-free clones called RL Bosche and R24. The latter, in

particular, has proved one of the stars of the recent replanting phase, not just here but throughout central Italy. The previous star, R10, though notable more for quantity than for quality, was also a Romagnan (R = Romagna).

The other quality grape of Romagna is Albana, whose proud boast is that it was the first white varietal to qualify as a DOCG (in April 1987). No one is still quite sure why Albana should enjoy such an accolade in its dry forms, though like the even less interesting Trebbiano, it does make very good sweet wine.

San Patrignano

Almost all of the wineries reviewed in this book are just that: wineries—maybe with a bit of oil production, or horse training, or agritourism added on; or in some cases they are adjuncts of other grander activities, like insurance or manufacturing, which are carried out elsewhere. San Patrignano is unique in that wine production is an incidental aspect of the principal on-premise activity, which is the rehabilitation of drug addicts.

The commune of San Patrignano was established in 1978 by one Vincenzo Muccioli, who, were he British, would by now be at least Sir Vincenzo if not Lord Muccioli (perhaps when he dies, Rome will canonize him). The idea is to take in drug-dependent persons ("Whoever asks us for help is like our child, to be loved in the same way," is their motto), and in some cases their spouses and children as well, to wean them off their particular habit and, when ready, to provide them with work training to enable them to find gainful employment eventually in the outside world. There are some 50 different opportunities for professional training in the commune of around 1,500 people, and in the gastronomic field alone one can choose to make cheese, salami, oil, honey, and, of course, wine. They estimate that 70 percent of returnees into society take work in the field in which they trained at San Patrignano, and they maintain that they have saved the state 35 centuries' worth of incarceration at a cost of more than €100 million. It is a deeply impressive place, and one of the most moving experiences I have had in my career in wine was joining hundreds of commune members for lunch in what they like to call their dining room.

I described wine as "an incidental aspect of the principal activity," and strictly speaking that is correct, though since San Patrignano began an important expansion in 1996, it has become a major player in quality production in Romagna,

Right: Some of the community's 1,500 members are trained in winemaking, which is now a major source of financial support

San Patrignano is unique in that wine is an incidental aspect of the principal on-premise activity, which is the rehabilitation of drug addicts. It has become a major player in quality production in Romagna

with numerous citations and awards for quality—to the extent that wine today accounts for a healthy chunk of the commune's income (it relies entirely on private donations, not wishing to be beholden to politicians and their parties). Since 1997, it has enjoyed the wisdom of one of Italy's most illustrious enological consultants, Riccardo Cotarella, who has guided it through a decade of planting and replanting (using massal-selected material in some cases, clones in others), so that today it has more than 100ha (247 acres) of vineyard on the Romagna slopes, average 656ft (200m) altitude, some 3 miles (5km) inland from the Adriatic in Rimini.

FINEST WINES

Avi Sangiovese di Romagna Superiore Riserva
This wine is dedicated to the founder of the San Patrignano community (Vincenzo Muccioli). A 100% Sangiovese that undergoes three weeks of maceration on the skins and 12 months' aging in tonneaux, it has a healthy line of typically Sangiovese acidity running right through it, as well as lots of ripe, soft, chewy tannins overlaid by bright, morello-cherry fruit.

Montepirolo Colli di Rimini DOC
An unusually convincing Bordeaux blend (the two Cabernets plus Merlot), this wine is aged for 12 months in barrique and, like Avi, for 18 months in bottle, before being sold unfiltered. Dense and concentrated, with lots of ripe tannins and a coffee/dark-chocolate finish, it has lots of chunky fruit and should age well. "This is Cotarella's specialty, and he does it well," I noted of the 2004★.

Noi Colli di Rimini DOC
This is another blend, this time of Sangiovese, Cabernet Sauvignon, and Merlot. Although not on a level with the top two wines described above, it has the kind of structure that should allow it to age nicely, despite seeming a bit tough in its youth. The name (which translates as "us") refers to the "passion, commitment, and pride" of all those in the commune involved in its making. [2006 V]

The numbers (150,000 bottles) are mainly made up by **Aulente Rosso**, an IGT Sangiovese del Rubicone, which is a pleasant drink but not a lot more.

Above: The barriques used to age Montepirolo, in the colorful barrel cellar decorated by members of the community

San Patrignano
Total area: 250ha (618 acres)
Area under vine: 105ha (259 acres)
Total production: 500,000 bottles
Via San Patrignano 53,
47852 Ospedaletto di Rimini, Rimini
Tel: +39 05 41 36 21 11
www.sanpatrignano.org

Fattoria Zerbina

It was in 1966, a golden time to acquire potentially fine central Italian wine properties at bargain prices, that Vincenzo Geminiani purchased a farm in the gently rolling foothills of the northern side of the Apennines, south of the small city of Faenza. The early wines of Fattoria Zerbina were the subject of some positive recognition in the context of those lean times. But it was only after Vincenzo's granddaughter Cristina, a qualified agronomist, took over in 1987 that the property began its transition to the leading position in the admittedly limited world of high-quality wines of Romagna that it enjoys today.

Cristina understood early on that "fine wine is made in the vineyard." She understood something else that is obvious now but was not then: that the future for quality Romagna wine lay with Romagna's principal varieties, Sangiovese and Albana. In those days, as still to some extent today, Sangiovese di Romagna as a generic wine was somewhat looked down upon as being mere mass-production plonk. With the aim of raising quality in the vineyard, she recruited the services of consultant agronomist Dr Remigio Bordini, with whom she works to this day, and they set about plotting the overthrow of the negative reputation of the zone's Sangioveses.

In 1990 they took a deep plunge with the planting of a vineyard, Vigna Pozzo, to *alberello* or free-standing bush—a system of Greek origin, still common in southern Italy (especially Puglia) but unknown at that time in northern Italy, though once (according to Cristina) widespread in Romagna. Today all their vineyards are planted to *alberello,* at up to 11,000 plants per hectare. Production is not more than 1kg per plant; the bunches are *spargolo* (loose); berries are small and thick-skinned.

At around the same time, Cristina began experiments with clonal selection that still continue, trying some from Tuscany, some from Romagna, and some from her own vineyards by massal selection.

Cristina is now a keen advocate of *zonazione* (mapping), meaning the identification of different soil types, not just from vineyard to vineyard but within vineyards, determining differing levels of vine vigor as well as of ripeness (measured by potential alcohol, acidity, and pH). It is a system that not only influences the use of clones and rootstock but also affects the timing of harvesting, so that a single vineyard may be picked, and separately fermented, in several phases.

When it comes to the cantina, Cristina, who has not employed a consultant for over a decade, is a believer in keeping things simple. There are no concentrators, no microoxygenators, and they do not resort to *salasso* (the bleeding of the tanks). Maceration lasts between 10 and 21 days, depending on the wine, and the better reds will complete the malolactic and do their aging in barrique, of which no more than 30 percent will be new.

A point of interest relevant not only to these wines but to all wines of central Italy today arose during a vertical tasting of Pietramora back to 1985, regarding the increase in alcohol from 12.5% to more than 15%. Climate change, Cristina explained, accounted for some of the increase. *Alberello,* too, played its part, giving greater concentration and ripeness to the berries. But the principal factor, she suggested, was the evolving policy of picking at polyphenolic ripeness, which can occur considerably later than technical (sugar) ripeness.

FINEST WINES

Cristina makes three Sangiovese wines at different quality levels, all Sangiovese di Romagna Superiore DOC. **Ceregio** is fresh and fruity, for early drinking.

Torre di Ceperano
The second, more complex wine is Torre di Ceperano, the top representative of Sangiovese (with small additions) in lesser years, built for medium- but not long-term aging. A vertical tasting back to 1993 showed that this wine can age reasonably well. Pick of the bunch was the potent, seductive 1999 [**V**].

Pietramora Riserva

The top wine, appearing only in top years and containing no French grapes but up to 5% of the indigenous Ancellotta, is Cristina's pride and joy. Pietramora started life as a cru, made from old vines of a north-facing vineyard. But since 2000, as the older vineyards were pulled up, it has been more of a selection of the best grapes and wines of the estate. It is a wine of depth and sometimes almost frightening power, yet one that, for all its concentration, never entirely forsakes elegance. In a vertical tasting back to 1985 the quality of some of the earlier wines (the original 1985 in particular) left no doubt that Romagna is just as capable as Tuscany of producing *vins de garde*, and the structure of some of the later editions suggests that, if anything, the potential for longevity is improving, though at present they tend toward imbalance due to excess alcohol. Perhaps 13.5–14% is about right, as in the excellent 1997 ★ (aromas of cherry liqueur and Christmas spices, tight but sweet fruit on the palate, great concentration and balance). But 15.5% as in the super-powerful 2001 ("Sangiovese on steroids," I noted) is surely too high.

Marzieno Ravenna Rosso IGT

Named for the local village (Marzeno, but Cristina was not allowed to used the name unchanged), this is predominantly Sangiovese, plus the best Cabernet, Merlot, and Syrah of the estate. It is another wine of concentration, intense fruit, and high alcohol. It is the wine preferred by "internationalists," Pietramora being the wine of "purists."

Scacco Matto

Cristina is every bit as proud of this dessert wine as she is of her top reds. Made from botrytized grapes, it is lighter and less oxidized than Vin Santo, having intense peach, apricot, and floral perfumes. It represents the otherwise modest Albana grape at its highest expression and somewhat unfairly tends to win Cristina more praise than even her reds.

Left: Cristina Geminiani, who has dramatically raised the reputation of her region, as well as that of her family winery

Fattoria Zerbina

Total area: 40ha (99 acres)
Area under vine: 35ha (86 acres)
Total production: 220,000 bottles
Via Vicchio 11, 48018 Marzeno, Faenza, Ravenna
Tel: +39 05 46 40 022
www.zerbina.com

Castelluccio

There is a sense of déjà vu about this estate, set amid the steep, sometimes dramatic slopes of the foothills on the other side of the Apennines from Tuscany. This is because, like Poggio Scalette in Chianti Classico, the farm (or 70 percent of it, at least) is owned by the family of illustrious consulting enologist Vittorio Fiore, a northerner who made his name in Tuscany. In charge now is the second of the four Fiore sons, Claudio, aided and supported by his wife Veruska.

Claudio offers a bit of history: "Castelluccio was established as a domaine by Gianmatteo Baldi, a film director with a passion for wine, in the 1970s. The first vineyards came into production in the early 1980s." Baldi, according to Claudio (other producers like Fattoria Paradiso may disagree), was the first producer in these parts to fix his sights on quality. He also had the idea, certainly the first in this zone, of

Castelluccio was one of the first producers in these parts to fix sights on quality, and certainly the first in this zone to divide production into crus

dividing production into crus, which he named after various *ronchi* (singular *ronco*), using the Romagnan name for hill (the equivalent of Tuscany's *poggio*). At that time there were three *ronchi*, two planted to Sangiovese *in purezza* and one to Sauvignon Blanc. This last, called Ronco del Re, rapidly became a cult wine and reached a retail price of 75,000 lire per bottle—a fortune if you recall that most Romagnan white could be had for pennies. Claudio continues: "In the late 1970s, Baldi persuaded my father to act as consultant, and he was here until 1990, when there was some kind of falling out. In 1999, the company that had taken over asked my father to return as consultant and even offered him some of the shares. Today my family owns 70 percent of the company."

"In 2000 my father offered me and Veruska [a Tuscan lass despite the name] the chance of taking charge, giving me the task of returning the azienda to the glory of earlier days. I jumped at it. I had a good memory of the place from when my father used to take me with him on his travels, and I knew from various tastings that the wine was capable of being outstanding. I had good experience behind me with Livio Felluga [in Friuli] and Castello di Meleto [Tuscany], and I was confident I could handle it."

What are the differences between the Tuscan operation and the Romagnan? Claudio opines that in many respects, in particular in relation to the vinification, the differences for them are not significant, since the presiding genius is Vittorio Fiore in both cases. The sole major difference is the soil and, more generally, the terroir. Here the predominant *terreno* is clay, which gives minerality, freshness, and structure, as distinct from the *galestro*, or flaky schistous rock, and sand of Poggio Scalette, which tends to deliver less power but rather more elegance.

As to the making of the wines, as indicated, Claudio sticks pretty much to the paternal principles, with certain modifications. Harvesting is in 44lb (20kg) boxes, and the fruit of different vineyards is rigorously kept apart. In an effort to get as much color as they can with a minimum of harsh tannin, they employ *délestage*, involving the total mixing of the skins with the juice, about four times in a total maceration period of five to seven days. Temperature control, of course, at 82–86°F (28–30°C); and malolactic fermentation immediately after the alcoholic fermentation, which, importantly, takes place in wood. The barrels are larger than barriques—350 liters instead of 225—and they try to limit the influence of oak aromas by using only 50 percent new barrels (for Ronco delle Ginestre) or only barrels already used at least once (for Ronco dei Ciliegi). The wines spend 12–14 months in barrel, then up to a year in bottle prior to release.

FINEST WINES

Ronco dei Ciliegi and Ronco delle Ginestre

Today, Claudio Fiore makes the same three crus as existed in the early 1980s. Of the two pure Sangioveses, **Ronco dei Ciliegi** is the elegant one, being grown on soil that contains less clay and more limestone than the more full-bodied **Ronco delle Ginestre**. I tasted five wines from each Ronco together, dating back to 1983 (Ciliegi) and 1982 (Ginestre). Ciliegi generally had characteristic tea-leaf and herb aromas, with hints of cherry and, in the older wines, leather. The 2001 was the star, but the 2002 was equally remarkable for the year. Ginestre was more mineral, almost medicinal, with some tar, as well as more concentration, a greater wealth of fruit, and distinctly more oak, which marred the otherwise deep, structured 2001, the smoother 2000, and the again surprisingly successful 2002.

Ronco dei Ciliegi

1983 Color aging, but not badly. Fairly fresh, tea-leaf and herb aroma, not strong. Lacks concentration but has definite Sangiovese character on the palate—leather, herb, tea leaf, dried cherry. Smooth tannins and good, firm acidity. Subtle rather than powerful, quite respectable, but slightly underwhelming.

1990 Garnet heart, orange rim. Nose clean and typical (tea-leaf and herb), but you have to search for it. A bit more concentration than the 1983, with firmer backbone. Still drinking well, but not particularly exciting for the vintage.

2000 Fairly deep, bright, youthful color. Cherry/berry fruit on the nose, and good follow-up on the palate, with ripe tannins, good acidity, and pretty good length. Fruit character develops with air, nothing hot or jammy, and no excess of oak. Nothing overstated, nicely balanced.

2001★ Tight-grained ruby. Fresh cherry fruit on the nose. Currently restrained on the palate, with firm structure; quite earthy. A superior wine needing time, now somewhat closed but promising to develop into a fine and elegant bottle.

2002 They made around 4,000 bottles instead of the usual 10,000–15,000. Deep, youthful hue. Attractive, cherry syrup/berry nose. Firm acid, tight-grained tannins, good concentration, no hint of rot. The best wine of this tasting. It needs time but will be extraordinary for the vintage.

Ronco delle Ginestre

1982 Light, aging color. Nose herbal, almost medicinal; mineral. Good tannin-acid structure, agreeable cherry fruit as well as dried herb. Elegant and balanced, with sweet fruit and mineral notes on the finish.

1990 Still lively color, medium deep. Mineral notes and yeast extract on the nose. Lively though not excessive acid, with more concentration than the 1982 but not more complexity. A slight disappointment for such an illustrious vintage.

2000 Deep, youthful, almost opaque color. Oak sits on the nose, blocking the fruit, an influence that runs right through the wine. Wine guides and point systems enter the mind, rather than individuality and terroir. Impressively rich and concentrated, but it lacks Sangiovese typicity. Perhaps with time...

2001 Deep, almost opaque. Oak influences the nose, but the fruit comes through, chunky and concentrated. Plenty of everything—tannin, acidity, cherry/plum fruit. Tight and closed, it needs time but should prove very good, even though it could do with a little less Massif Central.

2002 Perhaps the deepest color of all, tight-grained. Oak again predominates on the nose, though the concentration of fruit on the palate is impressive (plum and dark berry). Like the Ronco dei Ciliegi of the same year, this is another surprisingly good result for the vintage.

Sauvignon Blanc Ronco del Re

I have tasted this wine less often, but I am not convinced. It may be good for central Italy, but northern Italy, and certainly the Loire's Central Vineyards, can do a lot better.

Massicone

This Cabernet Sauvignon/Sangiovese blend was introduced relatively recently. It is quite rich and reasonably balanced, but for authenticity I would take the red Ronchi any time.

Castelluccio
Total area: 50ha (124 acres)
Area under vine: 12ha (30 acres)
Total production: 90,000 bottles
Via Tramonto 15,
47015 Modigliana, Forlì-Cesena
Tel: +39 05 46 94 24 86
www.ronchidicastelluccio.it

Marche

For several centuries between the Middle Ages and unification in 1860, when they were annexed by the Kingdom of Italy, Le Marche (The Marches) were a collection of small, semi-autonomous entities under the overall control of the Vatican. This may explain a certain lack of uniformity in wine and lifestyles—indeed a certain rivalry and antagonism between the upper half, influenced by its contiguity with Romagna, and the lower part, influenced in its turn by adjacent Abruzzo, which is often lumped together with Molise and Puglia as "south." To illustrate this, before Italian car license plates changed in the 1990s, the inhabitants of the province of Ancona, which is in the center but considers itself northern, upon spotting a number plate beginning MC (for Macerata) instead of their own AN, would with mock horror call out, "Morte Certa!"—certain death.

Le Marche (we will henceforth refer to it in the singular) is a region of dramatic landscape —rolling hills dividing a generally placid sea and a range of increasingly menacing, often snowcapped Apennine mountains as you head south. The distance between sea and peak is not great, and a view of all three from the same vantage point can be quite moving. No doubt thanks in large part to its fragmented history, this is agricultural country, no industry having been attempted until well into the 20th century, with the usual unfortunate 20th-century effect on local architecture. But the style of farming was subsistence, the land being quite unsuitable for the industrial version, while the hilly, stony terrain favored such crops as the vine and the olive.

Verdicchio: quality and versatility

By far Marche's most important contribution to the wine scene of central Italy is Verdicchio, the name of both the grape and the wine. Despite an outrageous *disciplinare* for the main denomination embracing Verdicchio—one that allows far too many grapes per hectare (equaling almost 100hl/ ha, double the amount that responsible quality winemakers impose upon themselves)—Verdicchio in the past 20 years has rightfully taken its place among the outstanding indigenous grapes of Italy and is arguably the best of the whites. Two denominations exist, actually, though the one called Verdicchio dei Castelli di Jesi, covering a much larger territory than Verdicchio di Matelica, is by far the more important in terms of both quantity and quality. That territory is inland from Ancona (a major fishing port) in a zone dominated by towns fortified (like castles) against potential raiders in earlier centuries. Incidentally, the name Jesi, or Iesi, refers not, as is often erroneously thought, in any way to Jesus, but to the pre-Roman settlement of Aesis, from which the local "torrent," the Esino, also derives its name. Matelica is farther inland, toward the mountains, and produces wines of greater bite and minerality.

The main strength of Verdicchio is its versatility, which rivals that of Chardonnay, the major difference being that you can get good to excellent Chardonnays from many parts of the wine world, whereas Verdicchio excels only here (with the possible exception of Lugana, where they call it Trebbiano di Lugana). Verdicchio from Le Marche can come sparkling or still, oaked or unoaked, dry or sweet, light and racy, or rich and fat, made for early drinking or for laying down. Even when produced at the exaggerated level permitted by the law, it is acceptable, and it can be truly outstanding.

Ancona: Conero and Rosso Piceno

In the north and center of the region, those parts nearest Romagna, the dominant red grape is still Sangiovese. But the wines are unremarkable, and by the time one arrives at Ancona, the Montepulciano grape has begun to take over, producing wines of considerably more convincing quality. Conero (DOCG) or Rosso Conero (DOC, with an even

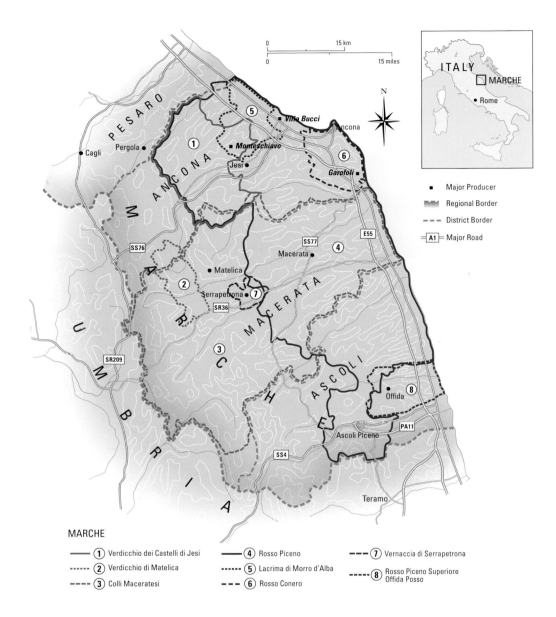

MARCHE

——— ① Verdicchio dei Castelli di Jesi   ······ ④ Rosso Piceno   ——— ⑦ Vernaccia di Serrapetrona

······ ② Verdicchio di Matelica   ······ ⑤ Lacrima di Morro d'Alba   ——— ⑧ Rosso Piceno Superiore Offida Posso

---- ③ Colli Maceratesi   ---- ⑥ Rosso Conero

higher permitted yield), the red wine from the hills behind the capital, must be at least 85 percent Montepulciano, and more often than not the best versions are 100 percent. Rosso Piceno, from the southern half of the region, or Rosso Piceno Superiore, from the extreme south, is the other important red wine of Le Marche, being a blend of Montepulciano and Sangiovese, the former taking on increasing importance as that of the latter diminishes. By the time one arrives in Abruzzo, of course, Montepulciano has taken over completely, and Sangiovese has disappeared.

Of the minor wines, the most notable is Lacrima di Morro d'Alba, an idiosyncratic, fresh, and aromatic red from a grape grown only in and around the commune of Morro d'Alba in Ancona.

Bucci

The concept of high-quality wine production is even more recent in Marche than it is in Tuscany, and Bucci has been in it longer than almost anyone—since the early 1980s. Ampelio Bucci, the principal, has done well dispensing financial advice to people in Milan, but he has also made sure that the family farm has thrived in the meantime. The Buccis have been here since the 18th century. They are passionate about agriculture in general and viticulture in particular, and like to boast that their vineyards are older (with an average age of around 25 years) and their staff younger (average age 22 years!) than anywhere else in Marche.

You get the impression, even just drinking the Bucci wines, that these are real products of terroir, and everything they say and do tends to confirm the impression. They are certified organic and have been for around ten years. They make sure—through careful massal selection (all replanting is from their own material) and severe green-pruning—that their vines are less bountiful than Verdicchio is wont to be (they get yields of around 70 quintals per hectare, as compared with the legally permitted 140). They also make sure that their vines are healthy and given maximum opportunity to dig their roots in deep for sometimes precious water supplies, as well as for mineral complexity. Soil makeup, they maintain, is essential to the welfare of the vine, clay playing an essential role in terms of water retention and pH, chalk regulating the plant's biochemical processes and helping to fix the acidity to which white wines owe their structure. They are looking, as they put it, for a "recognizable, or perhaps unique, style"—not one geared to the market but rather one toward which the market needs to orient itself.

Perhaps in no aspect of their production is this philosophy better exemplified than in their choice of enological consultant: the maverick from Bolzano in Alto Adige, Giorgio Grai. Grai is credited with having one of the sharpest, if most idiosyncratic, palates in Italy, and it is he who puts together the final blends, from the various parcels separately vinified according to provenance and vine age. Two whites and two reds are produced from seven different vineyards of between five and 45 years age, and at between 525 and 1,181ft (160–360m) elevation. All are aged in old oak *botti* of between 40 and 75hl.

FINEST WINES

Villa Bucci Verdicchio dei Castelli di Jesi Classico Riserva

Top of the tree is this Riserva, which as such must be aged two years before release. It comes from the oldest vines of the estate and is made only in the best years. The style includes a creamy texture combined with a mineral bite, something saline, and some very ripe, apple/pear fruit. Not a million miles from resembling a very fine white Burgundy and capable of aging in a similar way. [2006★]

Bucci Verdicchio dei Castelli di Jesi Classico

This is a blend of wines from the various vineyards. Grai's aim in blending it is to produce a consistent Bucci style, which could best be described as intense and bright, with a firm acidity running through from start to finish. Refreshing, firm, and quite long on the finish. For medium-term aging.

Tenuta Pongelli Rosso Piceno

A 50/50 blend of Montepulciano and Sangiovese, this is a wine that seemed irrelevant in the years when all the points were awarded to the big bruisers, being light and intense and so fresh it can be served slightly chilled, even with fish. [2005 V]

Villa Bucci Rosso Piceno

Being 70% Montepulciano and 30% Sangiovese, this is a deeper, richer wine than Pongelli but still with the accent on elegance rather than power.

Right: Ampelio Bucci has been able to indulge his passion for art but has always made his wines an even higher priority

Bucci
Total area: 400ha (988 acres)
Area under vine: 31ha (77 acres)
Total production: 140,000 bottles
Via Cona, 30, 60010 Ostra Vetere, Ancona
Tel: +39 07 19 64 17 9
www.villabucci.com

Garofoli

This is a family firm founded, under the present name, by Gioacchino Garofoli in 1901, though his father, Antonio, was already active in the production and sale of typical *marchigiano* wines from 1871. Gioacchino's sons Franco and Dante took over in the post-war period, and they were followed by Franco's sons Carlo and Gianfranco, who have run the show from the 1970s until the present day. Recently they have been joined by three of their offspring—Beatrice, Caterina, and Gianluca—so we are currently into the fifth generation.

The great merit of the house of Garofoli has been to follow tradition as long as it works but to be able to see when it needs an update. The wines have always—and I have known them since my first visit in the 1980s—been markers of their type and yet a

The great merit of the house of Garofoli has been to follow tradition as long as it works but to be able to see when it needs an update

bit more than typical. Certainly Garofoli was among the first in Marche, if not in central Italy, to embrace stainless-steel technology and barrique aging for its top wines, but it has consistently kept a tight rein on the horse while driving it judiciously forward. And the winery has always been the sort where you could eat your breakfast off the floor.

In the old days, the Garofoli family, like many merchants, were a *casa vinicola*—a winery that bought in grapes and transformed them into wine. The description still forms part of their official title, and the practice continues for the lesser wines, though one of the forward steps they took a while back was to start acquiring vineyards, from which all of their top wines of today are sourced. As for grape varieties, they stick to what Marche does best—Verdicchio and Montepulciano—and they are one of the few important *marchigiano* wineries that has not gone at least partially down the internationalist road.

FINEST WINES

Verdicchio dei Castelli di Jesi Classico Riserva Serra Fiorese
When first produced in the 1984 vintage, this was the first of a now-lengthening line of oak-aged Verdicchios. It took them a while to master the technique, but today it is a wine that benefits from the mellowing effect of small oak without too much in the way of wood or smoke aromas.

Verdicchio dei Castelli di Jesi Classico Superiore Podium
Nicely balanced between the freshness of firm acidity and the fullness of very ripe Verdicchio fruit, this is a wine for medium-term aging. It is given extra complexity, like the Serra Fiorese, by being kept on the fine lees for about nine months. Probably more for purists than for the international market, it evolves in a fascinating way. [2008★]

Brut Riserva Metodo Classico
This sparkling wine, first released in 1977, is a 100% Verdicchio made by the traditional method, with 48 months on the lees. Garofoli obviously takes it very seriously, and indeed it is a sparkler of finesse, though with a bolder, less subtle style than its French counterpart.

Conero Riserva Grosso Agontano
Made from 100% Montepulciano grapes and aged in barriques 12 to 18 months, this is a wine whose intrinsic power has been rounded and tamed by the passage in oak. Rich yet refined, it needs a few years in bottle to really come out.

Right: Brothers Carlo (*left*) and Gianfranco Garofoli, the fourth generation of this intelligently traditionalist firm

Garofoli
Area under vine: 50ha (124 acres),
Total production: 2 million bottles
Via Arno 9, 60025 Loreto, Ancona
Tel: +39 07 17 82 01 62
www.garofolivini.it

Monte Schiavo

Monte Schiavo is the property of the Pieralisi family. Or rather, I should say, one of the many properties of the Pieralisi family, which, apart from a four-star hotel, an airport, and a cosmetics business (not to mention a controlling interest in wineries in Abruzzo, Puglia, and Sicily), owns the world's largest manufacturer of olive oil processing equipment, with more than 80 percent of total global production. You might think, then, that the growing of grapes and the making of wine would occupy a rather peripheral place in their hearts. But the winery they have established in the center of the Verdicchio dei Castello di Jesi zone is one of the major players in Marche's private sector, with a staff dedicated to producing high-quality grapes and wines at commercial prices, and a consultant enologist of the highest caliber, Pier Luigi Lorenzetti.

The origins of the Pieralisi empire go back to the late 19th century, but it was in the 1960s, at a time of great economic hardship, that Giannino Pieralisi, a direct descendant of the founder Adeodato, began acquiring and planting vineyards. Until 1994, Monte Schiavo was a sort of private cooperative, dominated, but not entirely owned, by Pieralisi. But in that year they took it over completely, and have been driving it upmarket ever since, with Lorenzetti and managing director Luigi Calzetta in charge.

Today, in its recently completed, state-of-the-art winery, Monte Schiavo makes the full gamut of red and white wines of Marche, but its primary strength lies in its range of Verdicchios. Others may rival it, but no producer surpasses it in its ability to demonstrate the versatility of this remarkable grape.

FINEST WINES

From the humble Ruviano through the single-vineyard Coste del Molino, from the unfiltered Nativo to the Spumante, the oaked Il Bando di San Settimo and the sweet *passito* wine Ar Chè, Monte Schiavo's 100% Verdicchio wines all strike the taster as having a very specific and different personality. The most important, however, are the first two here.

Pallio di San Floriano Verdicchio dei Castelli di Jesi Classico Superiore [V]
The grapes for this wine (named for a medieval festival) are left on the vine 10–14 days longer than those for the lighter styles, and the juice is given six hours of skin contact after crushing. The result is a dry wine whose subtle opulence is balanced by a firm, fine line of acidity (there is no malolactic) that holds the multiple layers of flavor in place.

Le Giuncare Verdicchio dei Castelli di Jesi Classico Riserva ★
A single-vineyard wine named for a spring near the vineyard. Late-harvested in two passages, 25% fermented in tonneau with *bâtonnage*, the rest undergoing 15 hours of cold maceration; malolactic completed. As a riserva it must be aged two years, 14 months of which are on the fine lees. Le Giuncare is a complex wine capable of medium-term aging. The first vintage, 1998, is still going strong.

Adeodato Rosso Conero
Among the reds, pride of place goes to this wine, named for the founder of the Pieralisi empire. Made entirely from Montepulciano grapes, it has a very deep color and concentrated blackberry aromas, dark and brooding, with a compact palate and oaky, coffee and chocolate notes on the finish. In a good vintage, it is capable of aging 20 years, but it's slightly hard-going in youth.

Lacrima di Morro d'Alba
Now sourced from their own vineyards and macerated on the skins for a brief five days before aging in stainless steel, this is a summery red of low tannicity and almost Muscatty floral bouquet that can be drunk slightly chilled.

Left: Pier Luigi Lorenzetti (*left*) and Luigi Calzetta, who offer an unrivaled range of Verdicchios from Monte Schiavo

Monte Schiavo / La Vite
Total area: 350ha (865 acres)
Area under vine: 115ha (284 acres)
Total production: 1.6 million bottles
Via Vivaio, Località Monteschiavo,
60030 Maiolati Spontini, Ancona
Tel: +39 07 31 70 03 85
www.monteschiavo.it

Year by Year 2008–1990

Vintages in Italy are every bit as crucial to quality and, of course, to quantity as they are in France. Absurdly, people often judge Italian vintages according to what they know of the French zones, especially Bordeaux, so that, for example, 2005 may be looked on as marvelous, when in Tuscany it was average, and 2004 might be considered average, when in Tuscany it was marvelous. Similar inversions may be applied within Italy, confusing Tuscany with Piemonte, or Abruzzo with Sicily. The sole defense against this sort of muddled thinking is to check out the zones individually, year by year.

It is safe to assume that central Italy is reasonably homogenous in macroclimatic terms, though it is safer to make such assumptions for Tuscany and Umbria, both to the south and west of the Apennines, than it is for Tuscany and Le Marche, on opposite sides of the mountains.

I have indicated the success of the vintage with one to five stars, a final gray star signifying a half.

2008 ★ ★ ★ ★

Horrifically wet weather during late spring and early summer caused big problems with mildew and mud, but from late June the weather was hot and dry, with occasional showers, or rather storms, including some devastating hail (as south of Montalcino). In the end, a year of balance with some high notes.

2007 ★ ★ ★ ★

Assoenologi described 2007 as "heterogenous." Summer temperatures climbed to almost record heights, and there were fears of a repeat of 2003, when much fruit got baked in the sun's oven. But relief came in September when temperatures descended considerably, and nights in particular became cooler. Again, a good year with high notes.

2006 ★ ★ ★ ★

An unusually cool August gave way to warm, dry days in September and October, producing a crop good in both quality and quantity. Chianti, Vino Nobile, and Brunello all display classic character. A good year for whites, too—in particular Verdicchio Riserva, which came on the market in 2009.

2005 ★ ★ ★

A year for early pickers. Summer conditions were fine, and the vintage was shaping up nicely, but September rains led many to wait for the final flourish—a mistake, as it happened, because early October was very wet, so anything picked thereafter was either dilute or compromised by rot. Better on the coast than inland. Great for Merlot.

2004 ★ ★ ★ ★ ★

A year of moderation throughout: no excess heat, the right amount of rain, a gradual buildup of sugars, and good balance of components in the fruit. Vintage-time weather held steady to complete a perfect picture. The result: beautifully balanced wines, both for early drinking and for laying down.

2003 ★ ★ ★

All Europe will recall this year of heat and drought, which had berries shriveling on the vine. Wines emerged concentrated and often somewhat cooked, with unbalanced alcohol and acidity, more power than finesse. Cool-climate wines, from Montepulciano, Rùfina, and the heights of Classico, fared best in Tuscany. Generally poor for whites.

2002 ★ ★

Not quite as bad as 1992, this near-washout of a cold, freakish year was passed over by many producers in Montalcino and Classico for their top wines. Those presented tended to show marked Cabernet characteristics. Good for lesser wines like Rosso di Montalcino and non-riserva Chianti, into which would-be Brunello and cru quality were poured.

Right: Selvapiana's Chianti Rùfina is among the longest-lived of all Tuscan wines, though most Sangioveses age less well

2001 ★ ★ ★ ★ ★

After all the brouhaha attendant upon the Millennium wines, 2001's excellence tended to go almost unnoticed for a while. Although not particularly charming in youth, these wines have proved worthy performers with age, and the best are starting to open out very nicely.

2000 ★ ★ ★ ★

A hot year, and dry, but not so much as to make cooked wines as in 2003, unless growers were particularly inept with their canopy management. The wines are warm and supple, with lots of ripe fruit, but are probably not for the long haul.

1999 ★ ★ ★ ★

A classic year with some stars just beginning to shine at their brightest. Has legs.

1998 ★ ★ ★

The year seemed to be shaping up brilliantly until September, but vintage-time rains compromised the result. Beginning to slide.

1997 ★ ★ ★ ★ ★

Hailed as *the* great vintage by *The Wine Advocate* and *Wine Spectator*, it is certainly fat and juicy, but can tend to superficiality. Still an investment vintage, though.

1996 ★ ★ ★

An unmemorable year, now largely past its sell-by date, but a classic case of the need to avoid generalizations, since in Piemonte it was a top vintage for laying down.

1995 ★ ★ ★ ★

The opposite of 1994. The weather until mid-September was cool and wet, but a brilliant Indian summer richly rewarded those producers who were brave enough to wait.

1994 ★ ★ ★

Vintage-time rains diluted a promising crop. There are some good wines, but even these need drinking now.

1993 ★ ★ ★

Some decent wines but not a lot left.

1992 ★

One of the worst years ever. Steady downpour throughout September caused widespread rot.

1991 ★ ★ ★

A year of good, forward wines, most of which should have been drunk by now.

1990 ★ ★ ★ ★ ★

Supposedly the "vintage of the century," but all too many examples have proved unable to last the distance. Since this was before the big replanting flurry, we can only hope that the current clones have more staying power than the old ones.

Previous years with some excellent wines include 1988, 1985, 1982, 1975, 1971, 1964, 1955, 1947, and 1945.

Young and old

We have seen that one producer, Franco Biondi Santi of Greppo in Montalcino, maintains that wine made from Sangiovese is capable of great aging powers, though we have no evidence to back this up apart from a few bottles of Biondi Santi's own 1891, after which, barring his 1925, there exist no examples older than the 1945 that could even begin to demonstrate this thesis. Selvapiana's Chianti Rùfina 1947 can be amazing, depending on the bottle, but old bottles of Chianti Classico Badia a Coltibuono or Capezzana's Carmignano are more likely to be disappointing than delicious. You can find old fungi-covered bottles lurking in the nether depths of certain old *castelli*, but on the whole you would be well advised, should

you get your hands on them, to sell them rather than to drink them. As implied in my note on the 1990 vintage, the biotypes of Sangiovese that were planted in the 1960s and '70s were not generally built for long aging, and we can only wait and see what the recently developed clones bring us in this regard—from around 2030 on. One thing is certain: As a grape for making complex, vibrant wines of potentially great longevity, on currently available evidence, Sangiovese cannot compare with Cabernet Sauvignon or indeed Merlot, Pinot Noir, or Nebbiolo.

What Sangiovese can do is make exciting wines for mid-term drinking. In my experience, 15 or 20 years is normally about as far as it goes before terminal decline begins to set in. But again, the wines that I have tasted that are older than that are mainly from the old clones or, in the best scenario, from massal-selected fruit.

Above: Although the finest wines, including Lungarotti's Rubesco, require and reward time, older is not always better

Among other central Italian varieties, the one most likely to age well is Umbria's Sagrantino. But again, existing evidence is too sparse to prove the point, and we will just have to wait a few decades (or you will   I will be dead or gaga). Montepulciano, when made with aging in mind, as with Abruzzo's Valentini, can age at least as well as Sangiovese, possibly better. It pains me to say it, but it is the French grapes that stand the best chance of carrying youthfulness through the decades. Old bottles of Sassicaia, for example, can be fascinating.

In the white department, Verdicchio is far and away the best candidate for extended aging, but even that means only about 15 years. Some Tuscan and Umbrian Chardonnays can do it, too: I am thinking of Cervaro della Sala or de Marchi Collezione.

New Horizons

The Italian approach to wine is quite different from that of Anglo-Saxons. Wine is to be consumed as part of a meal, not principally as an alcoholic drink. That latter role is for beer or bittersweet apéritifs, or, in central Italy, perhaps Vin Santo. It follows from this that Italian wines will have certain "negative" characteristics in what Anglos might consider exaggerated form, while being lacking in others. Roundness, fruitiness, and softness are not generally attributes of Sangiovese-based wines, which tend more to acidity, tannicity, and savoriness. The clue is in the food.

As I said in the Preface, the typical Tuscan meal or *pranzo* (also the word for lunch, that being the main meal of the day), comes in three sections. The antipasto often features *fettunta*—thin slices of Tuscan bread toasted and salted (the bread itself is unsalted) and perhaps rubbed with garlic (you may prefer to rub it on for yourself, or not if you're due to discuss Uganda or have an interview with Silvio Berlusconi), and doused in extra virgin olive oil; and/or bruschetta—toast spread with chopped tomato and basil, or chicken liver pâté, or olive paste, or whatever; and/or *affettato misto*, a variety of salami and carpaccio-style meats, plus or minus cheese, or marinated fish, or preserved vegetables, or raw vegetables... The list goes on.

By this time you might think you'd be pretty stuffed, but remember: You're in Italy now, and you didn't have anything for breakfast but *caffè*/brioche, and you've been visiting dusty vineyards and musty cellars all morning, so you're ravenous. Indeed, technically, you haven't yet begun, because the "first dish" (*primo piatto*) is about to arrive, and it is usually pretty generous, and you will be expected to take an enthusiastic second helping if you don't want to fall out with your hostess. The *primo* generally takes the form of pasta or risotto or *zuppa*, and here's where the Tuscan/central Italian culinary creativity really kicks in. Many of these dishes do not contain meat, giving you a break between meat courses, like the

adagio that separates the allegro of a concerto from the presto. I know vegetarians who swear that Italy is the greatest place to eat in the world.

Then on to the *secondo piatto*, or second course, which is generally a fairly straightforward serving of roast or grilled protein, accompanied perhaps by vegetables from the *orto* or kitchen garden and perhaps some potatoes to die for, fried or roasted with extra virgin olive oil and sprinkled with rosemary. By this time, all you want to do is lie down in a dark place and snooze for the rest of the afternoon, but don't forget the cheese, and the dessert, and the *cantucci* with Vin Santo, followed of course by the ritual and by now essential *caffè* with chocolates (and easy on the grappa, mind).

Which brings us back to alcohol and the question of wine's place in the meal. This is not a cookbook, and I am not a cook, so I won't attempt a detailed explication of what goes with what. But Tuscan wine, properly chosen, will at every stage of the meal marry with the subtle and/or demanding flavors of the food—for the simple reason that the Tuscans have been at this for a long time and know what combines with what. Those tannins and acids that, taken in isolation, seemed to make for austerity or worse, when up against the combination of tomatoes, garlic, oil, and savoriness seem to blend right in, actually enhancing the smell/taste/touch experience. And if this is true of Tuscan food, it is equally so of many other types of cuisine.

So yes, the flavors of central Italian wines can be demanding. But once you get used to their challenge and realize their potential for matching with food rather than over- (or under-) whelming it, it is hard to go back to the alcoholic fruit-juice style that is so popular in countries like America, Britain, or Australia, where wine is the new beer. And if that sounds provocative, by all means feel provoked enough to prove me wrong by switching to Italian at mealtime. With an open mind, who knows how your horizons might be widened?

The Finest 100

Producers or wines appear in alphabetical order within their category.
A star (★) indicates what is, in my opinion, the finest of the fine.

Ten Market Leaders
Antinori ★
Banfi
Brolio
Folonari
Frescobaldi
Garofoli
Lungarotti
Ruffino
Saiagricola
Tenuta San Guido

Ten Great Sangioveses (non-Brunello)
Bucerchiale, Selvapiana
Il Carbonaione, Poggio Scalette
Cepparello, Isole e Olena
Flaccianello, Fontodi
Nocio dei Boscarelli, Boscarelli
Percarlo, San Giusto a Rentennano
Le Pergole Torte, Montevertine ★
Pietramora, Zerbina
Il Poggio, Monsanto (includes Canaiolo and Colorino)
Rància Chianti Classico Riserva, Fèlsina

Ten Outstanding Producers
Castello di Ama
Badia a Coltibuono
Biondi-Santi (Tenuta Greppo)
Capezzana
Caprai
Fontodi ★
Isole e Olena
Il Poggione
Querciabella
Soldera (Case Basse)

Ten Great Brunellos
Biondi-Santi Riserva
Brunelli Gianni
Lisini Ugolaia
Mastrojanni Schiena d'Asino
Palmucci Poggio di Sotto
Il Poggione Riserva
Salicutti Piaggione
Salvioni La Cerbaiola
Sesti (Castello di Argiano) Phenomena
Soldera Case Basse ★

Ten Rising Stars
Caiarossa ★
Camigliano
Casa Sola
Ghizzano
La Massa
Pian dell'Orino
Poggiopiano
Le Potazzine
Castello di Potentino
Sesti (Castello di Argiano)

Ten Top International Reds
Avvoltore, Moris Farms
Camartina, Querciabella
Lupicaia, Castello del Terriccio
Masseto, Ornellaia
Paleo Rosso, Le Macchiole
Il Pareto, Folonari
Redigaffi, Tua Rita
Sassicaia, Tenuta San Guido ★
Siepi, Castello di Fonterutoli
Solaia, Antinori

Ten Exciting and Unusual Wines
Il Caberlot, Il Carnasciale
Evoè, Panizzi
Lacrima di Morro d'Alba, Monte Schiavo
Pergolaia, Caiarossa
Piropò, Castello di Potentino
Pugnitello, San Felice
Sagrantino di Montefalco Passito, Adanti
San Lorenzo, Sassotondo
Suolo, Villa di Argiano
25 Anni Sagrantino di Montefalco, Caprai ★

Ten Great Sweet Wines
Calcaia Muffa Nobile, Barberani
Occhio di Pernice Vin Santo, Avignonesi
Recinaio Vin Santo di San Torpè, Sangervasio
Scacco Matto, Zerbina
Scalabreto, Moris Farms
Vin San Giusto, San Giusto a Rentennano ★
Vin Santo, Avignonesi
Vin Santo, Galiga e Vetrice
Vin Santo, Isole e Olena
Vin Santo, Rocca di Montegrossi

Ten Dry Whites of Excellence
Bàtar, Querciabella ★
Caiarossa Bianco, Caiarossa
Castagnolo Orvieto Classico Superiore, Barberani
Cervaro della Sala, Antinori (Castello della Sala)
Chardonnay Collezione de Marchi, Isole e Olena
Giuncare Verdicchio dei Castelli di Jesi, Monte Schiavo
Redenzione Vermentino Monterufoli, Saiagricola
Vernaccia di San Gimignano S. Margherita, Panizzi
Vernaccia di San Gimignano Ab Vinea Doni, Falchini
Villa Bucci Verdicchio dei Castelli di Jesi Classico
    Riserva, Bucci

Ten Really Good Value Wines
Barco Reale del Carmignano, Capezzana
Chianti Classico, Poggiopiano
Chianti Classico Riserva Poggio Rosso, San Felice
Chianti Classico, Rocca di Montegrossi
Chianti Rùfina, Galiga e Vetrice
Ciliegiolo, Sassotondo ★
Poderuccio, Camigliano
Rosso di Montalcino, Il Poggione
Verdicchio dei Castelli di Jesi Classico Superiore
    Pallio, Monte Schiavo
Vino Nobile di Montepulciano, Fattoria del Cerro

Glossary

abboccato/amabile somewhat sweet

agriturismo agricultural venue with holiday apartments

albarese rocky alkaline soil high in chalk content

alberello method of training the vine to stand independently or supported by a stake

annata vintage

appassimento drying of grapes for Vin Santo or other passito wines

assaggiatore taster

assemblage/assemblaggio blending of parcels of wine

autostrada motorway

azienda/aziende estate(s)

bando decree, as issued by Grand Duke Cosimo III in 1716

barrique/barricaia 225-liter barrel, usually but not always of French oak/barrel-room

base basic wine of an estate

bâtonnage stirring of the lees in barrel or tank

borgo hamlet

botte/botti large barrel(s) of around 7–100hl in capacity

bottigliere wine steward

cantina/cantine cellar(s)

caratelli very small barrels used for making Vin Santo

casa colonica traditional stone farmhouse

castello castle

Chianina indigenous breed of Tuscan cow raised for its meat

chiantigiani (inhabitants) of the Chianti zone

classico original or classic heart of a zone

comune commune, which may embrace several villages or *frazioni*

consorzio consortium, or grouping of producers

creta senese chalky-sandy soil of large sections of Siena province

cryomaceration soaking grape must on skins at low temperature

cru in Italian wine-speak, a special selection

coltura promiscua mixed cropping

délestage method of aerating fermenting wine by pumping it from tank to tank; rack and return

disciplinare the set of rules governing a denomination

enologo enologist

esca/mal dell'esca a common complex of vine diseases

fattoria farm

fiasco wicker flask

frazione part of a commune

frizzante slightly sparkling

fuori zona outside of the zone

fusto cask

galestro flaky, schistous soil

gallo nero "black cockerel"—symbol of the Chianti Classico *consorzio*

governo (all'uso toscano) largely outmoded way of boosting wine by refermentation with partially dried grapes (Tuscan style)

in purezza purely, entirely

invecchiamento aging

libero professionista freelance consultant

macchia Tuscan equivalent of Southern Rhône garrigue or scrub

madre in reference to Vin Santo, the part that is left behind to mingle with the new wine

maestro master

malolactic natural process (which may or may not be induced) whereby malic, or appley, acid is transformed into lactic, or milky, acid after alcoholic fermentation

marchigiano/i of Le Marche

massal selection propagation technique using cuttings from many vines

mezzadria/mezzadro sharecropping/sharecropper

normale unofficially, a wine that is not special—that is, not Riserva

opera d'arte work of art

orto/ortolano (of or from the) kitchen or vegetable garden

palazzo large imposing house

passito dried, as of grapes hung or laid out to dry for sweet wine; a wine from dried grapes

podere estate

poliziano/i of Montepulciano

promiscuous mixed

quintal 100kg (220lb)

rimontaggio pumping over of must/wine to oxygenate and break cap of solids

rinascimento renaissance

Riserva official and controlled designation of special wine, usually aged longer

ronco/ronchi in Romagna, hill(s)

salasso bleeding—that is, siphoning off part of a tank of must/wine, to concentrate the remainder or make rosé or both

sfuso bulk

spumante fully sparkling

stage (Fr.) training period

strada regionale regional road

Superiore official designation of special wine, usually because of higher grape sugar

superstrada major highway

Super-Tuscan top-end wine that does not, or did not, conform to the rules

tenuta/tenute holding(s)

terreno land, soil

tino/tini wooden barrel(s), usually conical, usually for fermenting

tipicità typicity, conformity to type

titolare owner

tonneau/-x oak barrel(s), 5hl in capacity, usually of French oak

tracteur enjambeur/macchina scavallante tractor designed to straddle a row of vines

tre bicchieri highest award in the Gambero Rosso/Slow Food guide

uvaggio (di vigneto) grape mix (the same mix but in the vineyard, not just in the wine)

vecchio old (no longer an official designation)

vigna/vigneto vineyard

vite vine (not to be confused with *vita* = life)

zonazione analysis of soil and other features of a patch of land in order to help in the decision of what and where to plant

Bibliography

ARSIA,
I Vigneti Sperimentali in Toscana (Agenzia Regionale per lo Sviluppo e l'Innovazione nel Settore Agricolo-Forestale [ARSIA], Florence; 2003)

ARSIA I,
Il Sangiovese
[Proceedings of the First International Symposium on Sangiovese, 2000]
(ARSIA, Florence; 2001)

ARSIA II,
Il Sangiovese Vitigno Tipico e Internazionale: Identità e Peculiarità
[Proceedings of the Second International Symposium on Sangiovese, 2004]
(ARSIA, Florence; 2006)

ARSIA III,
Modelli di Terroir per Vini d'Eccellenza
[Abstract of the Third International Symposium on Sangiovese, 2008]
(ARSIA, Florence; 2008)

Associazione Consorzi di Tutela di Montalcino,
Montalcino
(Edizioni Cantagalli, Siena; 1998)

Associazione Grandi Cru della Costa Toscana,
Grandi Cru della Costa Toscana
(Grotte di Castro)

Associazione Italiana Sommelier,
Duemilavini: Il Libro Guida ai Vini d'Italia
(Bibenda Editore, Rome; 2008)

Nicolas Belfrage,
Brunello to Zibibbo: The Wines of Tuscany, Central, and Southern Italy
(Mitchell Beazley, London; 2004)

Gigi Brozzoni & Daniel Thomases,
I Vini di Veronelli
(Veronelli Editore, Bergamo; 2008)

P Bucelli, A Piracci, F Giannetti & V Faviere,
Il Vin Santo in Toscana: Composizione e Caratteri Sensoriali
(ARSIA, Florence; 1998)

Antonio Calò & Angelo Costacurta,
Dei Vitigni Italici
(Matteo Editore, Treviso; 2004)

Antonio Calò, Attilio Scienza & Angelo Costacurta,
Vitigni d'Italia
(Calderini Edagricole, Bologna; 2001)

Compagnia Italiana Terreni Allevamento e Impianti,
Sassicaia
(CITAI Spa, Florence; 2000)

Consorzio del Vino Brunello di Montalcino,
Brunello: I Produttori
(Colli di Val d'Elsa; 2008)

Consorzio del Vino Nobile di Montepulciano,
Montepulciano
(Siena; 2000)

Ente Tutela Vini di Romagna,
I Colori, gli Odori e i Sapori del Sangiovese di Romagna
(Faenza; 2002)

Gualberto Grati,
"I Vini Toscani nel XVIII e XIX Secolo"
(Doctoral thesis submitted to the Università Commerciale Luigi Bocconi, Milan; 2004)

L'Espresso,
I Vini d'Italia
(Le Guide de L'Espresso, Rome; 2008)

Carlo Macchi,
Giulio Gambelli
(Veronelli Editore, Bergamo; 2007)

David Moore & Philip Williamson,
Wine Behind the Label
(BTL Publishing Ltd, London; 2007)

Kerin O'Keefe,
Franco Biondi Santi: The Gentleman of Brunello
(Veronelli Editore, Bergamo; 2004)

Pellucci,
Il Brunello e gli Altri Vini di Montalcino
(Vipsul Edizioni, Fiesole; 1999)

Ezio Rivella,
Io e Brunello
(Baldini Castoldi Dalai Editore, Milan; 2008)

Giacomo Tachis,
Il Libro del Vin Santo
(Bonechi, Florence; 1988)

Index

Author's Acknowledgments

The following deserve thanks for the help they have given me in various ways:
Roberto Bandinelli, Università di Firenze, Dipartimento di Ortoflorofrutticoltura;
Stefano Campatelli, Consorzio del Vino Brunello di Montalcino;
Silvia Fiorentini, Consorzio Vino Chianti Classico;
Mario Fregoni, Università Cattolica del Sacro Cuore, Piacenza;
Alessandra Gemmiti, ARSIA;
Paolo Solini, Consorzio del Vino Nobile di Montepulciano;
Franco Traversa;
Franco Ziliani.

A special thank you to Giusy Andreacchio of Vinexus Ltd for her unstinting efforts in the area of emailing, telephoning, and generally communicating with—indeed, badgering—producers; and to Domy Sette, her colleague, who helped her; and to Nick Bielak, for his patience.

Thanks also to the team at *The World of Fine Wine* magazine / Fine Wine Editions, especially the constantly encouraging Neil Beckett and the industrious Stuart George.

Photographic Credits